Wine Food

Wine Food

New Adventures in Drinking and Cooking

Dana Frank and
Andrea Slonecker

Photographs by Eva Kolenko

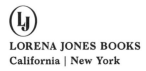

LORENA JONES BOOKS
California | New York

Introduction
9

How We Wine Food
10

Prefunk
26

Brunch with Benefits
57

Salad Days
88

The Big Veg
116

Picnics and Other Reasons
to Eat Outside
149

Uncommon Common Dinners
182

Cozy Night In
213

Resources
246

Acknowledgments
249

Index
250

Wine

Food

Wines + Recipes

Prefunk

Cava / Jamón and Peas 28

Blanc de Blancs Champagne / Golden Eggs 30

Muscadet / Oyster Bar, for a Shucking Good Time 32

Vermentino / Shrimp Aguachile 35

Albariño / Dips and Sticks 38

Chablis / Cast-Iron Skillet Mussels with Pancetta-Chive Butter 40

Provençal Rosé / Roasted Shallot Pissaladière 42

Rosé of Pinot Noir / Burrata with Strawberry Salad 44

Amontillado Sherry / Sherry-Cherry Chicken Liver Toast 46

Alpine Whites / Fête de la Raclette 50

Salad Days

Edelzwicker / A Sophisticated Hippie Salad 90

Arneis / Chop Chop 92

Dry-ish Riesling / Sweet-Sour-Salty-Crunchy Citrus Salad 94

Malvasia / Melon and Prosciutto with Radishes, Avocado, and Mint 96

Gewürztraminer / Tomato Chaat 98

Chenin Blanc / Little Louie Wedge 101

Sauvignon Blanc / Our Ideal Green Salad 103

Jurançon Sec / Roots Rémoulade with Smoked Trout 104

Corsican or Canary Islands Rosé / Fig Fattoush with Grilled Halloumi 106

Provençal Wines / Le Grand Aioli 110

Brunch with Benefits

Moscato d'Asti / Griddled Zucchini Bread with Moscato Peaches and Crème 58

Crémant / Biscuits and Morel Gravy 61

Franciacorta / Torta di Frittata with Spring Mushrooms and Stinging Nettles 63

Alsatian Pinot Blanc / Tropical Yogurt Parfaits with Seedy Cashew Crunch 66

Bugey-Cerdon / Pretzel Bagels and Lox 68

Pétillant Naturel Rosé / Falafel Waffles 72

Lambrusco / Leftover Beef Hash with Herby Poached Eggs 75

American Gamay / Pimento Cheese Soufflé 77

Riesling / Somm-Ssäm Throwdown 82

The Big Veg

Prosecco / Spring Fling 118

Sparkling Vouvray / Neon Coconut Curry with Paneer (or Tofu) and Greens 120

Verdejo / Stuffed Peppers with Sweet Corn, Herby Rice, and Possibly Too Much Cheese 122

Furmint / Carrot-Zucchini Latkes 125

Carignan / Ratatouille Gratin 128

Chianti Classico / Spaghetti Squash Parmigiano 130

Cabernet Franc / Wild Mushrooms and Baked Eggs, or Breakfast of Champignons 132

Southern Rhône Red / Pomegranate-Roasted Carrots with Lentils, Labneh, and Carrot-Top Zhoug 134

Zinfandel / Roots Tagine with Cauliflower "Couscous" 137

Georgian Wines / Georgian Supra 140

Picnics and Other Reasons to Eat Outside

Txakoli / Salt-and-Pepper Fried Chicken with General Tso's Dipping Sauce 150

Gemischter Satz / Spring Green Picnic Rolls 153

Greek White / Whole Grilled Fish with Herby Fennel Relish 155

Carricante / Flatbread alla Norma 158

Full-Bodied Rosé / Deviled Ham Hand Pies 160

Rossese / Big Boule Sandwich with Roast Beef, Pickled Beets, and Gorgonzola 162

Glou-Glou / Glou-Glou Thai BBQ 164

Oregon Pinot Noir / Campfire Cassoulet 167

Northern Rhône Syrah / Tomahawk Steaks with Grilled Radicchio and Cherry Tapenade 171

Spanish Wines / Paella and Porrons 176

Uncommon Common Dinners

Grüner Veltliner / Forbidden Rice Bowls with Slow-Roasted Salmon and Those Sweet-and-Sour Cucumbers Everyone Loves 184

Croatian White / Cod and Clams en Papillote 186

Aligoté / The New Tuna Noodle 189

Tempranillo / Summer Piperade with Fried Eggs 190

Beaujolais / Spatchcock Roast Chicken with Schmaltzy Potatoes and Cabbage 192

Barbera / Borscht Risotto 195

Dolcetto / Delicata Crostata with Fennel Sausage, Ricotta, and Buckwheat Honey 198

Aglianico / Butternut Lamb Chili 200

Oloroso Sherry / Caramelized Onion and Bread Soup with Brûléed Blue Cheese 201

Sicilian Reds / Sunday Sauce 206

Cozy Night In

White Burgundy / Our Chicken Pot Pie 214

Orange Wine / Porcini Mushroom Stroganoff 218

Red Burgundy / A Giant Stuffed Pumpkin for Harvest Time 220

Trousseau / Coq au Vin Jura 223

Corsican Red / Seafood Stew with Aromas of the Maquis 225

Balkan Red / Romanian Cabbage Rolls with Lots of Dill 228

Barolo / Slow-Braised Lamb Ragù with Rigatoni and Whipped Ricotta 230

Cahors / Vietnamese Beef Stew (Bò Kho) 233

Red Bordeaux / Indian-Spiced Duck Breast with Burst Grapes and Glazed Cipollini 236

Champagne / Crabs and Mags 240

Introduction

Our idea of a great Saturday night begins that morning with a bottle of wine already in the fridge and a trip to the farmers' market to pick up ingredients for dinner. Armed with a shopping list, we set off with a plan, but often get distracted by vegetables we didn't expect to find or herbs that are so fragrant that we can't not buy them. Between visiting with our favorite farmers and our weekly catch-up with friends, we're thinking about that bottle of wine back at home and what flavors will go with it. Beyond the food, we consider where we'll be eating, and with whom, whether that means we'll be at the kitchen table reflecting on the past week with our families or in the backyard with a mess of friends. The details of these moments define how we drink and eat.

When we travel, we experience culture through the lens of wine and food. We don't always speak the local language, but we can communicate at the table because the pleasure of drinking and eating is universal. Those moments expose us to new wines and influence our cooking.

One of our favorite places to visit is Morgon, a village in Beaujolais, France, where the vines grow wildly, reaching out from the rugged terrain like claws from the underworld. Because the vines are old and know just what to do, the winemaker's sole purpose is to shepherd the grapes through their natural fermentation. Nothing needs to be done to them to make wines that taste alive and real. At the table, last vintage's wine is poured for a humble cuisine: country cheeses, rustic charcuterie, lentils stewed with chunks of smoky cured pork, and a glistening, crispy-skinned roast chicken. The juices drip down chins between sips of bright, fruity red wine.

Off the coast of Croatia, we fell in love with the hundreds of tiny islands that dot the shoreline. Turquoise water laps the rocky beaches while fishermen clean their daily catch and families sunbathe nearby. Fresh fish drenched in olive oil, a handful of little clams, tomatoes, and wild thyme are tucked into a paper packet and steamed. Wines come from the house up the street, where an old man, who tends his graševina vines overlooking the sea, makes simple wines for his family and sells some around the village, too.

It was over a bottle of frappato and a bowl of pasta at an Italian cafe in Portland, Oregon, where we live, that we decided to write this book. Because of our shared interest in travel, learning about wines we'd never heard of, and cooking dishes that complement them, we knew it would be an adventure to get in the kitchen and cook together.

As we came up with the recipes, we enjoyed them at the table with friends and family, surrounded by interesting and exceptional wines. Comments about the nuances in the wines and how they worked with the flavors in the food led to conversations about politics, everyday life, family, desires, and the future. And what we were left with were memories of many great meals, having learned more about the world around us.

What we've realized in the process is that these moments of drinking and eating are more dynamic when shared with friends and loved ones. We are more interested than ever in continuing to explore the wine and food of diverse places, sharing what we learn along the way. In many ways, the adventure feels like it's just beginning.

How We Wine Food

Our favorite wines to enjoy with food are lower in alcohol, higher in acidity, fresh- and alive-tasting, and are made by vintners who allow the grapes to speak louder than their winemaking methods. There are exceptions, of course. A grilled steak needs a bigger wine with deeper fruit flavors, like Northern Rhône syrah. A slow-cooked tagine with dried fruit is perfectly suited to the zinfandel grape that's baked in the California sun.

When we're thinking about wine food, we want balance first and foremost. Neither the wine nor the food should outweigh the other. Some wines are complemented best by foods with similar flavors. Think freshly shucked oysters with briny Muscadet. Other wines benefit from some contrast, like a rich, cheesy soufflé with high-toned gamay.

Most food can be wine food. Outside of super-spicy or overly acidic dishes, there's a wine to match pretty much anything you want to eat. Try lots of different wines with the food you cook. The recipes and recommended wines that follow are merely starting points.

How to Use This Book

In the following pages, you'll uncover recipes that aren't typically partnered with wine, but deserve to be, as well as updated classics that beg for a good bottle on the table. Each recipe is a fresh introduction to a type of wine, with information about where it comes from, a few producers who are making exemplary versions to seek out, and commentary on how and why the wine's flavors work so well with the dish. The wines and recipes are grouped into chapters based on occasions, seasons of the year, and times of the day, whether you're hosting an afternoon barbecue or an evening "prefunk" before you go see a show. Interspersed are feasts for gatherings, with full menus meant for celebrating a specific type of wine; we recommend you invite friends to each bring a bottle to share. Also sprinkled throughout are pairing guides that cover everything from takeout food to ten of the most beloved pastas of Italy.

Our approach to matching wine and food spans both special and everyday reasons to open a bottle and cook something that will taste great with it. Many of the recipes are geared toward cooking simple, everyday dinners, but we think it's important to consider any and all opportunities to drink wine and enjoy a good meal, from weekend brunches to cozy winter suppers to those times when all you want to do is pop a cork and pull something from the pantry.

Recommended Wines and Producers

As you thumb through this book, you may be surprised to see some of the grape varieties and regions we've included. For far too long, Americans have been on a limited wine diet, drinking wines made only from the most popular ten or so grapes that all come from the five highest-producing countries. What a shame. Italian pinot grigio, for example, is one of the most-consumed wines in the United States, but there are hundreds of other tasty varietals grown in Italy that you've probably never heard of. Our goal is to introduce you to more of the vast assortment of grapes and the countries that grow them.

In addition, we highlight emerging categories, such as *pétillant naturel* ("pét-nat"), biodynamics, and orange wine (see page 218); a shift toward lower alcohol styles; and a new appreciation for wines made naturally.

The producers we've recommended all make natural wines. While the term *natural* can be quite controversial and doesn't have a solid, agreed-upon definition in winemaking, it generally means that the grapes are grown without the use of herbicides or pesticides and the vineyards are organically or biodynamically farmed, regardless of whether they are certified as such. The wines ferment by way of their own wild yeasts, instead of commercial yeast strains, and they're made without any additives except for little or no sulfur, which is naturally occurring in grapes and is often a necessary preservative. Seems pretty straightforward, right? Sadly, there's a laundry list of legally approved additives that can be used in winemaking—everything from colorants to tannin softeners to fish bladders—without any requirement to list them on a wine's label. The producers we highlight are some of our favorite winemakers from around the world, and you can have confidence that their wines are not only delicious, but also fit in the spectrum of naturally made wines.

This is a book for everyday wine drinking, so for most of the styles we recommend, you'll be able to find a bottle for less than $25, with the occasional splurge.

A Note on Cooking with Wine

You may have heard the saying "Cook with a wine you'd be happy to drink." While the thought of cooking with the same wine that you'll be drinking with dinner is a nice notion, sometimes that means sacrificing half a bottle of said wine. We buy an extra bottle for cooking special meals like coq au vin, when the wine is a star component of the dish. But most of the time we keep half-drunk bottles in the refrigerator for a week to ten days for the purpose of using them in our cooking. In our recipes, we call for "dry red" or "dry white." We're not saying to pour a bottle of plonk into your pot, but we are saying that it is okay to use the dregs in the bottom of a bottle that's been sitting on your counter a little too long (assuming that it was a tasty wine to begin with).

How to Buy Wine

Before you can drink wine, you have to buy it, and for most people, that's an entirely intimidating experience that includes a wall of wine, shelves full of bottles, a million different label designs, foreign languages, and wildly different prices. And if it's intimidating enough, you'll probably just walk down the wine aisle of your grocery store, scan for prices, grab a label that appeals to you, and then maybe stick with that bottle every week until the store doesn't have it anymore and you're forced to choose a new wine. For something so delicious and exciting, that doesn't sound like fun at all. Here are our tips to make finding and buying wine a more enjoyable experience.

Befriend a Shopkeeper

We're often asked for advice on how to decipher good wine from bad. Well, lots of reading and tasting will help. But the most surefire way is to buy your wine at a shop where you can build a personal relationship with the shopkeeper. Maybe such a place doesn't exist in your town, but there are numerous online retailers who sell fantastic wines and, even virtually, they will happily help you choose what to buy. Think of that person as a steward, a sherpa, a guide to get you to the wines you want to drink. Most people don't have enough time in their lives to learn the intricacies of wine. But that sherpa has time, so you may as well take advantage of her wisdom. Start by telling her what you like and, equally as important, what you don't like. Be forthright about how much you'd like to spend on a bottle. Let her choose a few wines for you to take home to drink. Take notes or photos of the wines you enjoyed and go back in a week or two for another round of bottles. Drink. Repeat. Over a month or two, that shopkeeper, now your friend, will have a really good idea of what you like to drink. We challenge you to go beyond the grocery-store wine department and discount outlets. Sure, they're convenient, but the selection is often limited to wines that will help the store meet a bottom line, and the prices at an independent shop aren't necessarily higher. For a list of some of our favorite retailers around the country, many of whom have online shops, see the Resources (page 246).

The Price Is Right . . . or Is It?

Our lives very much revolve around our day-to-day expenses. And while wine isn't a necessary expense, it is necessary . . . know what we mean? Our hope is that you'll start to think about wine in the same way that you think about food, namely, that you get what you pay for. That doesn't mean you have to pay $40 to drink a great bottle, or even $25. Price doesn't always correlate to quality in the world of wine. We've had mind-blowing bottles that cost us less than a takeout dinner for two, and shockingly bad bottles that were the same price as a new cashmere sweater. Sure, certain wines just cost more because of where they're from. Red Burgundy, for example, will always be more expensive than Languedoc-Roussillon wines, because of their prestige. That being said, you don't have to choose the priciest bottle of Burgundy to drink well. On the flip side, heavily manipulated wines made at factory wineries typically will be inexpensive because they are mass-produced. In general, you'll be hard-pressed to find a good-quality bottle for much less than $15. Of course, there are exceptions, but if you use that as your benchmark, you'll be able to find good wines priced for everyday drinking. If you have $20 to spend, you're in a totally different category with many more options. We recommend that you stick to what you want to spend on a bottle but stay flexible about the types of wines you're willing to drink for the money.

Bottle, Box, Can, or Keg?

We say buy the bottle, 100 percent of the time. There are great merits to a box of wine in your fridge with an easy-access spout. Since it's not exposed to air, you don't have to drink it right away. Canned wine is awesome chilled in a cold creek after a long hike. And kegs have saved wineries the expense of bottles and labels and made wine more accessible by popping up in places like bars. But we're traditionalists on this subject, and we most enjoy wine out of a bottle. We don't love the idea of our wine sitting in the plastic bag that lines a box, nor do we like how wine tastes coming through keg lines. A canning line is much too expensive for a small winery, so it's almost certain that canned wines come from large-scale operations where the quality won't be as high. That being said, this is purely a subject of personal preference, so feel free to experiment.

Label Lexicon

How many times have you, or someone you know, bought a wine because of the label? The age-old adage "Don't judge a book by its cover" comes into play here. We can't emphasize this enough. There are marketing geniuses who create amazing artwork for terrible wines, and, conversely, some of our favorite bottles have labels that look like they came off a home printer. Don't get wooed by critter labels—those with roosters or dogs on bikes—or fancy letterpress, or gold-leaf embossing. They might be cute, or even very beautiful, but they don't give an indication of what's inside the bottle. Deciphering labels written in a language you don't read can be tricky. Even trickier is the fact that every country has its own rules for how wines need to be labeled. Three of the most common labeling styles to know are French, German, and Italian, but keep in mind there are many variations from region to region.

The Bigger the Bottle the Better

187.5 ml: Split

375 ml: Half

750 ml: Standard
(5 glasses of wine)

1.5 L: Magnum
(2 standard bottles)

3 L: Double magnum
(4 standard bottles)

4.5 L: Jeroboam
(6 standard bottles)

6 L: Imperial or
Methuselah
(8 standard bottles)

9 L: Salmanazar
(12 standard bottles,
1 case of wine)

12 L: Balthazar
(16 standard bottles)

15 L: Nebuchadnezzar
(20 standard bottles)

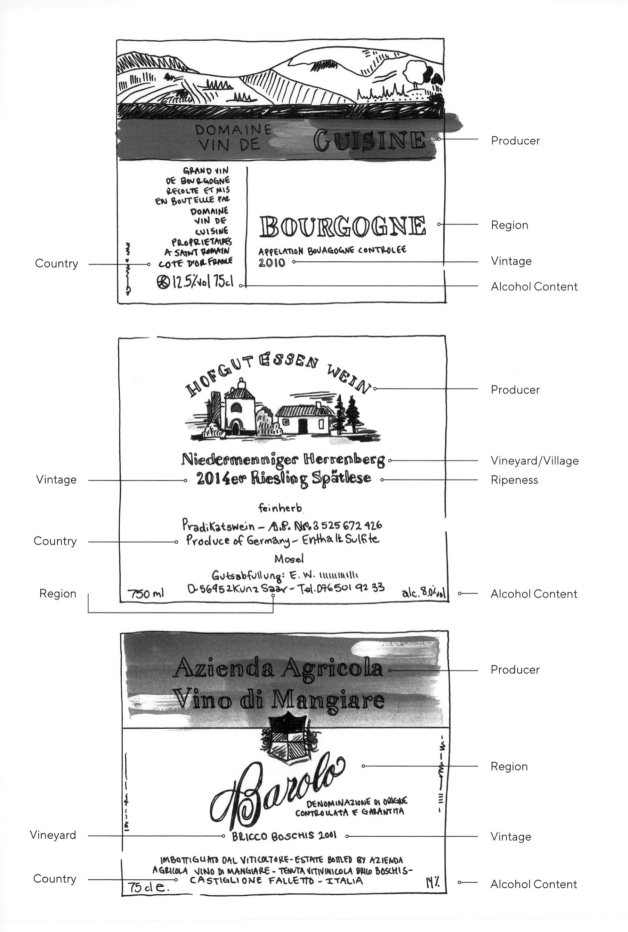

Producer

Region

Vintage

Alcohol Content

Country

Producer

Vineyard/Village

Ripeness

Vintage

Country

Region

Alcohol Content

Producer

Region

Vineyard

Vintage

Country

Alcohol Content

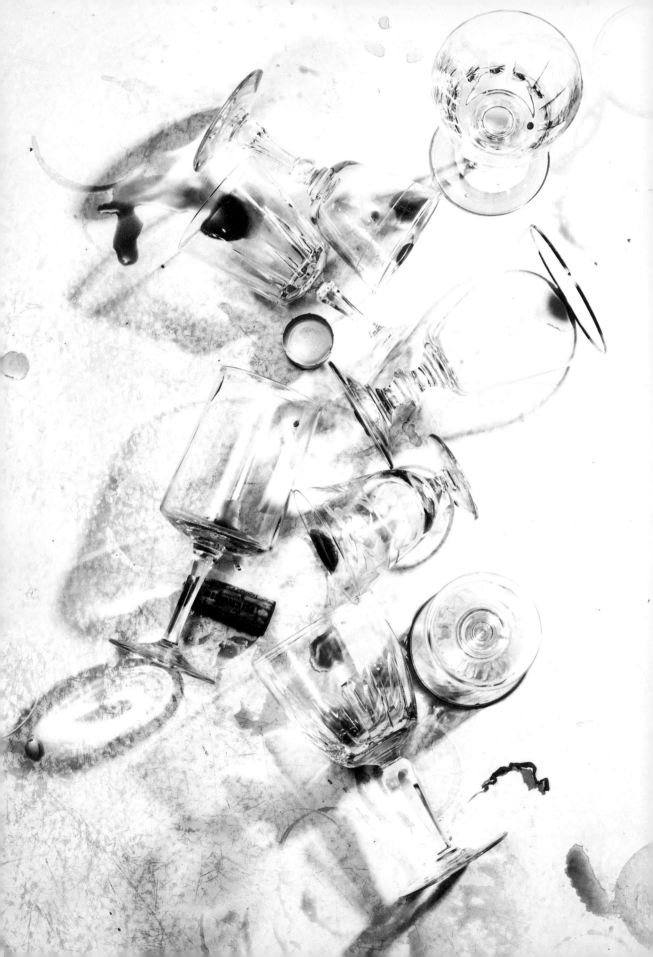

Serve like a Sommelier

Sommeliers dedicate innumerable hours learning the finer points of fine-dining service and infinite details about grapes, regions, and styles of wine. It's admirable, but not something most people are interested in pursuing. You don't need to study for years or pass an intensive exam to serve wine at home. What follows are our suggestions for opening and sharing a bottle at your next party or for a quiet dinner tomorrow night.

Opening Act

The corkscrew—you can't open a bottle without one. Well, you can, but it involves a shoe, or a book, or a pair of pliers. There are big, bulky cork pullers, like the rabbit-style, and electric bottle openers that take up too much space on a kitchen counter. There are fancy corkscrews with wings that cantilever the cork from the bottle, and the classic two-pronged ah-so that most people can't figure out how to use. What you really need is available at almost every corner market or in your grocer's wine department: an inexpensive waiter's corkscrew, which folds up to fit easily in your pocket or kitchen drawer and will cost you less than $4. Some professionals swear by similar, but pricey, versions from companies like Laguiole, but for us, a stash of the cheapies works great. They have a short blade at one end to cut the bottle's foil, and a screw, or "worm," that folds in and out. There are single-hinged and double-hinged styles, and both work well. The double-hinged generally pulls corks out a little easier, but a lot depends on personal preference.

Musings on Glassware

It's easy to be allured by the vast selection of wine glasses on the market. You can now have separate glasses for specific grape varieties. Instead of a plain ol' white wine glass, you can have a riesling glass, an oaked chardonnay glass, an un-oaked chardonnay glass, and a viognier glass. And by the time you have all of those glasses, you don't have room in your cupboards for anything else. All a marketing game? Not necessarily. Science has proven that certain varieties smell and taste better when drunk from certain shapes of glassware. However, we recommend having a tight selection of glasses that suit your storage space and the types of wines you tend to drink.

If you're only into having one style, no problem. We'd recommend a standard 13-ounce white wine glass. In fact, that's our everyday glass, regardless of what we're drinking. It works just as well for a nice Barolo or a sparkling wine as it does for a simple white. You could add a second style, such as an 18-ounce Burgundy glass with more of a bowl shape, if you want something for those special bottles you open from time to time. But for us, that's about all we use. Stemless glasses, tumblers, and, heck, even plastic cups, are useful for rosé at the park or txakoli (CHA-ko-lee) on your front porch, but most of the time we prefer to use a glass with a stem so the wine isn't warmed by our hands. Champagne flutes can be festive and fun, but we'd rather use a standard glass for bubbles. A flute can be a little tricky to drink from, and it's hard to get your nose in there to smell the wine. The most important takeaway is that you don't need to spend a lot of money on glassware. Choose a simple, rounded style (no need for angular glasses, or bowls with big, curved lips), and, because glasses break, have a few extra on hand.

Keep It Cool

While we believe wine drinking should be fun and easy, there are a few things that we take very seriously about the whole matter, temperature being one of them. It'a always a bummer to be served a lukewarm bottle of red at a restaurant, or a white that's so cold your teeth ache when you drink it. Getting the temperature right for your bottle is something we always encourage. We prefer sparkling wines and fruity, light whites to be quite cold, between 40°F and 50°F. A short dunk in a bucket of ice water will get these wines truly cold if they haven't had enough time in your refrigerator. Richer white wines, rosés, and orange wines are best between 50°F and 60°F. Red wines are definitely best at or below room temperature, so drink them anywhere from 60°F to 65°F, and serve lighter reds slightly cooler than full-bodied reds.

Store your bottles somewhere cool and dark, and lying on their sides. The top of the fridge or that cabinet above your stove are decidedly the worst places for wine, as is the closet next to your furnace. Basements and other temperature-controlled areas are ideal, and a small wine fridge is a worthwhile investment.

To Decant, or Not

You don't need to be drinking fancy or expensive wine to use a decanter. While we don't use one often, it's a helpful tool for separating the sediment from older wines, or getting some air into a bolder red. And a decanter is fantastic for orange wines, as they can always use some time to open up. If you're decanting for sediment, pour the wine slowly so any deposits at the bottom of the bottle don't end up in the decanter. You'll leave a tiny amount of wine behind, full of gritty bits you wouldn't want to drink anyway. If you're decanting for air, you can glug the wine right into the decanter, no need to be gentle about it. Depending on the wine, you can decant and drink right away—the wine will open up as you enjoy it—or let it sit for an hour or two first. Be aware that some old wines are just too old to decant. Pouring them out of their bottle will expose them to too much air and they'll fall apart immediately. If you don't want to buy a decanter, other household items, such as a water pitcher, will work just as well. A large Erlenmeyer flask is another alternative, and it doubles as a great conversation piece.

Breathing Room

In many cases, you can pop a bottle and get to drinking it right away. Sometimes, though, you'll want to open your wine ahead of time and let it breathe, either in the bottle or in a decanter. If it's tannic or quite bold, some hang time with the cork pulled will make a big difference in how the wine tastes. Grippy tannins will relax a bit, and you'll avoid most of the harsh, "furry" sensation that big wines leave on your palate. Leave those big wines to open up for an hour or two. Pay attention to how your wine tastes as you enjoy the bottle. You'll likely notice a clear evolution from first sip to last drop, and that's all due to how much air has come into contact with the wine.

Taste like a Pro—Swirl, Sniff, Swish, Swallow

You don't have to know a lot about wine to enjoy drinking it. In fact, sometimes knowing too much makes it less enjoyable. But if you are armed with just a couple of tips for tasting wine and detecting flaws, you'll always be able to drink a great bottle and not have to think about it too much.

While you'll most likely want to just get down to the business of drinking, we recommend one proper swirl, sniff, swish, and swallow to make sure your wine isn't flawed. The first thing you should do when you pour yourself a glass is swirl. Set the foot of your glass on a counter or table and give it a gentle circular swoosh to release some of the aromas of the wine. As it settles down, you should next sniff, but don't hold your nose an inch above the wine glass. Tip the glass and really get your nose in it. Take a deep breath with your mouth closed and then open your mouth to exhale. You've now gotten the wine's beautiful aromatics through your nasal passage, against the back of your throat, out over your tongue, and hit so many taste receptors along the way. Time to taste and swish. Now, the swish can be a bit annoying for casual drinking, but we encourage just one go at it when tasting a newly opened bottle to ensure it tastes okay. Take a medium-size sip of your wine and either swish it around like mouthwash, or purse your lips and draw in a small amount of air to make a gurgling or slurping noise before swallowing. Either way you do it, the point is to make sure the wine touches every part of your mouth so you can really taste it. If you don't detect any flaws (read on for more about that), you've survived tasting your wine and you can now just drink it.

Common Faults

Since wine, at its simplest, is an agricultural product, and very much alive and constantly evolving, it's no surprise that any number of faults could be present in a bottle. Some of the common flaws that you could possibly find in your wine, such as reduction, can be easy to ignore and might "blow off," or disappear as the wine sits open. Others will have left their mark on the wine and, no matter what you do, will not improve. If you suspect your wine is flawed, take it back and ask your wine shop to exchange it for another bottle. Please don't use it for cooking, which will only concentrate the off flavors you're detecting.

Why Does This Wine Smell like Wet Dog?
Corked (trichloroanisole, or TCA) wines are a result of a tainted cork that leeches musty basement and wet dog flavors into the wine. Smelling the cork is one way to check for TCA; however, some corks smell corked even though the wine is actually perfectly fine, so be sure to taste to confirm. Corked wines cannot be recovered.

Why Does This Wine Smell like Nail Polish Remover?
Ethyl acetate (EA) is a reaction between the naturally occurring acetic acid and ethyl alcohol that is created during fermentation, and it is very hard to get rid of once a wine is bottled. There's not much that can be done to save a bottle with EA.

Why Does This Wine Smell like Vinegar?
Volatile acidity (VA) is caused by bacteria in the wine that creates acetic acid, which is the same acid that gives vinegar its aroma and tangy flavor. Small amounts of VA are okay, and even add an interesting component to a wine when not overpowering.

Why Does This Wine Smell like Rotten Eggs?
Reduction is a hydrogen-sulfur compound and can occur when a wine isn't exposed to enough oxygen in a closed container, be it a tank, barrel, or bottle. In small amounts, time in a decanter will allow some reduction compounds to dissipate. In large amounts, they're likely there to stay. It doesn't necessarily render a wine undrinkable; you just have to decide how much rotten-egg taste you can handle.

Why Does This Wine Smell like a Barnyard?
Brettanomyces, or Brett, as it's commonly called, is a microbial fault that, like reduction, can be tolerated in small doses by most people. Once it lives in a winery, Brett is very hard to get rid of and causes a range of flavors from pigpen to horse manure to Band-Aid.

Why Does This Wine Look Brown?
Oxidation is the process by which a wine is exposed to too much air before or after bottling, and the wine changes color, loses its vibrancy, and starts to taste flat. Red wines will appear to have lost their lustrous color and white wines will start browning. These wines are past the point of no return. It's good to note that some styles of wine, such as oloroso sherry and marsala, take well to oxidation and are purposely exposed to air.

Why Does this Wine Taste like Salami/a Mouse Cage/Corn Chips?

Mousiness is a flaw that people perceive in many different ways. Dana refers to it as "salami mouth," but others taste a distinct corn chip or mouse-cage flavor. Mousiness is a lactic microbial flaw that is nearly impossible to detect by nose, but is obvious on the palate. It's not a totally understood fault, and there is plenty of debate about whether it can go away once it's in a wine. It's most commonly detected in natural wines made without sulfur, and may not be recognizable until a wine has been in contact with air for a few hours.

Why Is This Still Wine Fizzy?

Re-fermentation can occur when a wine is accidentally bottled with just the tiniest bit of sugar and it starts to ferment all over again. These bottles will have a fizzy texture to them, and will bubble around the edge of a wine glass. Of note are wines that are bottled with a touch of carbon dioxide as an alternative preservative to sulfur. Such wines might have the slightest prickle that quickly disappears, and no bubbling in the bottle or glass. That trapped CO_2 generally goes away once the wine sits in the glass for a few minutes.

Why Does This Wine Smell like Dried Fruit?

A "cooked" (heat-damaged) wine has been exposed to temperatures above 75°F for a prolonged time, and gives off notes of dried and stewed fruits. The wine will taste flat, devoid of acid, and like someone laced it with brown sugar. You may be able to spot a heat-damaged wine if you notice that the foil cap is stuck in place or the cork has started to push out of the bottle. Some cooked wines experience seepage through the cork, but leaking wine isn't always a result of heat damage.

Prefunk

Cava

JAMÓN AND PEAS

Makes 4 to 6 servings

Producers to Look For

Recaredo
Suriol
Via de la Plata
Vinyes Singulars

Cava is Spain's claim to fame in the world of sparkling wine. It's made predominantly in the northwestern region of Catalonia, although there are delicious bottlings that come from other parts of the country as well. Generally composed of the grapes macabeo (ma-ca-BAY-o), parellada (par-AY-yah-da), and xarel-lo (sha-REH-lo), cava is just as bubbly as Champagne, and can age incredibly well, but costs a fraction of its French counterpart. In fact, the wines are made in the same way: the second fermentation—the one that makes the wine sparkling—takes place in the bottle. Just as for Champagne, very specific laws dictate how long the cava must age on the lees, those spent yeast cells that hang out in a wine, adding all kinds of interesting flavors, such as baking bread, nuts, and dry hay. The basic wines simply labeled *cava* spend at least nine months on the lees. They are easy drinking with citrus and nutty flavors. Reserva cava must be aged a minimum of fifteen months on the lees, which compares roughly to nonvintage Champagne, and offers a little more texture and developed flavors than the basic. And at the top end, comparable to a vintage Champagne, is Gran Reserva cava, which needs at least thirty months on the lees to be labeled as such. They're a splurge, but worth it for their bready, yeasty aromatics and long, complex finish. While you're more than welcome to buy a really cheap cava and mix it with orange juice for Sunday morning mimosas, we'd point you toward a bottle that's a few dollars more, but wonderful on its own. You don't have to drop the money for a Gran Reserva bottle (although you really should sometime) to drink great cava.

Cava and ham, specifically Spanish *jamón*, are very good friends. Jamón has an inherent nuttiness, along with being ever-so-slightly gamey. It's also fatty and salty, and when you combine these characteristics, you have something that was always meant to be enjoyed with bubbly wine. Cava is also a fantastic wine to enjoy with sweet green vegetables, such as fresh peas. This is a winning combination of umami-rich Spanish cheese, fresh mint, and a hint of lemon, all smashed together with barely cooked spring peas. Mound the mash alongside a pile of shaved jamón and some toasted hazelnuts and you've got a beautiful snack or light lunch.

2 pounds fresh English peas, shelled, or 2 cups frozen peas (no need to defrost)

½ cup shaved hard Spanish cheese, such as Zamorano, Garrotxa, or aged Manchego, plus more for garnish

2 tablespoons extra-virgin olive oil, plus more for drizzling

1 tablespoon chopped fresh mint, plus torn leaves for garnish

1 teaspoon grated lemon zest

Kosher salt

Freshly ground black pepper

2 tablespoons fresh lemon juice

⅓ pound thinly sliced dry-cured Spanish ham, such as Serrano or Ibérico

½ cup toasted hazelnuts (see Note)

Grilled bread, for serving

Bring a large pot of salted water to a boil. Add the peas and cook until tender but still bright green, 1 to 3 minutes. Drain, then rinse briefly under cold water, just to stop the cooking. While the peas are still slightly warm, put all but ¼ cup of them in a mortar and add the cheese, oil, mint, lemon zest, a couple big pinches of salt, and several grinds of pepper. Pound them with a pestle to a very coarse but spreadable mash. Stir in the lemon juice, taste, and adjust the seasoning. (The pea spread can also be made in a food processor, but the texture won't be as silky and the flavors will be less intense.)

Spoon the pea spread onto one side of a large platter or serving bowl and spread it in a freeform circle that's about ¾ inch thick. Top the spread with the reserved whole peas, more cheese, torn mint leaves, and freshly ground pepper. Drizzle with oil. Loosely fold the ham slices on the other half of the platter and scatter the hazelnuts over and around them. Serve with grilled bread.

The pea spread will keep, covered, in the refrigerator for up to 1 day. Assemble and add the garnishes just before serving.

Note
To toast the nuts, preheat the oven to 350°F. Spread the nuts on a baking sheet and roast in the oven until golden brown and aromatic, 8 to 12 minutes. Set aside to cool.

Blanc de Blancs Champagne

GOLDEN EGGS

Makes 8 servings (16 egg halves)

Producers to Look For

Jacques Lassaigne
Larmandier-Bernier
Pascal Doquet
Pierre Moncuit
Ulysse Collin

Champagne is the ultimate wine indulgence. Labor-intensive and needy, Champagne takes her sweet time to get from the vineyard to your glass, and she comes with a price tag to reflect all that work. Champagne is based primarily on pinot noir, pinot meunier (MOO-ñay), and chardonnay grapes all grown in Champagne, France. They have to first be made into a still wine, then bottled with a bit of sugar and yeast to ferment a second time under a crown cap. During this second fermentation, the yeast eats the sugar and creates fantastic tiny bubbles that are trapped in the bottle. Once the wine finishes fermenting, it spends a year to three or more on the retired yeast in the bottle, picking up flavor and texture. After that, any sediment is expelled and the wine gets topped off. The winemaker decides how much sugar to add in the topping wine: no sugar for brut nature–style wines, small amounts of sugar for extra-brut and brut, and more sugar for extra-dry, dry, demi-sec, and doux. The bottle is closed with a cork and metal cage and the wine is left to age for anywhere from a few weeks to a few years. Only then is it ready to drink . . . nearly two years after the grapes were picked and fermented not once, but twice. Worth every penny.

Since you'll be splurging on Champagne, you might as well pick up a jar of caviar, too. Then elevate everyday hard-cooked eggs to party status with a golden beet turmeric brine and top with a dollop of crème fraîche and the decadent caviar. These eggs are a sexy snack meant for a serious bottle of bubbles. We recommend a chardonnay-based Champagne that packs a chalky, bright punch to balance the rich texture of the eggs and the saltiness of the caviar. If you really want to go for it, choose osetra caviar, but don't be afraid to use the more affordable sturgeon caviar, or even salmon roe for a colorful bite.

8 extra-large eggs, at room temperature
4 sprigs dill, plus torn dill fronds, for garnish
1 golden beet, trimmed, peeled, halved
    lengthwise, and thinly sliced into
    half-moons
¾ cup Champagne vinegar
1 tablespoon honey
1 tablespoon kosher salt

2 teaspoons dill seeds
1 teaspoon ground turmeric
½ teaspoon black peppercorns
2 cups water
2 tablespoons plus 2 teaspoons
    crème fraîche
1 ounce caviar or salmon roe
Coarse sea salt, for garnish

Fill a bowl with ice water. Bring a medium pot of water to a boil over high heat. Decrease the heat to maintain a gentle simmer and slowly lower the eggs into the water using a slotted spoon. Cook for 8 minutes, then remove the eggs with the slotted spoon and plunge them into the cold water to stop the cooking.

To peel, gently tap and roll the eggs against the countertop, making tiny cracks all over like a mosaic. Peel the eggs under cool water, beginning at the thickest end. Put the eggs in a tall, heatproof container that will be large enough to hold them plus the pickling brine, such as a 1-quart canning jar. Nestle in the dill sprigs around the edges of the container.

In a small saucepan, combine the beet slices, vinegar, honey, kosher salt, dill seeds, turmeric, peppercorns, and water and bring to a boil over medium-high heat, stirring occasionally. Decrease the heat to maintain a low simmer, cover, and cook until the beet slices are tender, about 15 minutes.

Pour the hot brine, beet slices and all, into the jar over the eggs and push the eggs down to submerge. Cool to room temperature, then cover and refrigerate for 6 to 8 hours for the eggs to absorb the color and flavor. (Don't leave them in the brine much longer than 8 hours, because the egg whites become rubbery if they're pickled too long. Out of the brine, the eggs will keep in a covered container in the refrigerator for 3 days.)

Cut the eggs in half lengthwise and arrange them on a platter. Top each with ½ teaspoon of the crème fraîche, slightly off-center of the yolk, followed by a small spoonful of caviar. Sprinkle with a pinch of coarse salt and a few torn dill fronds and serve.

Muscadet

OYSTER BAR, FOR A SHUCKING GOOD TIME

Makes 6 to 8 servings

Muscadet is the classic pairing for oysters. Made from the melon de bourgogne grape, Muscadet is replete with mineral and saline notes, so it makes sense that it partners with briny bivalves. Until recently, most Muscadet wines were made without malolactic fermentation, or "malo," the second fermentation that many wines go through, in which harsh malic acids are converted to softer lactic acids. The lack of malo kept Muscadet bright, zippy, and full of acidity. But we've found that some of the best Muscadet for our oyster bar are the newer bottlings that undergo malo. The wines have just a touch of richness and body to them, and the typical sharp acid is toned down a tiny bit. Here, we recommend producers of both styles.

If fresh oysters intimidate you, let this oyster bar wash you of your fear once and for all. (Some shops even sell them pre-shucked now.) You needn't save oysters for a special occasion at a restaurant. You can shuck an oyster without stabbing your hand and racing to the emergency room. Oysters used to be the food of the working class, and were only elevated to "fancy" at the beginning of the twentieth century. And, last, what's intimidating about standing around in your kitchen, slurping oysters and drinking wine with your friends? Think of this as party food—the precursor to sitting down to a delicious dinner.

Since this is party food, set yourself up for success: invest in two oyster-shucking knives—they're inexpensive. The granita can be made at up to a month in advance, the mignonette three days ahead, and the relish a few hours before people arrive. And when they show up, give a shucking tutorial, enlist your friends to help, keep everybody's glasses full of Muscadet, and never be afraid to eat oysters at home again.

Cucumber-Grapefruit Granita

½ large (about 6 ounces) cucumber, peeled, seeded, and very coarsely chopped
Juice of 1 ruby red grapefruit, strained
¼ cup dry white wine, preferably Muscadet
1 tablespoon sugar

Ginger Mignonette

2 teaspoons minced ginger
2 teaspoons minced shallot
3 tablespoons rice vinegar
¾ teaspoon fish sauce

Fennel-Apple Relish

1 small fennel bulb
1 small tart green apple
1½ to 2 tablespoons fresh lemon juice
1 teaspoon coarsely crushed pink peppercorns
Sea salt

Freshly grated horseradish
Small lemon wedges
Hot sauce of your choice
36 oysters

continued

To make the granita: Combine the cucumber, grapefruit juice, wine, and sugar in a blender and blend until smooth and frothy. Pour the mixture into a shallow baking dish or pie plate and place it in the freezer. When it just begins to freeze, after about 30 minutes, give it a stir. Return the pan to the freezer. Continue stirring every 30 minutes or so, creating a slushy texture as it freezes. Once frozen, use a fork to rake the mixture to get a fluffy, icy granita. Cover tightly with plastic wrap and keep in the freezer until ready to serve, or for up to 1 month.

To make the mignonette: In a small bowl, stir the ginger, shallot, vinegar, and fish sauce. Cover and refrigerate until ready to serve, or for up to 3 days.

To make the relish: Trim the fennel bulb and cut it into ⅛-inch cubes. Core the apple, leaving the skin on, and cut it into ⅛-inch cubes. In a medium bowl, gently stir the fennel, apple, 1½ table-spoons of the lemon juice, the pink peppercorns, and a nice pinch of salt. Taste and adjust the seasoning, add-ing more lemon juice or salt as needed. Cover and refrigerate until ready to serve, or for up to 4 hours.

Transfer the granita, mignonette, and relish to small serving bowls or rame-kins, along with grated horseradish and lemon wedges. Have the hot sauce on hand. Prepare a large serving plat-ter of ice. Shuck the oysters, arranging them on the ice as you go, and serve immediately.

Note

To shuck oysters, lay the oyster on a kitchen towel with the flatter part facing up. Fold the towel over the oyster with the hinge exposed. Holding the oyster securely, use an oyster knife to find the notch in the hinge between the top and bottom shells. Apply moderate pressure to insert the tip of the knife through the notch, angling it slightly downward to avoid stabbing the meat. Twist the knife until the shell pops open. Run the knife around the edge of the upper shell to release it. Once open, run the knife under the oyster and flip it over in the shell, taking care not to pour out the juices. Carefully wipe away any shell fragments and grit. Slurp, sip, repeat.

Vermentino

SHRIMP AGUACHILE

Makes 4 to 6 servings

Producers to Look For

Bisson
Cardedu
Clos Marfisi
Domaine de Majas
Ryme Cellars
Terenzuola

Vermentino grows along the coastlines of Italy, but also has a home in Southern France, where it's called *rolle*. The Italian versions are found in Liguria, on the Tuscan coast, and in Sardinia, and they tend to be refreshing, lighter-bodied wines with a lush fruitiness and touch of salinity. When grown in Tuscany, vermentino takes on more richness than in other parts of Italy, but retains its freshness all the same. In France, rolle is grown widely in Provence, as well as the Languedoc-Roussillon, bottled on its own, or sometimes blended into rosé. Vermentino is the yin to our aguachile's yang, bringing a mouthwatering saltiness and bold herbaceousness to the citrus-and-coconut-bathed shrimp.

If you've had ceviche, you've basically had aguachile. The idea is the same: raw shrimp or chunks of fish are quickly "cooked" in a citrus marinade. The difference is that there's spicy chile water mixed with the citrus in aguachile. One of Dana's favorite versions comes from Mexico, where she vacations with her family every year, and that's what inspired this recipe. Joe Jack's Fish Shack, right in the heart of Puerto Vallarta's old town, serves an aguachile with gorgeous, plump white shrimp and curls of fresh coconut swimming in chile-laced lime juice. It's served with perfectly fried, extra-salty chips. This recipe takes those shrimp and tosses in some juicy mango, crunchy jicama, and avocado. Because you'll be drinking vermentino with this aguachile, we've dialed back the jalapeño so that the heat doesn't fight with the acidity in the wine. You can always add more if you prefer it spicier. It's imperative that you buy the freshest shrimp possible since you'll be eating them just one step away from raw.

1 pound medium shrimp, peeled, deveined, and quartered

Sea salt

Vegetable oil, for frying

16 (3-inch) corn tortillas (sometimes labeled "street tacos" or "taqueria-style")

⅓ cup fresh lime juice

3 tablespoons coconut water

1 large jalapeño chile, seeded and coarsely chopped

⅓ cup diced jicama

⅓ cup diced avocado

⅓ cup diced mango

⅓ cup chopped cilantro, plus torn cilantro leaves, for garnish

continued

One to two hours before serving, put the shrimp in a medium bowl and season them with 1 teaspoon salt. Cover and refrigerate.

Just before serving, fill a large skillet with about ½ inch of oil and place it over medium heat. Line a large baking sheet with paper towels and set it near the stove. The oil is ready for frying when a small piece of tortilla dropped in sizzles rapidly on contact. At that point, slide in 3 or 4 tortillas, or as many as will fit in the pan with a little overlap, and fry until very crisp and golden brown, turning to cook on both sides, about 2 minutes. Transfer the tostadas to the prepared baking sheet and immediately sprinkle them with salt. Repeat until all of the tortillas are fried.

Blitz the lime juice, coconut water, jalapeño, and ¼ teaspoon salt in a blender until the chile is completely pulverized. Add the chile water to the bowl of salted shrimp, along with the jicama, avocado, mango, and cilantro. Let sit for 2 to 4 minutes, until the shrimp turns opaque and is just barely "cooked." Taste and adjust the seasoning.

Transfer the aguachile to a serving bowl and garnish with cilantro leaves. Break each tostada into 3 or 4 jagged pieces and serve immediately.

Albariño

DIPS AND STICKS

Makes 6 to 8 servings

Producers to Look For

Bodegas Albamar
Bodegas Corisca
La Clarine Farm
Nanclares y Prieto

Some wines are quietly impressive. They don't leap out of the glass giving you everything they've got right away. They hang around, being really delicious in a shy kind of way. They're like the talented wallflower at the school dance, standing by the punch table, watching everyone else until the moment strikes them and they take center stage. Albariño is one such wallflower. Hailing from Northwestern Spain's Rías Baixas region, great albariño is a little demure on the nose, not flowery or fruity or overtly aromatic, instead showing mineral and citrus. Truly delicious albariño has a bit of weight to it—it's not always meant to be an easy quaffer, but instead a touch more serious, and that's what's so charming about it. Buried in albariño is a genuine expressiveness that's a bit saline and savory and a touch lemony. Avoid versions that are described as oaky (a real bummer) or highly aromatic (a result of commercial yeast). There's a lot of tropical tutti-frutti–tasting albariño out there. Definitely skip those.

We love having snacks waiting for guests when they come over for dinner. They're a great icebreaker, and everyone can stand around with a glass of wine and something to nibble on while you finish cooking. No one feels hungry, and it takes the pressure off. With very little effort, you can take your snack tray from hummus and carrot sticks or chips and salsa to an all-out dip extravaganza of paprika-laced chorizo butter, creamy tuna mayo, and tangy pistachio yogurt. These are three super-easy recipes that can be buzzed up in a food processor, one after another, and chilled until about an hour before your guests arrive. Chop up whichever crunchy vegetables you have on hand, or choose from what's in season at the farmers' market to make your sticks.

Whipped Chorizo Butter

6 ounces dry-cured Spanish chorizo, skin removed and discarded, meat coarsely chopped

¼ cup cold unsalted butter, cubed

¼ cup water

2 tablespoons sherry vinegar, or to taste

½ teaspoon kosher salt, or to taste

½ teaspoon freshly ground black pepper, or to taste

¼ teaspoon smoked Spanish paprika, or to taste

Tonnato Dip

2 (4-ounce) cans tuna in oil, drained

¼ cup mayonnaise

¼ teaspoon kosher salt, or to taste

¼ cup extra-virgin olive oil

4 teaspoons fresh lemon juice, or to taste

Pistachio-Yogurt Dip

1 cup unsalted shelled pistachios

⅓ cup water

1 teaspoon kosher salt, or to taste

⅓ cup plain Greek yogurt

2 tablespoons fresh lemon juice, or to taste

Dipping Sticks

French breakfast radishes, leaves intact if they are fresh, bulbs halved or quartered lengthwise

Baby carrots, tops trimmed with 1 inch of stem intact

Broccolini, trimmed and steamed for about 5 minutes, until tender-crisp

Belgian endive spears

Asparagus spears, trimmed and steamed for 3 to 5 minutes, until tender-crisp

Fennel bulb, cut lengthwise into batons

Snap peas

Grissini (Italian crispy, thin breadsticks)

To make the Whipped Chorizo Butter: Put all the ingredients in a food processor and buzz until blended and relatively smooth, like a pâté, scraping down the sides as needed. Taste and add more vinegar, salt, pepper, or paprika, as needed. Transfer the dip to a small bowl or jar, cover, and refrigerate for up to 1 week. Bring to room temperature about 1 hour before serving.

To make the Tonnato Dip: Put the tuna, mayonnaise, and salt in a food processor and buzz until smooth. With the processor running, drizzle in the oil and lemon juice and continue processing until creamy smooth, scraping down the sides as needed. Taste and add more lemon juice or salt as needed. Transfer the dip to a small bowl or jar, cover, and refrigerate for up to 3 days. Bring to room temperature about 1 hour before serving.

To make the Pistachio-Yogurt Dip: Put the pistachios in a food processor and buzz until very finely chopped and almost pasty. With the processor running, drizzle in the water, add the salt, and continue processing until creamy, scraping the sides and bottom as needed. Add the yogurt and lemon juice and process to combine. Taste and add more lemon juice or salt as needed. Transfer the dip to a small bowl or jar, cover, and refrigerate for up to 3 days. Bring to room temperature about 1 hour before serving.

To serve, put the dips on a large platter and arrange the dipping sticks around them in a bountiful, colorful presentation.

Store the assembled platter, covered, in the refrigerator for up to 1 day.

Chablis

CAST-IRON SKILLET MUSSELS WITH PANCETTA-CHIVE BUTTER

Makes 4 servings

How do we properly extol the delicious virtues of Chablis? Grown on limestone-rich Kimmeridgian soils in the northernmost part of Burgundy, we'd argue that Chablis is chardonnay at its finest. The region itself is closer in proximity to Southern Champagne than the rest of Burgundy, and you might be able to tell by the flinty, minerally notes that are hallmarks of both Champagne and good Chablis. Some producers use oak barrels, while others abstain, relying on stainless steel for fermentation and aging. Either way, we suggest a wine that flaunts its pretty fruitiness and lip-smacking acidity—your mussels will love it.

We love slurping steaming hot mussels in their shells and sopping up their buttery, briny sauce right out of the pan they were cooked in. No utensils needed, just some napkins and glasses full of Chablis. A prefunk doesn't get more hands-on than that. This recipe is ideal, whether your table is on the back patio next to the grill or in the kitchen near the oven. It's just as appropriate to serve as a party starter, or with a simple salad for a weeknight dinner. Don't be afraid to change up your compound butter. No pancetta? Use bacon. Like your mussels more herby? Add fresh thyme or dill. And there will be enough butter to make two rounds of the mussels, so if you'd like to feed more than four, pick up a couple more pounds of mussels and cook them in batches.

½ cup unsalted butter, at room temperature
6 ounces pancetta, cut into ¼-inch dice
1 large shallot, minced
3 large cloves garlic, minced
⅓ cup minced fresh chives

1 lemon, zest finely grated
Freshly ground black pepper
Sea salt
2 pounds mussels, debearded, scrubbed, and drained well
Grilled or toasted bread, for serving

Melt 1 tablespoon of the butter in a large skillet over medium heat. Add the pancetta and cook until it's browned and crispy on the outside but still a little meaty within, 5 to 10 minutes. Pour the pan's contents through a fine-mesh strainer set over a bowl. Set the pancetta aside to cool. Add about 2 tablespoons of the rendered fat back to the pan and return it to medium heat. Add the shallot and garlic and cook until fragrant and just softened, 1 to 2 minutes, then transfer them to a medium bowl. Add the remaining 7 tablespoons butter and the chives, lemon zest, and several grinds of pepper to the bowl. Mince the pancetta quite finely—like the size of bacon bits—and add that to the bowl too. Mix and mash with a fork until the butter is uniformly flecked with the other ingredients. Taste and add salt, as needed. If the butter is too warm to hold shape at this point, set it in the refrigerator for a few minutes to harden slightly, removing it while it is still pliable.

Spoon the butter down the center of a sheet of parchment paper and shape and roll it into a cylinder about 6 inches long. Twist the parchment paper at the ends to seal. Refrigerate until firm, at least 1 hour and up to 3 days before using. (The butter can be wrapped tightly in plastic wrap and frozen for up to 3 months.)

Preheat the oven, or a covered gas or charcoal grill, to 500°F with a 12-inch cast-iron skillet inside. Once preheated, add the mussels to the hot skillet in an even layer. Roast or grill, with the cover closed, until the mussels are open, about 5 minutes, shaking the pan once about halfway through.

Meanwhile, cut the lemon in half and char the halves, cut-side down, on either the grill grate or the stove top, in a heavy skillet set over medium-high heat, until deeply browned, 2 to 3 minutes.

When the mussels are open, remove the pan and add about half of the butter, dotting slices of it around the pan. Toss and stir as the butter melts into the mussels, creating a brothy sauce in the bottom of the pan. Squeeze the charred lemon over the top and serve piping hot with the bread for sopping up the sauce.

Provençal Rosé

ROASTED SHALLOT PISSALADIÈRE

Makes 12 servings

Producers to Look For

Chateau Peyrassol
Domaine de Sulauze
Domaine de Terrebrune
Domaine du Bagnol
Domaine Hauvette

Provence hugs the southeastern coastline of France, and includes the well-known cities of Marseilles, Nice, and Saint-Tropez. Well over half of the wine made there is rosé, and a lot of it is from large producers who put quantity over quality. If you look beyond the big guys, this is one of the best places in the world for pink wines. Grapes such as cinsault (SAHN-so), grenache, and mourvèdre (mohr-VED-dra) dominate the region, but outliers, like tibouren (TEE-boh-rahn), are worth seeking out. They're bottled in the spring and we start seeing them on the shelf by early summer.

Sometimes you just can't mess with a classic. But here, we did. Pissaladière, the onion tart studded with anchovies and olives and synonymous with Provençal cuisine, is one of our favorite dishes of all time, but we wanted to shake it up just a bit. We swapped the traditional sweetly stewed onions for slow-roasted shallots, and Niçoise olives for their intense oil-cured cousins. Rosé from Provence, with its signature sea salt and fresh-red-fruit aromatics, is exactly what we want to drink with meaty little anchovies, briny olives, and a shatteringly crisp crust.

2 pounds shallots, peeled
¼ cup extra-virgin olive oil, plus more for drizzling
1½ tablespoons apple cider vinegar
Kosher salt
Freshly ground black pepper
4 thyme sprigs
1 (17.3-ounce) box puff pastry dough, thawed according to package directions
12 oil-packed anchovy fillets
12 oil-cured olives, torn in half and pitted

Preheat the oven to 450°F with a rack positioned in the bottom third.

Cut the larger shallots into wedges, quarter the medium ones, and halve the small ones. Toss the shallots in a 9 by 13-inch baking dish with the oil, vinegar, 1 teaspoon salt, several grinds of pepper, and the thyme sprigs. Roast until very tender and lightly browned, stirring every 10 minutes, about 30 minutes. Discard the thyme sprigs.

Line a large rimmed baking sheet with parchment paper. Place the 2 square sheets of puff pastry on a clean countertop. Brush an edge of one of the squares with water and press an edge of the other one in. Essentially, you want to merge the two sheets into one. Trim off one of the sections of the pastry at the fold, and use a rolling pin to smooth out the seam and fold lines, so you have a 9½ by 15-inch rectangular sheet of pastry. Transfer the pastry to the prepared baking sheet and use a fork to poke holes all over it. Spread the shallots in an even layer over the pastry, leaving a ¾-inch crust. Arrange the anchovies and olives so that there will be 1 anchovy fillet and 2 olive halves on each slice when the pissaldière is cut into 12 squares. Generously drizzle the whole thing with oil.

Bake until the pastry edges are deep golden brown and the shallots have some caramelization on top, about 20 minutes. Cool and then cut it into 12 squares and serve.

Rosé of Pinot Noir

BURRATA WITH STRAWBERRY SALAD

Makes 4 servings

Producers to Look For

Analemma
Beckham Estate Vineyard
The Eyrie Vineyards
Gentle Folk
Scribe
Swick Wines

Oregon has an obsession with pinot noir. Its winemaking history began in 1966 when David Lett of the Eyrie Vineyards planted the first cuttings of pinot in Northwest Oregon's astonishingly fertile Willamette Valley. Over the next fifty-plus years, the growing region has come to include vineyards in the far southern reaches of the state, as well as up north along the Columbia River Gorge. Pinot noir is as much a part of Oregon as anything else that defines its people and landscape. And when the rosé craze came to a head in the United States in the mid-2000s, Oregonians happily jumped on board, producing pink wine from various grapes, from tempranillo to, of course, pinot noir. Interestingly, you won't find much rosé of pinot outside of the States. Sure, there's plenty in Champagne, and some in California and Australia, but Oregon has the market cornered with these fruity, blushy summertime wines. With a range of colors, from barely salmon to pale magenta, pink pinot noir begs for fresh food, dinner on the porch, and 9 PM sunsets.

And what's better to pair with a highly seasonal wine than equally seasonal fruit? Remember, we mentioned that the Willamette Valley is incredibly fertile. The growing season is long, for grapes, hazelnuts, flowers, and all types of produce. In good growing years, strawberries start appearing at the farmers' market in early June and can continue on until mid-September. Burrata is a Southern Italian specialty, a thick skin of mozzarella stretched around a creamy interior. It's rich and salty, and our favorite way to enjoy it is with a small salad like this one, with its juicy, deep-red strawberries, crisp celery hearts, and tarragon. Very ripe berries and rosé are an age-old pairing, and not only do we love the match of color between wine and berries, but also the nearly perfect complement of flavors.

½ cup sliced strawberries

¼ cup very thinly sliced celery hearts and leaves

2 tablespoons extra-virgin olive oil, plus more for drizzling

1 tablespoon white balsamic vinegar

2 sprigs tarragon, leaves picked

Flaky sea salt

Freshly ground black pepper

2 (4-ounce) balls burrata cheese

Grilled or toasted bread, for serving

In a small bowl, toss the strawberries, celery hearts and leaves, oil, vinegar, and tarragon leaves. Season with salt and pepper.

Place the burrata in a shallow serving bowl or on a plate and tear it open, loosely, to expose the creamy center. Sprinkle the top with salt and pepper and drizzle generously with oil. Spoon the salad to either side of the burrata and serve with the bread.

Amontillado Sherry

SHERRY-CHERRY CHICKEN LIVER TOAST

Makes 6 servings

Producers to Look For

Bodegas Alba Viticultores
El Maestro Sierra
Emilio Hildalgo
Valdespino

Amontillado is the style of sherry that has spent part of its life under *flor*, the magical yeast that's unique to Jerez, Spain. That flor gives sherry its nutty, yeasty aromatics but also protects the wine from oxidizing (see page 24). Unlike fino and manzanilla sherries that stay under flor—and therefore maintain their briny character—amontillado is only under flor until the yeast dies, while the rest of its aging is in a barrel for two to eight years, putting the focus on building complexity and oxidization. The end result? A much more complex, richer style of sherry that is dry and loaded with notes of toasted nuts, orange peels, sea salt, and warm spices. It's an especially exciting style of sherry because it achieves the balance of an aged wine with the deep flavors of the flor. Drink all of that with this chicken liver toast and you have yourself one helluva umami-spiked snack.

Sherry and liver is perhaps one of the most spot-on pairings in the wine world. And while we're certainly not the ones to invent it, we are the ones to shout about it from the rooftop. Old-school chopped chicken liver gets a new lease on life with sherry-soaked dried cherries and caramelized shallots. Everything gets roughly mashed together and piled on a slice of crispy country loaf, as the juices ooze into the bread while the crust holds its crunch. Here you have all of the savory, earthy flavors of liver with the almost exotic notes of the wine, paired up in a, dare we say, magical way.

½ cup dried cherries, coarsely chopped
⅓ cup amontillado sherry
1 pound chicken livers, lobes separated and trimmed of connective tissue
5 tablespoons extra-virgin olive oil, plus more for drizzling
Kosher salt

Freshly ground black pepper
2 medium shallots, minced
¼ cup chopped fresh flat-leaf parsley
6 (¾-inch-thick) slices country bread, such as levain or whole grain
1 clove garlic, halved

In a small bowl, soak the cherries in the sherry until plump, about 10 minutes.

Rinse the livers and pat them dry. Heat 3 tablespoons of the oil in a 10-inch skillet over medium-high heat. Cook the livers in two batches until firm but still pink inside, turning once, 3 to 5 minutes. (Overcooked livers are dry and have a chalky texture, so don't let them cook too long.) Transfer the livers to a cutting board, leaving the drippings in the pan off the heat. Coarsely chop the livers to get some larger chunks (about ½ inch) and some smaller crumbly bits. Place the chopped livers in a medium bowl and season with a big pinch of salt and several grinds of pepper while still hot. Toss and gently mash some of the mixture briefly, so that it is kind of bound, like a really chunky paste. Set aside.

Preheat the broiler.

Place the skillet back over medium-high heat, add the shallots, and cook them in the pan drippings until browned, about 4 minutes. Add the soaked cherries and excess sherry and deglaze the pan, scraping the bottom and sides for about 1 minute. Pour this into the bowl with the livers. Add the parsley and 1 tablespoon oil to the bowl and toss to combine. Taste and adjust the seasoning with more salt and pepper.

Meanwhile, drizzle the bread slices with the remaining 1 tablespoon oil and place them under the broiler, turning once, until deeply toasted and charred along the edges of both sides, about 5 minutes total. Rub the hot toasts with the cut sides of the garlic clove and top with the warm chicken liver mixture. Cut the toasts in half on a bias, if you like. Drizzle with more olive oil, finish with a few grinds of black pepper, and serve.

Store the chicken liver mixture, covered, in the refrigerator for up to 2 days. Bring to room temperature before serving.

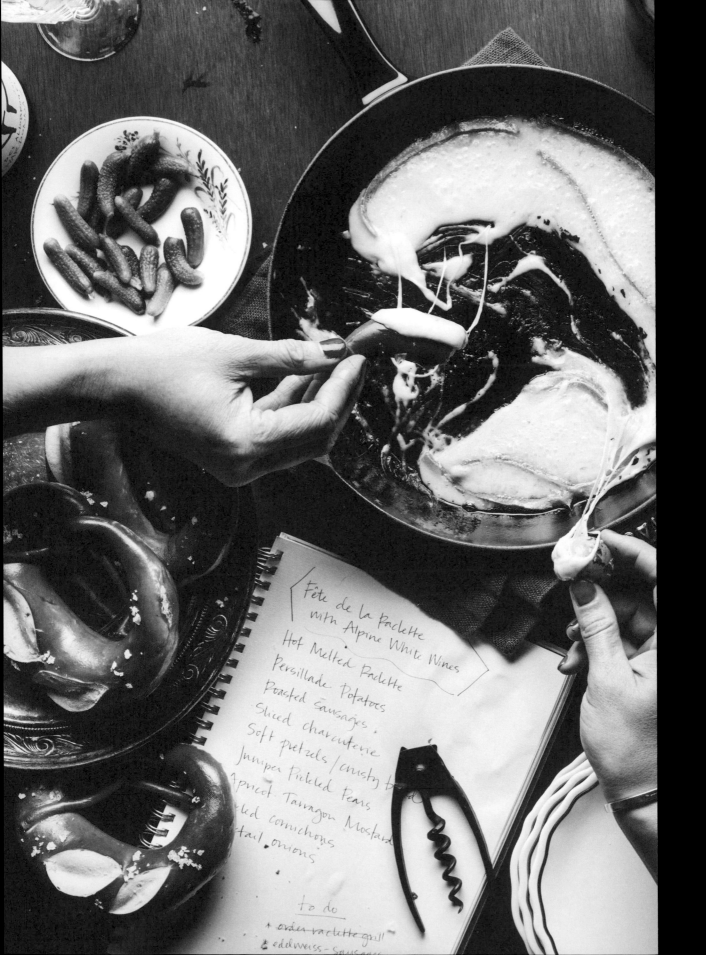

Fête de la Raclette
with Alpine White Wines

Hot Melted Raclette
Persillade Potatoes
Roasted Sausages
Sliced charcuterie
Soft pretzels / crusty bread
Juniper Pickled Pears
Apricot Tarragon Mustard
~~led~~ cornichons
~~tail~~ onions

to do
* order raclette grill
* edelweiss sausages

Alpine Whites

Producers to Look For

Cave Caloz	Foradori
Domaine Louis Magnin	Franco Noussan
Dominique Belluard	Les Vignes de Paradis
Ermes Pavese	Manni Nössing

For most people, the word *alpine* evokes visions of magnificent snow-covered peaks, a chalet with a Bernese Mountain Dog out front, fur-trimmed coats, and après-ski cocktails. For us, alpine means wine. Crisp white wines that immediately transport us to where the spring waters are icy cold and crystal clear, and the vines share space with abundant wildflowers. There are a wide variety of white wines from the alpine regions of France's Savoie, Switzerland's Valais, and Italy's Valle d'Aosta, Trentino, and Alto Adige, and nearly all of them will be the quintessential pairing for your cheese-filled fête. Task your guests with a wine treasure hunt—they should look for grapes such as petite arvine, altesse (all-TESS), gringet (GRAHN-jzay), chasselas (SHAH-se-la), nosiola (no-zee-OH-la), kerner, and prié blanc, all wines rich with stony minerality and vibrant fruity notes reminiscent of Meyer lemons and baked apples, apricots, and yellow plums. While they won't be the most common white wines on the shelf, they're definitely worth seeking out. Keep in mind that Swiss wines, although relatively unknown outside of Europe and the most expensive of the bunch (as is life in Switzerland), are unbelievably delicious and not to be missed.

The fondue trend may have gone with the eighties, but thankfully the hot melted cheese party isn't over. We consider raclette to be the fondue of our generation. For very little money, you can purchase or rent a raclette grill, or for no money you can use a hot skillet and your oven to get to melted cheese nirvana. Raclette, like Gruyère and Comté, is a slightly stinky alpine cheese with a smooth paste and great melting capabilities. Like all melted cheese–based meals, this one is best shared with a group of friends. Imagine a cold winter day with snow on the ground and your fireplace ablaze. Throw some pillows on the floor, with your cheese feast splayed out on the coffee table and the wines on ice nearby to keep the glasses filled.

The following menu reflects our favorite bites to smother, but feel free to go rogue using these guidelines, plus tips for serving:

1. Plan on 4 ounces of raclette cheese per person. If baking the raclette in an oven, melt the cheese in batches to keep it hot and fresh.

2. Always have an array of salty cured meats and smoked sausages on the table.

3. Fruits in various forms are a no-brainer, as they bring their sweetness to balance the tang. Consider pickled or dried fruits in addition to fresh.

4. Boiled new potatoes make this feel more like a meal than a giant snack.

5. Soft pretzels and hearty whole-grain breads are wonderful vessels for scooping up the cheese.

6. Scrape the hot melted cheese over the warm persillade potatoes, sausages, charcuterie, and soft pretzels and breads, with pickled pears, mostarda, cornichons, and cocktail onions served on the side.

FÊTE DE LA RACLETTE

Hot Melted Raclette
(page 52)

Persillade Potatoes
(page 52)

Juniper-Pickled Pears
(page 53)

Apricot-Tarragon Mostarda
(page 53)

Roasted Sausages

Sliced Charcuterie (landjager,
summer sausage, smoked ham,
and/or speck)

Soft Pretzels and Crusty Bread

Pickled Cornichons and Cocktail Onions

HOT MELTED RACLETTE

Makes 8 to 10 servings

2 to 2½ pounds raclette cheese, cut
    into ¼-inch-thick slices by your
    cheesemonger

If you have a tabletop raclette machine,
use it to let your friends each melt
slices of raclette in the little trays. If
not, preheat a cast-iron skillet (or two)
in the oven at 400°F.

When the oven and the skillet are preheated, remove the skillet and add
enough slices of the cheese to cover
the bottom in a single layer. Bake the
cheese until melted and bubbling around
the edges, 4 to 5 minutes. Repeat to
melt the remaining cheese in batches
after the first round is eaten.

PERSILLADE POTATOES

Makes 8 to 10 servings

3 pounds small German Butterball or
    Yukon gold potatoes
2 tablespoons plus 1 teaspoon kosher salt
2 tablespoons unsalted butter, at room
    temperature
1 cup loosely packed flat-leaf parsley leaves,
    finely chopped
3 large cloves garlic, finely minced

Put the potatoes in a large saucepan
and add enough cold water to cover
them by at least 2 inches. Season the
water with 2 tablespoons of the salt
and bring it to a boil over high heat.
Decrease the heat to maintain a gentle
simmer and cook until the potatoes
are tender when pierced with a fork,
15 to 20 minutes, depending on their
size. Drain the potatoes in a colander,
then return them to the pot. Immediately add the remaining 1 teaspoon
salt and the butter and toss gently to
melt the butter, coating the potatoes
thoroughly without mashing them.
Sprinkle the potatoes with the parsley
and garlic and toss again. Serve
immediately.

JUNIPER-PICKLED PEARS

Makes 8 to 10 servings (2 pints)

2 ripe or slightly underripe Bosc pears
1¼ cups apple cider vinegar
1 cup water
6 tablespoons honey
2 teaspoons kosher salt
2 teaspoons juniper berries
2 bay leaves

Halve and core the pears, then cut each one lengthwise into 12 spears. Pack the spears into 2 wide-mouth, pint-size canning jars. Combine the vinegar, water, honey, salt, juniper berries, and bay leaves in a medium saucepan and bring to a boil over medium-high heat, stirring until the honey and salt are dissolved. Boil for about 2 minutes. Pour the boiling-hot brine into the jars to completely cover the pears, about 1 cup per jar. Cover the jars with lids and set aside to allow the brine to slowly cool to room temperature as it pickles the pears, about 4 hours. When completely cooled, either use the pickled pears immediately, or refrigerate them for up to 1 month.

APRICOT-TARRAGON MOSTARDA

Makes 8 to 10 servings

½ cup packed finely chopped dried apricots
½ cup golden raisins, half left whole and
    half finely chopped
1 shallot, minced
½ cup dry white wine
½ cup water
3 tablespoons white wine vinegar
3 tablespoons yellow mustard seeds
1 tablespoon dry mustard
½ teaspoon kosher salt
1½ tablespoons finely chopped
    fresh tarragon

In a medium saucepan, combine the apricots, raisins, shallot, wine, water, vinegar, mustard seeds, dry mustard, and salt and bring to a boil over medium-high heat. Decrease the heat to maintain a gentle simmer, cover, and cook until the liquid is absorbed, the fruit is softened, and the mostarda is the texture of chunky compote, 15 to 20 minutes. Uncover and stir in half of the tarragon. Set aside to cool and allow the flavors to come together. Once cooled, stir in the remaining tarragon. (Add a splash of water if the mostarda has become too thick.) Set aside until ready to serve, or refrigerate for up to 2 days. Serve at room temperature.

Pairing Cheat Sheet
Wine and (Grilled) Cheese 101

SAUTERNES / STILTON

SANCERRE / AGED GOAT + FIG JAM

RIOJA / MANCHEGO + QUINCE PASTE

JURA CHARDONNAY / COMTÉ

ARNEIS / ROBIOLA

CHAMPAGNE / CAMEMBERT

NEBBIOLO / TALEGGIO

RED BURGUNDY / ÉPOISSES

SONOMA COAST CHARDONNAY / HUMBOLDT FOG

FINGER LAKES RIESLING / VERMONT CHEDDAR + APPLE BUTTER

IROULEGUY ROUGE / P'TIT BASQUE + CHERRY PRESERVES

SPÄTLESE RIESLING / LIMBURGER + RAW SWEET ONION

Brunch
with
Benefits

Moscato d'Asti

GRIDDLED ZUCCHINI BREAD WITH MOSCATO PEACHES AND CRÈME

Makes 6 to 8 servings

Producers to Look For

Cascina Barisel
G.D. Vajra
Marco Bianco
Vittorio Bera e Figli

Moscato d'Asti may very well be the wine of angels. It's lightly fizzy, low in alcohol, and an explosion of peachy notes on the nose. Many years ago it was known as Asti Spumante, and quickly gained a reputation for being a sweet dessert wine that was incorrectly lumped into the same category as Champagne. The two wines could not be more different: Champagne's elegance, fine bubbles, and varying levels of dryness make it a much, much more serious distant relative of Moscato d'Asti and her fruity sweetness. Moscato is a great choice for brunch because it's low octane. You can drink a few glasses and won't be tanked by 2 PM, and with the bubbles, acidity, and ripe fruitiness, your palate feels fresh.

Given its beautiful aromatics, Moscato d'Asti is a natural partner for peaches, nectarines, and apricots. This is a summery brunch dish, perfect for soft, yielding stone fruit, a bit of tangy crème fraîche, and warm-weather zucchini. Cinnamon and cardamom replace the baking spices commonly found in old-fashioned zucchini breads, and this one is loaded with as much zucchini as it can handle. We also use good olive oil, which adds its own layer of fruitiness. Bake the bread the day before you're planning to enjoy it, and the next morning the dish will be so simple to put together while sipping coffee in your robe.

Zucchini Bread

⅔ cup extra-virgin oil, plus more for greasing the pan
12 ounces zucchini, shredded (about 3 cups)
1⅔ cups sugar
4 large eggs
2 teaspoons pure vanilla extract
2 teaspoons baking soda
1 teaspoon baking powder
1 teaspoon kosher salt
1 teaspoon ground cinnamon
1 teaspoon ground cardamom
3 cups all-purpose flour

Moscato Peaches

1½ pounds peaches, or a mix of peaches, nectarines, and/or apricots
½ cup Moscato d'Asti
2 tablespoons sugar, plus more as needed

About ¼ cup unsalted butter
Crème fraîche, for serving

To make the Zucchini Bread: Preheat the oven to 325°F with a rack positioned in the lower third. Grease an 8 by 4-inch loaf pan with oil.

Whisk the oil, zucchini, sugar, eggs, vanilla, baking soda, baking powder, salt, cinnamon, and cardamom in a large bowl. Add the flour and stir just until combined. Pour the batter into the prepared pan.

continued

Bake until a toothpick inserted in the center comes out clean, about 1½ hours. Set the pan on a wire rack to cool for about 5 minutes, then run a knife along the edges of the bread and invert to unmold it. Return the bread to the rack to cool completely before slicing, 3 to 4 hours. After cooling, it can be wrapped tightly and stored at room temperature for up to 3 days, or refrigerated for up to 1 week.

To make the Moscato Peaches: Pit the peaches and cut them into thin wedges. Put them in a large bowl, pour in the Moscato, and sprinkle with the sugar. Toss to combine. Taste and add more sugar, if needed. Set the bowl aside until the peaches soften and give up some of their juices, at least 30 minutes and up to 8 hours.

Preheat the oven to 200°F. Line a large rimmed baking sheet with a wire rack and place it near the stove.

Trim the crust from each end of the zucchini bread. Cut the loaf into 8 slices, each about 1 inch thick. Heat a large cast-iron griddle pan or skillet over medium heat. Add 2 tablespoons of the butter and swirl it around to coat the griddle. Once melted, add as many slices of the zucchini bread as will fit comfortably in the pan. Cook, turning once, until both sides are nicely browned and crisp, 2 to 3 minutes per side. Decrease the heat if they seem to darken too quickly. Add another pat of butter if the griddle becomes dry after the first sides are cooked. Place the griddled slices on the prepared baking sheet and keep them warm in the oven while the rest are cooked. Repeat to cook the remaining slices, adding more butter to the pan as needed.

Serve one slice of hot griddled bread per person, each drizzled with crème fraîche and topped with a big spoonful of the peaches and Moscato syrup.

Crémant

BISCUITS AND MOREL GRAVY

Makes 8 servings

Producers to Look For

Celine & Laurent Tripoz
Domaine des Marnes Blanche
Domaine Philippe Tessier
Domaine Pierre Frick

Life doesn't always call for a bottle of wine on a Champagne budget. We believe that sparkling wine should be enjoyed all the time, not just for special occasions, so it's great that the world of bubbles is so vast, and you can spend as much (or as little) as you want. Crémant is found all over France, and is made in the same method as Champagne, which is to say that its second fermentation (the one that creates the bubbles) happens in the bottle. That's generally one very big indicator of a quality sparkling wine. Crémant's bubbles tend to be a little easier on the palate, and you'll find crémant made from a wide variety of grapes, such as chardonnay in Burgundy, chenin blanc in the Loire Valley, and pinot blanc in Alsace. Look for crémant from Limoux, Bordeaux, Die, and the Jura as well.

Our biscuits and gravy is a highbrow version of a lowbrow dish. Morels, which only appear for a short season each spring and fall, are wonderfully earthy with a delicate chew, and a great substitute for the typical crumbled sausage found in most breakfast gravies. We amped up our sauce with lots of fresh thyme and Creole seasoning for a touch of heat and found that a wide variety of crémants are fantastic with those flavors. The wine's bubbles help cut through the richness of the gravy while also making the biscuit taste more biscuity. And if you'd like a fried egg on top, we wouldn't talk you out of it.

Biscuits

4½ cups all-purpose flour, plus more
    for dusting
1 tablespoon plus 1 teaspoon baking powder
1 teaspoon baking soda
1 teaspoon kosher salt
1 teaspoon sugar
¼ cup minced fresh chives
1 cup cold unsalted butter, cubed
2 cups cold buttermilk, shaken
Heavy cream, for brushing

Gravy

1 pound morel mushrooms
6 tablespoons unsalted butter
⅓ cup all-purpose flour
1 quart whole milk
1 tablespoon Cajun-Creole seasoning blend
2 teaspoons kosher salt
2 tablespoons chopped fresh thyme

Sweet paprika, for garnish

To make the biscuits: Preheat the oven to 400°F. Line a rimmed baking sheet with parchment paper.

In a large bowl, whisk the flour, baking powder, baking soda, salt, and sugar together. Whisk in the chives. Add the butter cubes and toss to coat them in the flour mixture. Using your fingertips, rub the butter into the flour mixture, working quickly to avoid melting, until the butter is evenly distributed and the flour-coated bits are about the size of peas. Pour in the buttermilk and gently toss with a fork until moist clumps form. Turn the clumpy dough out onto a lightly floured work surface and gather it together. Very gently pat it into a round mass, about 1½ inches thick. It should still be clumpy and uneven

continued

and just barely hold together. For the most ethereal biscuits, take care not to overwork the dough; it's really just patted together, no kneading required. Cut biscuits from the dough using a 3-inch biscuit cutter, dipping it in flour between cuts to prevent sticking. Gather the scraps and gently pat them together to cut out as many biscuits as you can; you should be able to make 8 biscuits.

Arrange the biscuits on the prepared baking sheet, spacing them 1 inch apart, and brush the tops lightly with cream. Bake until the tops and bottoms are golden brown and crunchy, about 30 minutes. Extra biscuits will keep at room temperature for 1 day, or in a sealed container in the refrigerator for up to 3 days. To freeze, wrap the biscuits individually in plastic wrap and then freeze them together in a zip-top bag for up to 1 month.

To make the gravy: Put the morels in a colander and rinse them under cool running water, rubbing lightly to remove all the grit. Drain well. Slice the large ones crosswise into rings, but keep the smaller ones whole.

Melt 4 tablespoons of the butter in a large skillet over medium-high heat. When the foam subsides, add the mushrooms and cook until their liquid releases and mostly evaporates and the mushrooms are tender, 5 to 7 minutes.

Decrease the heat to medium and add the remaining 2 tablespoons butter, stirring to melt. Sprinkle in the flour and stir until it's completely dissolved into the mushrooms and butter, about 1 minute. Pour in 1 cup of the milk and cook, stirring, until it looks smooth and velvety with no visible lumps, about 1 minute. Add the remaining 3 cups milk, the Cajun-Creole seasoning, and salt and increase the heat to bring the mixture to a simmer. Decrease the heat to maintain a very gentle simmer and cook until the gravy is thickened to the consistency of a creamy soup, with no gritty raw flour taste, stirring often, about 10 minutes. (Keep in mind that the gravy will get much, much thicker on the plate, so keep it a bit thin in the pan.) Stir in the thyme and taste and adjust the seasoning.

To serve, split open the biscuits and spoon the gravy over the bottom halves. Set the tops over the gravy and sprinkle with the paprika to garnish.

Franciacorta

TORTA DI FRITTATA WITH SPRING MUSHROOMS AND STINGING NETTLES

Makes 6 servings

Producers to Look For

Arcari + Danesi
Cà del Vént
Elisabetta Abrami
1701 Franciacorta
SoloUva

Franciacorta might be one of the most delicious sparkling wines you've never drunk, although it's been produced in Northern Italy's Lombardy region since the sixteenth century. Franciacorta's recent history starts in the early sixties when an enthusiastic young cellar apprentice tried his hand at making a small lot of fizzy wine. His experiment was an instant success, with production growing massively in the following years. We can now thank Franciacorta for an annual production of nearly seven million bottles of delicious Italian bubbles for our drinking pleasure. Chardonnay reigns supreme in the region, composing the makeup of many of the wines, while some are blended with small percentages of pinot noir and pinot blanc.

While it's not necessarily a bargain compared to Champagne, you could really dazzle your friends by choosing the queen of Italian sparkling wine over the king of French bubbles for this brunchy gathering. Franciacorta's grapes grow in the ancient glacial flows of the ice age, packed with mineral-rich sand and silt. Think white fruits like peaches and pears, as well as toasted nuts, and fragrant cherry blossoms; perfect flavor companions for a morning of garlic-scented mushrooms and springtime nettles sandwiched into an impressive (and simple-to-make) frittata cake. We certainly don't want to talk anyone out of Champagne, ever, nor would we scoff at a bottle of inexpensive prosecco, but there's something to say about going off the beaten path of bubbles.

1 teaspoon kosher salt, plus more
    for seasoning
8 ounces stinging nettles, or stemmed
    and chopped kale leaves
2 tablespoons plus 2 teaspoons
    extra-virgin olive oil
8 ounces mixed spring mushrooms, such
    as chanterelle, hedgehog, matsutake,
    maitake, hen of the woods, or oyster,
    sliced or torn into bite-size pieces
Freshly ground black pepper
3 tablespoons minced green garlic,
    or 2 cloves garlic, minced
8 large eggs
¼ cup finely chopped fresh flat-leaf parsley
¼ cup finely grated Parmigiano-Reggiano
    cheese
6 ounces Fontina Val d'Aosta cheese,
    rind trimmed, grated

Preheat the oven to 375°F. Line a baking sheet with parchment paper and set aside.

Bring a large pot of water to a boil over high heat and season it generously with salt. Set a colander in the sink. Using tongs, add the nettles to the water (be careful, they do "sting" before they're cooked!) and cook until the leaves are wilted and the stalks are tender, 3 to 5 minutes. Skim any murky foam that rises to the top. Drain the nettles well in the colander, pressing with the back of a large spoon to squish out excess water. Transfer the nettles to a large cutting board, spreading them out to continue to dry as they cool. When cool enough

continued

to handle, trim away any thick, tough stalks. Coarsely chop the nettles and set aside.

Meanwhile, in an 8-inch nonstick skillet, heat 2 tablespoons of the oil over medium-high heat. Add the mushrooms, 1 teaspoon salt, and several grinds of pepper and cook until the mushrooms release their liquid and lightly brown, 8 to 10 minutes. Stir in the garlic and cook until it's aromatic and softened, about 1 minute more. Transfer the mushroom mixture to a bowl and set aside.

Wipe the skillet clean and set it over medium heat. Add ½ teaspoon oil and swirl to coat the bottom and sides of the pan. Beat 2 of the eggs in a medium bowl. Season with a pinch of salt and stir in 1 tablespoon of the parsley and 1 tablespoon of the Parmigiano-Reggiano cheese. Pour the egg mixture into the hot pan and quickly swirl to coat the bottom in an even layer. Cook until the eggs are set on the bottom but still a little undercooked on top, about 1 minute. Slide the frittata out of the pan and onto the center of the prepared baking sheet, with the undercooked side up.

Spread half of the chopped nettles over the frittata, all the way to the edges, and sprinkle with about one-third of the Fontina cheese.

Cook another 2-egg frittata in the same manner. Slide it out of the pan and on top of the first one, with the undercooked side up. Spread all of the mushrooms over the top of this one and sprinkle with half of the remaining Fontina cheese.

Cook another 2-egg frittata in the same manner as the first two. Slide it out of the pan and on top of the frittata stack, undercooked-side up. Spread the remaining nettles over the top and sprinkle with the remaining Fontina cheese.

Repeat to cook a final 2-egg frittata. Slide it out of the pan and on top of the frittata stack, undercooked-side up.

Bake the frittata cake until the cheese is melted and the eggs are just set, about 10 minutes. Allow it to cool for a few minutes, then carefully transfer it to a large round plate or cake stand. Serve warm or at room temperature, cut into large wedges.

Store, covered, in the refrigerator for up to 2 days. Bring to room temperature before serving.

Alsatian Pinot Blanc

TROPICAL YOGURT PARFAITS WITH SEEDY CASHEW CRUNCH

Makes 6 servings

Producers to Look For

Albert Mann
Domaine Léon Boesch
Domaine Ostertag
Laurent Barth
Meyer-Fonné

Not all pinot blancs are created equal, and styles can vary wildly from easy drinking (and kind of boring) to a bit more serious, with exotic aromatics and vibrant freshness. Although pinot blanc is not one of the four noble varieties in Alsace, France, it is widely planted and more of a simple, everyday wine in the region. It has fruity aromatics reminiscent of apricots, yellow plums, and a hint of smoke, and makes drinking midmorning a cinch with its not-too-zippy acidity. It's also a spot-on pairing for a yogurt parfait bursting with tropical fruit, drizzled with bold honey, and sprinkled with a seedy cashew crunch.

Since we really wanted to go tropical with our parfait, and decadent, because it's brunch, we mixed the yogurt with coconut cream for an extra hit of flavor. The crunch is a bit like a brittle, but healthy, using coconut oil and honey to bind the seedy bits. You can use an everyday honey for the brittle since it gets baked into the crunch, but we recommend using a good, aromatic honey for the yogurt and drizzling, as it will definitely complement the aromatics in the wine. Choose a colorful assortment of fruit to play off the white yogurt, and make sure you pick fruits that are ripe and juicy to balance the yogurt's tartness. And though we think this is just the dish to serve during a lazy weekend brunch, you could certainly have it as a dessert instead.

Seedy Cashew Crunch

¼ cup honey

2 teaspoons coconut oil

½ teaspoon sea salt

1½ cups raw cashews, coarsely chopped

¼ cup raw pumpkin seeds

¼ cup mixed seeds, such as sesame, chia, sunflower, and/or poppy

3 cups whole-milk plain Greek yogurt

¾ cup (one 6.8-ounce box) coconut cream (see Note)

2 tablespoons floral honey, such as wildflower or orange blossom, plus more for drizzling

3 cups mixed chopped or sliced tropical fruit, such as pineapple, mango, dragon fruit, papaya, star fruit, passion fruit, banana, guava, and/or kiwi

½ cup coconut flakes, toasted

To make the cashew crunch: Preheat the oven to 350°F. Line a rimmed baking sheet with parchment paper.

Combine the honey, coconut oil, and salt in a small saucepan and melt over medium heat. Remove from the heat and add the cashews, pumpkin seeds, and mixed seeds, stirring to coat well. Spread the sticky mixture in an even layer in the center of the prepared baking sheet. Bake until the cashews are peanut-butter brown, 20 to 25 minutes, stirring once about halfway through. Set aside on a wire rack until completely cooled and brittle, then break into small, bite-size clumps. (The crunch will keep for about 1 week in an airtight container at room temperature.)

In a large bowl, whisk the yogurt, coconut cream, and honey to combine. Scoop about ⅓ cup of the yogurt mixture into the bottom of 6 footed glass parfait dishes or small bowls. Top each with ⅓ cup of the mixed fruit, then another ⅓ cup of the yogurt mixture. Top with the remaining fruit, dividing it evenly. Sprinkle with the cashew crunch, followed by the toasted coconut flakes. Finish with a sassy drizzle of honey, and serve.

Note
Until recently you'd have to extract the thick layer of coconut cream that settles in a can of coconut milk, but now canned coconut cream is readily available at most Asian markets and even at general markets like Whole Foods and Trader Joe's.

Bugey-Cerdon

PRETZEL BAGELS AND LOX

Makes 8 servings

Producers to Look For

Domaine Balivet
Domaine de la Dentelle
Domaine Renardat-
Fâche
Raphaël Bartucci

Brunch is one of the best times to drink off-dry wines. We're not talking sticky dessert wines here, but wines with just a touch of sweetness and lots of fresh, fruity notes. A still wine works, but a fizzy bottle is even better. If you don't know about Bugey-Cerdon, we're very happy to introduce you. Bugey-Cerdon comes from the mountainous region in Eastern France halfway between Lyon and Geneva, Switzerland, and it's made entirely from gamay or a blend of gamay, probably borrowed from the neighboring Savoie, and poulsard (POOL-sard), borrowed from the neighboring Jura. While there are both red and white still wines made in other parts of Bugey, those labeled Cerdon will always be pink, bubbly, and slightly sweet. They also clock in at a smooth 8 to 9% alcohol, which is pretty much perfect for day drinking. If the juiciest raspberry-rhubarb-grape juice just isn't your thing, well then, we're not sure what to say. We have yet to meet anyone who doesn't love Bugey-Cerdon.

This recipe is a nod to Andrea's first book, *Pretzel Making at Home*. When you think about it, pretzels and bagels are very similar breads, the only difference being that bagels are boiled in water and pretzels are dipped in a lye solution before baking. And then there's the matter of shape, of course, with ring versus knot. This is an iconic bread mash-up for the best of both: bagels that taste like soft pretzels. (Or are they soft pretzels that look like bagels?) That pretzelized crust is traditionally created using food-grade lye, a naturally occurring alkaline substance. This extreme alkaline is what produces the leathery texture, deep brown color, and mineral flavor found in authentic pretzels, but most home cooks aren't up to the challenge of sourcing and working with lye. A suitable alternative is baked baking soda. By placing baking soda in a low oven for about an hour, the pH is slightly altered, making it behave similarly to lye. That's what we recommend you use. The "everything" topping mix is completely optional. The bagels will be delicious with any of the seeds exclusively, or even just flaky salt. Slice up some juicy tomatoes and a sharp red onion, pick some fragrant dill, and rinse a jar of capers. The effort here is in the bagels, so your accoutrements should be really easy to put together.

continued

Dough

1 (¼-ounce) envelope (2¼ teaspoons) active dry yeast
½ cup warm water (between 100°F and 115°F), plus more as needed
1 tablespoon barley malt syrup (see Note) or dark brown sugar
3¼ cups unbleached bread flour, plus more as needed
½ cup cold pilsner or lager beer
2 tablespoons unsalted butter, cubed, at room temperature
2 teaspoons kosher salt
¼ cup baking soda
Nonstick cooking spray

Everything Topping

1 teaspoon fennel seeds
1 teaspoon caraway seeds
1 teaspoon sesame seeds
1 teaspoon poppy seeds
1 teaspoon flaky sea salt
1 egg yolk
1 tablespoon water

Pretzel Bagel Bar

16 ounces cream cheese, softened
1 pound salmon lox
1 bunch fresh dill
2 large tomatoes, thinly sliced
2 loosely packed cups microgreens or sprouts
1 cucumber, thinly sliced
1 small red onion, thinly sliced
1 (3.5-ounce) jar capers, rinsed and drained
Flaky sea salt
Freshly ground black pepper

To make the dough: In a large bowl, or the bowl of a stand mixer, sprinkle the yeast over the warm water. Stir in the barley malt syrup or brown sugar until dissolved. Let the mixture stand until the yeast blooms and is a little foamy, 5 to 7 minutes. Add the flour, beer, butter, and kosher salt to the yeast mixture and stir to form a shaggy mass. Begin kneading with the dough hook on medium-low speed or on a lightly floured countertop with your hands. After about 1 minute, the dough will form a smooth ball. It should be quite firm and may be slightly tacky but not sticky. If it is sticky, add a little more flour, about 1 tablespoon at a time, and knead it in until the dough is smooth. If the dough is too dry to come together, add more water, 1 teaspoon at a time. Continue kneading the dough on medium-low speed or by hand until smooth and elastic, 5 to 7 minutes. Transfer the dough to a large, lightly greased bowl, cover with plastic wrap, and refrigerate for at least 8 hours and up to 24 hours, for optimal flavor.

Meanwhile, preheat the oven to 250°F.

Spread the baking soda in a small baking dish and place it in the oven for 1 hour. Remove from the oven and let cool. Store the baking soda in an airtight container until ready to use.

When you are ready to shape the bagels, line 2 large baking sheets with aluminum foil and coat them well with nonstick cooking spray.

Turn the dough out onto an unfloured work surface and firmly press it down to deflate. Cut the dough into 8 equal portions. Working with one piece of dough at a time and keeping the rest covered, firmly pat the dough down into a rough rectangle, then tightly roll it up lengthwise into a cylinder. Pinch the seam together. Shape the dough into a

10- to 12-inch rope by rolling it against the work surface, applying mild pressure and working from the center of the dough out. (If it's sticky, dust the surface very lightly with flour. If you need more friction, spray the surface with a little water from a squirt bottle or drizzle with a few drops of water and spread it with your hand.) Overlap the ends of the rope by about 1 inch, creating a ring. Press and pinch the seams together. Place your hand through the center of the ring and roll it against the work surface, smoothing the seams and working it into an even thickness. Place the dough ring on one of the prepared baking sheets and cover with a damp kitchen towel. Repeat with the remaining dough, spacing the rings out on the baking sheets 1 inch apart.

Let the dough rise at warm room temperature until increased in size by half, about 30 minutes. (The pretzel bagels can be covered tightly with plastic wrap and refrigerated for up to 8 hours at this point.)

Preheat the oven to 500°F with racks in the upper and lower thirds.

To make the topping: In a small bowl, combine the fennel seeds, caraway seeds, sesame seeds, poppy seeds, and flaky salt. In a separate small bowl, whisk the egg yolk with the water to make an egg wash. Set the topping mixture, the egg wash, and a pastry brush near the stove.

Select a large, wide stainless-steel pot. (Avoid nonstick and other metals, such as aluminum and copper, which may react with the baking soda.) Turn the hood vent on high and put on a pair of rubber dishwashing gloves.

Next, make the soda water, taking care to avoid getting it on your skin or in your eyes. Put the baked baking soda in the pot and pour in 6 cups water. Bring the water to a low simmer over high heat, stirring gently to dissolve the baking soda. Decrease the heat to maintain a very gentle simmer. Using your gloved hands or a large skimmer, gently dip the pretzel bagels in the simmering liquid, one or two at a time. Leave them in the solution for about 20 seconds, carefully turning once after about 10 seconds. Use the skimmer to lift and strain them from the liquid, allowing the excess to drip off, and return the pretzel bagels to the baking sheets, again spacing them 1 inch apart as you work. If the ends come detached, simply reconnect them.

Quickly brush the tops of the pretzel bagels lightly with the egg wash and sprinkle with the topping mixture.

Immediately place the pretzel bagels in the oven and bake until deep brown in color, 9 to 12 minutes, rotating the pans from front to back and top to bottom halfway through the baking time. Transfer the pretzel bagels to a wire rack to cool for about 10 minutes before serving. They are best enjoyed the day they are made, ideally warm from the oven or within an hour of being baked.

To set up the bagel bar: Put all the components on platters and in small bowls at the table. Split the pretzel bagels in half and toast them, if desired.

Note

Barley malt syrup is a thick, dark syrup with a malty, bittersweet flavor that will give your dough complexity. Look for it in the baking aisle at natural food stores.

Pétillant Naturel Rosé

FALAFEL WAFFLES

Makes 4 servings

Producers to Look For

Day Wines
Fuchs und Hase
Frantz Saumon
Les Capriades
Lucy Margaux Vineyards
Vina Štoka

Pét-nat is the natural wine world's love letter to sparkling wine. Essentially the absolute easiest way to make a wine bubbly, *pétillant naturel,* as it's known by its full name, is a wine that finishes fermenting in the bottle, generally under a metal crown cap rather than a cork. As the yeast turns the grape's sugar into alcohol, it off-gasses carbon dioxide bubbles. That little crown cap keeps the bubbles in the bottle along with any sediment that occurs during fermentation. So what you're left with is a fizzy, sometimes cloudy wine that's easy drinking and just a little bit wild. We chose pink pét-nat here, for its lightly kissed raspberry and tart cherry notes that complement the cumin and coriander in the falafel and the freshness of the salad.

It's no secret that we're waffling with wild abandon these days. A hot waffle iron can stand in for a toaster oven or a panini press, and can cook everything from omelets to pizza to falafel. The convenience of a wipe-clean appliance, and the humor of putting anything other than breakfast batter in it, was enough to get us thinking about the intersection of the crust and spice of a perfect falafel with the toasty fluffiness of a Sunday-morning waffle. In an effort to create a brunch dish that's fresh and healthy, we tossed together an herby tomato-cucumber salad with chunks of salty feta to pile on top of the waffles. A perfect soft-cooked egg added just the right amount of richness to make it a complete brunch.

Falafel Waffles

¾ cup dried chickpeas
½ yellow onion, coarsely chopped
1 cup fresh flat-leaf parsley leaves
     and thinner stems
½ cup fresh cilantro leaves and
     thinner stems
¼ cup extra-virgin olive oil, plus more
     for brushing
¼ cup plain regular or Greek yogurt
Juice of ½ lemon
3 cloves garlic
1 tablespoon ground cumin
2 teaspoons kosher salt
1½ teaspoons baking soda
1½ teaspoons ground coriander
½ teaspoon freshly ground black pepper
¼ teaspoon cayenne pepper
¾ cup all-purpose flour

Topping

1 cucumber, peeled, cut lengthwise into
     quarters, and thickly sliced
1 pint cherry tomatoes, halved
6 radishes, thinly sliced
½ cup coarsely crumbled feta cheese
¼ cup fresh mint leaves
¼ cup fresh flat-leaf parsley leaves
2 green onions, thinly sliced
3 tablespoons extra-virgin olive oil,
     plus more for drizzling
Juice of ½ lemon
Kosher salt
Freshly ground black pepper

Plain yogurt
4 soft-cooked eggs (see Note), warm

continued

To make the waffles: Place the chickpeas in a large bowl and fill it with enough cold water to cover them by about 3 inches. Set aside to soak overnight and up to 24 hours, adding more water to cover if needed at any point.

On the day of cooking, drain and rinse the chickpeas well under cold running water. Transfer the chickpeas to a food processor along with the remaining waffle ingredients, except the flour. Process until very fine and well combined. It'll be a coarse paste, not smooth at all. You'll need to stop the machine periodically to scrape down the sides and bottom with a rubber spatula to ensure that everything is mixed. Add the flour and pulse to combine. Set aside.

To make the topping: In a medium bowl, toss the cucumber, tomatoes, radishes, cheese, mint, parsley, and green onions. Add the oil and lemon juice and toss again. Season with salt and pepper.

Brush the waffle iron with oil. Spoon the batter onto the iron, dividing it evenly to make 4 waffles. Cook until deeply browned and crisp on the outside.

Top the waffles with big spoonfuls of yogurt, followed by a generous pile of the topping. Tear the eggs in half and nestle them in the topping. Sprinkle the eggs with salt and the whole thing with pepper. Drizzle with oil and serve.

Note

To soft-cook eggs, fill a medium saucepan two-thirds full with water and bring it to a boil over high heat. Prepare a bowl of ice water and place it next to the stove. Decrease the heat to maintain a gentle simmer and slowly lower the eggs into the water. Cook for 6 minutes, then lift the eggs from the water with a slotted spoon and plunge them into the ice water to stop cooking, about 2 minutes. To peel, gently tap the eggs with the back of a spoon, making tiny cracks all over the shells like a mosaic. Peel the eggs under cool water, beginning at the thickest end. To rewarm before serving, dip the peeled eggs back into a pot of barely simmering water for about 1 minute.

Lambrusco

LEFTOVER BEEF HASH WITH HERBY POACHED EGGS

Makes 4 servings

Producers to Look For

Cà de Noci
Cantina Paltrinieri
La Collina
Lamoreasca
Saetti
Vittorio Graziano

When thinking about beef, hearty red wine is what most people tend to reach for. That makes perfect sense in many instances, but no one wants to be weighed down by beefy hash and a big red wine before noon. Lambrusco to the rescue! And not that Lambrusco that your parents partied with when they were youngsters. These fizzy, dry reds, mostly from Italy's famed Emilia-Romagna region, have the tannin and dark fruit to hang with red meat, but they're bubbly and served chilled, which makes them the quintessential brunch wine. You'll find two distinct styles of dry Lambrusco: those that are pink and fruity, generally made from the Lambrusco di Sorbara variety, and those that are deeply red and made predominantly from Lambrusco Grasparossa and Lambrusco Salamino. Stick with the reds for this dish, as the beef will need something to stand up to.

People seem to be very divided when it comes to leftovers. You'd be hard-pressed to find anyone who's just sort of neutral about yesterday's dinner repurposed into today's breakfast. You've probably found yourself in this situation: a hunk of meat left from dinner, not enough for a second meal on its own, so it sits in the back of the fridge until someone finally tosses it into the garbage. Instead of letting it go to waste, turn it into a brunch hash with creamy potatoes, caramelized onions, and the subtle heat of horseradish cream. Those of you who struggle with egg poaching will love this technique: The egg is tied up in a heat-safe sheet of plastic wrap, like a tiny purse, and cooked in simmering water. After poaching, the plastic is snipped and the egg emerges, with the whites all frilly and imprinted with herbs. They are adorable, impressive, and so simple to get right.

1 pound sweet potatoes, peeled and cut into ¾-inch chunks

1 pound (unpeeled) red-skinned potatoes, cut into ¾-inch chunks

Kosher salt

½ cup sour cream

1 tablespoon finely grated fresh horseradish or prepared horseradish

2 teaspoons fresh lemon juice

¼ cup extra-virgin olive oil

1 small red onion, halved and thinly sliced

8 ounces any leftover beef, such as pot roast, smoked brisket, or steak, torn or cut into bite-size pieces

¼ cup lightly packed fresh marjoram or oregano leaves, roughly chopped

Freshly ground black pepper

Herby Poached Eggs

Extra-virgin olive oil, for brushing

¼ cup chopped fresh herbs or whole tender leaves, such as marjoram, oregano, dill, parsley, chives, or tarragon

4 large eggs

1 bunch watercress or 2 packed cups baby arugula leaves

continued

Put the sweet potatoes and red-skinned potatoes in a medium pot and cover with water by 1 inch. Season with a few big pinches of salt and bring to a boil over high heat. Decrease the heat to maintain a gentle simmer and cook until the potatoes are tender when pierced with a fork, 5 to 8 minutes. Drain well and spread them on a kitchen towel to dry.

In a small bowl, mix the sour cream, horseradish, lemon juice, and ½ teaspoon salt. Taste and adjust the seasoning, then set the sauce aside.

Heat 2 tablespoons of the oil in a 12-inch skillet, preferably cast-iron, over medium-high heat until it just begins to smoke. Add the onion and cook until tender and evenly nicely browned, even slightly charred at the edges, 5 to 6 minutes. Season with salt and transfer the onion to a small bowl.

Heat the remaining 2 tablespoons oil in the same pan. When it just begins to smoke, add the potatoes and toss them to coat in the oil, then spread them out in a single layer. Let the potatoes cook on one side, without moving, to develop a crust, 2 to 4 minutes. Stir, scraping any sticky bits off the bottom, and cook for another 2 minutes. Add the beef and continue cooking, gently turning the mixture occasionally, until the potatoes are evenly browned and crusty and the meat is heated through, 2 to 3 minutes more. Mix in the onion and marjoram, season with pepper, and continue cooking for about 1 minute. Remove the pan from the heat, taste, and adjust the seasoning.

To make the eggs: Cut out eight 6-inch squares of heat-safe plastic wrap and stack 2 together, one on top of the other, laying them out flat on the countertop. Brush the top layer of plastic with a very light coating of olive oil, in a circle that's just big enough for an egg. Sprinkle with some of the chopped herbs or fan out whole leaves over the oil and gently press them to stick. Line a small bowl with the double layer of plastic wrap, herb-side up, and crack an egg into it. Gather the edges of the plastic wrap and twist it as close to the egg as possible, then tie it with kitchen twine. Repeat to make 3 more egg purses.

Choose a pot that will comfortably fit all the eggs and fill it with about 3 inches of water. Bring to a boil, then decrease the heat until the water is at a very gentle simmer. Lower in the eggs, pressing the plastic wrap into the water so that the eggs are completely submerged, and cook for 3 to 5 minutes, until the whites are set but the yolks are still runny. (It can be difficult to judge the doneness of the whites right around the yolk, so if a little creamy, not-completely-set white encircling the yolk bothers you, keep them in for the full 5 minutes. For softer poached eggs, 3 to 4 minutes is good.) Remove the eggs from the water and snip the twine to free the eggs. Voilà!

Toss the watercress into the warm hash briefly, then spoon the hash onto warmed plates. Top with big dollops of the horseradish cream. Place the eggs on top of the sauce, garnish with a little pepper, and serve.

American Gamay

PIMENTO CHEESE SOUFFLÉ

Makes 4 to 6 servings as a main dish, or 6 to 8 as a first course

Producers to Look For

Bow & Arrow
Brick House Vineyard
Division Winemaking Company
Eminance Road Winery
Lo-Fi Wines

We are two lucky ladies; we each live with an Oregon winemaker: Andrea with Tom Monroe of Division Winemaking Company, and Dana with Scott Frank of Bow & Arrow. Both guys are cshampions of gamay, the über-drinkable grape of France's Loire Valley and Beaujolais. It has been planted in Oregon's Willamette Valley since 1987, when Myron Redford of Amity Vineyards put cuttings in the ground, and it's becoming one of the most sought-after varieties in the pinot-rich valley. The enthusiasm for American gamay is in full swing, with beautiful wines coming from Oregon, as well as California and New York. They're inspired by Beaujolais with its easy-drinking fruitiness, but also by Loire Valley gamay with its savory tartness. Winemakers love it because it's less expensive to grow and make, and ready to drink sooner than pinot. And wine drinkers love it because it's effortlessly delicious. While you can certainly drink a French gamay with this soufflé, we encourage you to go American.

Making a soufflé is actually very easy. You don't need cream of tartar to beat egg whites to beautiful, billowy, glossy peaks. You can open the oven occasionally to check on your soufflé's progress, and this one won't dramatically deflate if you do. It can be one big, impressive soufflé, but individual portions are fun when you're feeling fancy. A soufflé can be made in just about any straight-sided dish or even a 2- to 3-quart saucepan, but it's imperative that there is no slope to the sides or the soufflé won't rise. Now that that's out of the way, let's focus on this mash-up of Southern-inspired pimento cheese lightly whipped into an eggy batter. Studded with bits of pimento peppers and minced chives, this is perfect for brunch with Our Ideal Green Salad (page 103), or just as great for dinner. A fruity American gamay with a slight chill on it is just what this dish needs to highlight the tangy sharp Cheddar and hint of Dijon mustard. This soufflé, like any other, is best served when the puff is most dramatic, piping hot and fresh out of the oven, so have the table set and everyone ready to eat when it comes out.

3 tablespoons unsalted butter, plus more for greasing

3 packed tablespoons all-purpose flour

1¼ cups whole milk

6 ounces extra-sharp Cheddar cheese, finely shredded

¼ cup freshly grated Parmigiano-Reggiano cheese

1 (6-ounce) jar diced pimento peppers, drained

¼ cup sour cream

3 tablespoons minced fresh chives

1½ teaspoons Dijon mustard

1½ teaspoons plus a pinch of kosher salt, or to taste

½ teaspoon sweet paprika

6 large eggs, separated, plus 1 large egg white

continued

Preheat the oven to 375°F with a rack in the bottom third. Generously grease a 2½-quart straight-sided soufflé dish or saucepan (or 6 to 8 individual soufflé dishes) with butter.

Melt the butter in a medium saucepan over medium heat. Add the flour and cook, whisking constantly, for about 2 minutes. Pour in the milk, whisking to prevent lumps, and bring the mixture to a simmer. Decrease the heat to medium-low and simmer until the mixture is very thick and smooth, whisking the bottom and edges of the pan often, 2 to 3 minutes. Remove the pan from the heat and whisk in the Cheddar cheese until completely melted and velvety smooth. Next, add Parmigiano-Reggiano cheese, pimento peppers, sour cream, chives, mustard, 1½ teaspoons of the salt, and paprika, whisking until smooth. Stir in the 6 egg yolks. Taste and adjust the seasoning; the flavor should be very robust, cheesy, fairly salty, and positively delicious. Set aside.

Using an electric mixer and a very clean, grease-free bowl, beat the 7 egg whites with the pinch of salt to firm, glossy peaks, meaning that when the whisk is drawn from the whites a peak forms and the tip just barely curls back on itself. Using a flexible spatula or wooden spoon, fold one-quarter of the beaten egg whites into the cheesy base sauce to lighten the mixture, then fold in the rest until just barely incorporated, scooping and gently rolling the two together to preserve as much volume as possible.

Scrape the soufflé mixture into the prepared dish, filling it no more than an inch from the top. (If you have too much of the mixture, see Note below.) Wipe clean the exposed inside edge of the dish and place the soufflé on a rimmed baking sheet. Bake until the soufflé is puffed high, deeply browned on top, and still quite jiggly, 30 to 35 minutes (or 15 to 20 minutes for individual servings). Serve right away, as everyone marvels at its beauty.

Note

If you have too much soufflé mixture to fill your dish just an inch from the top, you have two options: Either butter a smaller dish and bake a second, mini soufflé alongside the big one, or make a foil collar extension for the dish. To do that, tear off a sheet of heavy-duty aluminum foil that is about 4 inches longer than the circumference of the dish. Fold it lengthwise so that you have a 4- to 5-inch-wide strip of foil. Grease one side generously with butter. Wrap the foil strip around the outside of the dish, with the greased side facing in, so that at least 2 inches extends above the rim. Fold the ends together until the foil strip is taut and snug against the outside of the dish. Bake the soufflé as directed.

RIESLING! Somm – Seam Throwdown

Start w/
Oyster Bar

Dinner:
- Bossám +
  - Bossám Ssám Sauce
  - Riesling Ssám Sauce
- Two Quickle Kimchi
- Steamed short-grain heal...
- Twe Cucumbers, etc...

Riesling

Producers to Look For

Bellwether Wine Cellars
Nikolaihof
Ovum
Weingut Brand

Weingut Julian Haart
Weingut Hirsch
Weingut Keller

We are firm believers that riesling is one of the greatest wines in the world, and that it's a perfect partner for spicy food. So it was a no-brainer to throw a party dedicated to riesling, invite a handful of sommelier friends who also love the grape, and make a feast of Korean bossäm. We left the parameters wide open: bring a bottle of riesling from anywhere in the world, any style. We popped wines from Germany, Austria, Australia, Oregon, Washington, British Columbia, and New York, but definitively agreed that the best match for the umami-rich pork and kimchi were the wines with a bit of residual sugar in them, no matter their origin. The super-dry, almost steely rieslings didn't stand up to the explosive flavors of the food, but those with more ripeness, more tropical fruit, and just a touch of sweetness were absolutely perfect. You can look for German rieslings labeled *kabinett* (KAHB-ee-net) or *spätlese* (SHPATE-layzah), indicating slightly more sugar and much more ripeness in the bottle, however, there are plenty of fantastic producers who don't label according to ripeness level. For Austrian wines, try rieslings from the Wachau region labeled *Smaragd*; again, they'll be rich and fruity and just the thing for your bossäm. New World rieslings are an excellent match, but you'll want to avoid anything labeled *dry*. You can also shop for your riesling based on alcohol percentage; remember, the lower the alcohol (think 9 to 11% alcohol by volume [ABV]), the more sweetness in the wine. But don't let that sweetness scare you. Most rieslings, even the sweet ones, are replete with acidity, which is one of the qualities that make it such great wine. You'll want that acid to keep your palate fresh and perky and balance out any sweetness.

When you make it through the complexity that is riesling, you'll be hungry for dinner. What's more exciting than a glistening hunk of roasted meat carried from the oven and set in the middle of a table full of friends and wine? And while the roasted-meat tradition is long and deep the world over, we sure love this take on the Korean ode to the year's first kimchi. True Korean bossäm is boiled pork, generally neck or belly, sliced and served with any number of accompaniments, including freshly shucked oysters and the season's "fresh" kimchi before it's left to ferment.

Here, we've riffed on the now-famous recipe from Chef David Chang of New York's Momofuku: a sugar-and-salt-coated pork shoulder slow-roasted until it forms a crackling crust encasing meltingly tender meat. As impressive as it looks and tastes, it could not be more simple to prepare. We serve ours with a delicious Riesling Ssäm Sauce and Two Quickie Kimchis: one apple-kohlrabi, and one that utilizes the kohlrabi greens and excess leaves from a head of Napa cabbage, the inner leaves having been salt-cured to serve as the bossäm wrap. *Ssäm* is the Korean word for "wrapped," wherein your juicy shredded pork gets stuffed into the salted cabbage leaves, with warm short-grain rice, herbs, kimchi, ssäm sauce, and sliced cucumbers and chiles. This is a true feast that involves eating with your fingers, lots of napkins, and flowing cold, fruity riesling to keep your palate refreshed.

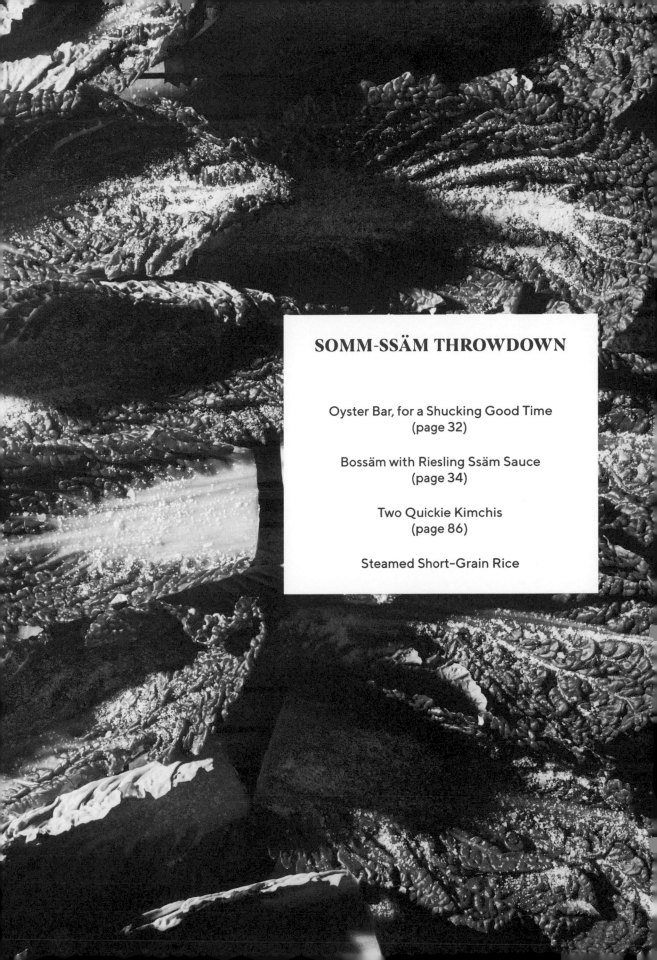

SOMM-SSÄM THROWDOWN

Oyster Bar, for a Shucking Good Time
(page 32)

Bossäm with Riesling Ssäm Sauce
(page 34)

Two Quickie Kimchis
(page 86)

Steamed Short-Grain Rice

BOSSÄM WITH RIESLING SSÄM SAUCE

Makes 8 to 10 servings

Slow-Roasted Pork Shoulder

1 (8- to 9-pound) whole bone-in pork
    shoulder
½ cup kosher salt
½ cup sugar

Salted Cabbage Leaves

1 (3- to 4-pound) head Napa cabbage
About 5 tablespoons kosher salt

Riesling Ssäm Sauce

1 bunch scallions, both white and green
    parts, thinly sliced
¾ cup riesling
⅓ cup dwenjang (Korean fermented
    soybean paste)
¼ cup gochujang (Korean red chile paste)
1 tablespoon unseasoned rice vinegar
1 tablespoon toasted sesame seeds
2 teaspoons toasted sesame oil

1 pound Little Gem or hearts of romaine
    lettuces, leaves separated, washed,
    and dried
Herb sprigs, such as cilantro, mint, and shiso
Sliced cucumbers
Sliced red chiles
Hoisin sauce
Two Quickie Kimchis (page 86)
4 cups steamed short-grain white rice

To make the pork: Place the pork shoulder in a large roasting pan. In a small bowl, stir the salt and sugar. Spread the mixture all over the pork, coating the top, bottom, and sides. Cover tightly with plastic wrap and refrigerate for at least 6 hours and up to 24 hours.

Preheat the oven to 300°F. Remove the pork from the refrigerator and pour off any juices from the bottom of the pan.

Roast the pork, fat-side up, until the meat is pull-apart tender and a nice brown crust forms on the exterior, about 6 hours. Once juices have accumulated in the bottom of the pan, after about 1½ hours, begin basting with the pan juices every hour or so.

Transfer the roast to a large platter, cover loosely with foil, and set aside at room temperature for up to 1 hour before serving.

wine food

To make the salted cabbage: Trim the bottom of the head of cabbage and separate the leaves. Reserve the larger outer leaves and the smaller innermost leaves to make kimchi. Layer the medium-size leaves on a large rimmed baking sheet, sprinkling each leaf evenly with a generous dusting of salt between each layer. Set aside at room temperature until the leaves are wilted and pliable and have given up some of their liquid, about 2 hours. Rinse the leaves well under cold water to remove excess salt, then pat dry. Wrap the leaves in plastic wrap and refrigerate for up to 1 day.

To make the ssäm sauce: In a small bowl, whisk the scallions, riesling, dwenjang, gochujang, vinegar, sesame seeds, and sesame oil. (The sauce will keep, covered, in the refrigerator for up to 3 days.)

Arrange the salted cabbage leaves, lettuce leaves, and herb sprigs on a large platter. Put the ssäm sauce, sliced cucumbers and chiles, and hoisin sauce in small bowls, and the kimchis and steamed rice in medium bowls. Place the pork shoulder in the center of the table with two large forks for shredding the meat from the bone. Let everyone build their own wraps, filling the salted cabbage and fresh lettuce leaves with shredded meat and accompaniments.

TWO QUICKIE KIMCHIS

Makes 8 to 10 servings

1 large kohlrabi, preferably with fresh-looking greens attached

1 large Granny Smith apple

1 to 1¼ pounds Napa cabbage leaves, halved lengthwise and cut crosswise into 1-inch-wide strips

¼ cup kosher salt

¼ cup plus 1½ tablespoons sugar

½ cup chopped (2-inch pieces) garlic chives or regular chives

¼ cup coarsely ground gochugaru (Korean red chile flakes)

2½ tablespoons fish sauce

1 (1½-inch) piece ginger, peeled and sliced

3 cloves garlic, peeled

3 to 4 tablespoons water

Black or white sesame seeds, for garnish

Trim the kohlrabi, reserving any greens. Peel the bulb and cut it into 2-inch-long by ¼-inch-thick rectangular sticks (like french fries). Peel and core the apple and cut it the same way. Remove the thick stems from the kohlrabi greens, if using, and cut the leaves in half lengthwise, then crosswise into 1-inch-wide strips.

Combine the kohlrabi and apple sticks in a large bowl and the cabbage and kohlrabi greens in a second large bowl. In a small bowl, mix the salt and ¼ cup of the sugar. Sprinkle the salt-sugar mixture over the contents of each bowl, dividing it evenly, and gently but thoroughly massage it in.

Set the bowls aside at room temperature until the apple mixture is tender and pliable and the cabbage mixture is wilted and both have given up a lot of juices, 20 to 30 minutes, tossing once about halfway through to evenly cure the vegetables and fruit. Drain off the accumulated juices from each bowl. One at a time, rinse each mixture in several changes of cold water, then drain well and squeeze out as much moisture as possible. Place each mixture back in its respective bowl and add the garlic chives to the apple and kohlrabi.

Process the remaining 1½ tablespoons sugar with the gochugaru, fish sauce, ginger, garlic, and 3 tablespoons of the water in a food processor to a smooth paste. Add the remaining 1 tablespoon water, as needed. Wearing disposable gloves, if you have them, mix about half of the paste into the apple-kohlrabi mixture and the other half into the cabbage, using your hands to work it in well.

The fresh kimchis can be enjoyed immediately, or kept in containers with tight-fitting lids in the refrigerator for up to 1 month. Sprinkle with sesame seeds before serving.

Pairing Cheat Sheet
Cheap and Easy (aka Takeout Time)

CHIANTI / PIZZA

SYRAH / BEEF AND BROCCOLI

ROSÉ / CHICKEN TIKKA MASALA

GRÜNER VELTLINER / SUSHI

CAVA / PAD THAI

GERMAN RIESLING / UDON

CHARDONNAY / ROTISSERIE CHICKEN

CABERNET FRANC / GYROS

BEAUJOLAIS / BURGERS

RIOJA / TACOS

Salad Days

Edelzwicker

A SOPHISTICATED HIPPIE SALAD

Makes 4 to 6 servings

We thought we'd really go for it with a slightly hippie but totally delicious salad packed with crunchy kohlrabi and chewy grains, and pair it with our favorite wine you've never heard of: Edelzwicker. Yes, Edelzwicker. It's that easy-drinking, fruity white blend from Alsace. It's fun and refreshing, often sold in liter bottles, and not meant to be a serious wine. But that doesn't mean it's not fantastic. Made from a blend of any number of grapes grown in Alsace, Edelzwicker comes from *Edel*, or "noble," and *Zwicker*, or "blend." It refers to the noble varieties that are used: riesling, gewürztraminer, pinot gris, pinot blanc, Sylvaner, muscat, and others. Like many wines (here's looking at you, Lambrusco and rosé), Edelzwicker has gotten its fair share of bad press. For many years it was considered cheap country wine, made from inferior grapes, and bottled for bulk consumption. As a result, some top producers have forgone the word *Edelzwicker* on their label so as not to tarnish their reputation.

In support of the collective effort to eat more salads—and salads that aren't just based on leafy greens—this one is substantial enough to be a vegetarian dinner, but certainly makes a fantastic starter, too. It screams texture, and is both hearty and playful. Edelzwicker has the perfect balance of fragrant white flowers and a touch of waxy richness to play off the vibrant dressing and earthy grains. If you can't find a bottle of Edelzwicker, well, that's a shame, but any Alsatian wine labeled *Gentil* would also work, although it will cost you a few dollars more.

Carrot-Ginger Dressing

8 ounces carrots, coarsely chopped
¼ cup water
Juice of 1 large lemon
2 tablespoons tahini
2 teaspoons honey
1 (½-inch) piece of ginger, peeled
    and coarsely chopped
1 small clove garlic
1 teaspoon kosher salt, or to taste
½ cup extra-virgin olive oil

Salad

¼ cup extra-virgin olive oil
1 large clove garlic, smashed
¼ teaspoon red pepper flakes
1 cup wheat berries
2 cups water
1 bay leaf
Kosher salt
5 large kale leaves, stemmed
1⅓ pounds kohlrabi
Toasted pumpkin seeds, for sprinkling

To make the dressing: In a blender, combine the carrots, water, lemon juice, tahini, honey, ginger, garlic, and salt and blend on high speed until smooth. With the blender running, drizzle in the oil until it's fully incorporated and the dressing is thick and smooth. Taste and adjust the seasoning. (The dressing can be made up to 5 days in advance and kept chilled.)

To make the salad: In a small skillet, heat 2 tablespoons of the oil with the garlic and red pepper flakes over medium heat. Soon you'll hear a gentle sizzle. Decrease the heat to medium-low and cook, stirring occasionally, until the garlic is aromatic and light golden brown, 3 to 5 minutes. Add the wheat berries and toast, stirring often. They will begin to pop after 5 or 6 minutes, but keep stirring until they smell toasty and several begin to pop at once, 1 to 2 minutes more. Pour in the water, throw in the bay leaf, and season with 1½ teaspoons salt. Bring to a boil, then decrease the heat to a gentle simmer, cover, and cook until the wheat berries are tender but still quite chewy, 40 minutes to 1 hour. Drain well and spread the wheat berries on a rimmed baking sheet, mashing up the bits of garlic and stirring them in. Set aside to cool.

Meanwhile, preheat the oven to 400°F.

Tear the kale into bite-size, uneven pieces no larger than 2 inches or so. Toss them on a rimmed baking sheet with 1 tablespoon oil and ½ teaspoon salt until well coated, then spread them out evenly. Bake until crispy, 8 to 10 minutes.

Trim, peel, and halve the kohlrabi. Slice them paper-thin using a mandoline, or as thinly as you can using a sharp knife. Toss the slices with the remaining 1 tablespoon oil and a good pinch of salt.

Just before serving, add the crunchy kale to the kohlrabi and toss gently, without crushing the kale too much. Smear a couple spoonfuls of the dressing in a big circle in the center of each plate. Spoon the wheat berries over the dressing and pile the kohlrabi and kale on top. Sprinkle with pumpkin seeds and serve.

Arneis

CHOP CHOP

Makes 4 to 6 servings

Producers to Look For

Azienda Agricola Negro
Angelo e Figli
Cascina Val del Prete
Idlewild
Ruth Lewandowski
Valfaccenda

The Piedmont region of Northwest Italy is known for Barolo and Barbaresco, the names of two villages and two wines, both made from nebbiolo grapes. Yes, barbera and dolcetto grapes are also grown throughout Piedmont, making it a red-heavy area. But let's not forget about arneis (ar-NAYZS), one of Italy's great white wines. If grown in the sandy white soils of the Roero part of Piedmont, arneis has a little more structure and citrusy edge. But coming from the clay-based soils of the Langhe (the heart of nebbiolo country), arneis is more striking and rich. Believe it or not, arneis used to be a blending grape, added to nebbiolo to make it just slightly more approachable and drinkable. That all went out the window at the beginning of the twentieth century and arneis quickly fell out of fashion. It wasn't until the mid-eighties that a handful of growers showed a renowned interest in it.

This is our ultimate version of an Italian-American chopped salad. A textural mash-up of crisp lettuces, crunchy chickpeas, and slow-roasted tomatoes makes for a delicious new take on an old favorite. It's fairly easy to toss together, and you might even have many of the ingredients on hand. But with lemon, vinegar, oregano, and spicy pickled peppers in the mix, this classic salad presents a pairing predicament. Initially we thought a pinot grigio would do the trick, but that proved to be acid overload. We found that arneis has an inherent floral quality and enough fruit to balance the acidity and heat of the salad. Although we're not usually fans of too-cold white wines, this is one you'll want to have very chilled so that the flavors are zingy and pop against the robust salad.

½ cup extra-virgin olive oil
2 tablespoons dried oregano
2 tablespoons red wine vinegar
1 tablespoon fresh lemon juice
2 cloves garlic, minced
Kosher salt
Freshly ground black pepper
½ cup thinly sliced red onion
1 (15-ounce) can chickpeas, drained
  and rinsed
1 heaping pint cherry tomatoes, preferably
  a mix of colors

½ small head radicchio, thinly sliced
1 head romaine lettuce, chopped into
  1-inch pieces
4 ounces Piave or Parmigiano-Reggiano
  cheese, cut into ¼-inch cubes
4 ounces soppressata salami, cut into
  matchsticks
⅓ cup pickled hot red peppers, such as
  cherry bomb or Hungarian, sliced
  into rings

Preheat the oven to 400°F.

Whisk ¼ cup of the oil with the oregano, vinegar, lemon juice, garlic, 2 teaspoons salt, and several grinds of pepper in an extra-large salad bowl. Add the onion, tossing to coat the slices in the vinaigrette, and set aside to marinate while you prepare the rest of the salad, or for up to 1 day.

Pat the chickpeas dry with paper towels, toss them with 2 tablespoons oil, and season with a big pinch of salt and lots of pepper. Spread them on a rimmed baking sheet and roast until nicely browned and crispy, 25 to 35 minutes. Set aside to cool.

Halve the cherry tomatoes and toss them with the remaining 2 tablespoons oil and a big pinch of salt. Spread the cherry tomatoes and excess oil in a baking dish that fits them snuggly in an even layer and then roast until wilted and juicy (some may be blistered in spots), 20 to 25 minutes. Set aside to cool. (The cherry tomatoes can be roasted at the same time as the chickpeas.)

While the chickpeas and cherry tomatoes are in the oven, prepare a large bowl of ice water. Soak the radicchio for at least 20 minutes and up to 1 hour in the ice water to reduce some of the bitterness and crisp it up a bit. Drain well and dry in a salad spinner or between kitchen towels.

Add the romaine lettuce, radicchio, cheese, salami, and pickled peppers to the bowl of vinaigrette and onions and toss. Add the roasted tomatoes and juices and oil from the roasting pan and toss again to coat everything well. Top with the crunchy chickpeas and serve family-style at the table.

Dry-ish Riesling

SWEET-SOUR-SALTY-CRUNCHY CITRUS SALAD

Makes 4 to 6 servings, or 8 to 10 as part of a feast

Producers to Look For

Beurer
Hofgut Falkenstein
J.B. Becker
Weingut Brand
Weingut Clemens Busch
Weingut Peter Lauer
Weingut Weiser-Künstler

The world of German riesling is large and confusing. Riesling has far too often been thought of as only sweet. It's suffered a vicious history with the devastating root louse phylloxera and living through both World Wars. The heart of German riesling, the Mosel, is home to incredibly steep vineyards that are nearly impossible to farm. Add to all that impossible-to-decipher wine labels and the result is riesling is misunderstood and underappreciated by most of the world. Because riesling is one of our favorite grapes, we want to make it a tiny bit easier to get on board: German rieslings are generally labeled by their ripeness level, using the *Qualitätswein* and *Prädikatswein* scales. Keep in mind that this doesn't indicate how sweet the wine will be, but instead how fruity and rich it will be. Look for words like *feinherb*, *halbtrocken*, and *kabinett* to get you into a bottle that is just off-dry, which is the sweet spot (no pun intended) for people who say they don't like riesling. Wines labeled *spätlese* and *auslese* will be progressively riper and much fruitier and start getting into sweet-wine territory. Beware that there are some phenomenal producers who do not label according to the ripeness scales but make wines that would technically fall into the "dry-ish" category. Buying riesling is the perfect opportunity to utilize your shopkeeper's knowledge to find the style you're looking for. For this bright citrus salad, be sure to choose something on the dry-ish side, as anything too rich and sweet will just drown out the umami of the fish sauce and shallots.

Admit it: by January, you get sick of kale salad. We do. Months of hearty greens, winter roots, and storage veggies have us begging for something vibrant, forward, and decidedly not heavy. Enter the orbs of citrus stacked at the market. Juicy and bright grapefruits, oranges, and mandarins are the saviors of a long, cold winter. And while you can just peel and eat them as is, why not toss them into a Burmese-inspired salad with a simple drizzle of fish sauce and lime juice and a sprinkling of crunchy fried shallots and toasted coconut. It's a great way to enjoy citrus for a winter dinner. Serve this salad as a component in the Crabs and Mags feast (page 241), an accompaniment to the tamarind-glazed ribs in our Glou-Glou Thai BBQ (page 164), or alongside grilled shrimp for a lighter meal.

1¼ cups thinly sliced (into rings) shallots

1 cup peanut, canola, or vegetable oil, plus more as needed

2 pounds oranges, such as Valencia or Cara Cara

2 pounds grapefruit

½ cup fresh Asian or Italian basil leaves, torn

¼ cup roasted salted peanuts

Juice of ½ lime, or to taste

1 tablespoon fish sauce, or to taste

2 teaspoons minced red or green jalapeño chile

1 teaspoon sugar, or to taste

¼ cup toasted unsweetened coconut flakes

Place a fine-mesh sieve over a small bowl and place it near the stove. Combine 1 cup of the shallots and the oil in a small saucepan and place over medium heat. Once the shallots begin to sizzle, about 5 minutes, decrease the heat to medium-low and gently fry the shallots, stirring often, until deep golden brown and crisp, 30 to 35 minutes. Drain the shallots in the sieve, collecting the infused oil in the bowl. If not using immediately, store the fried shallots and shallot oil at room temperature in separate sealed containers for up to 1 month.

Meanwhile, soak the remaining ¼ cup shallots in a bowl of cold water for about 20 minutes to release some of their pungency.

Working with one orange at a time, cut a slice from the top and bottom to reveal the flesh. Stand the orange upright and slice away the peel from the sides in wide strips, cutting downward, following the contour of the fruit, and removing all the white pith. Holding the orange over a bowl, use a sharp paring knife to cut along both sides of each segment, releasing the segments and allowing them and the juice to drop into the bowl beneath. (These citrus segments are called suprèmes.) Pick out the seeds as you go. Squeeze any remaining juice from the pith into the bowl. Repeat with the remaining oranges and the grapefruit. Drain the juice from the suprèmes, reserving it for another use (or just drink it on the spot).

Drain the shallots from the water and add them to the bowl of citrus suprèmes. Add the basil, peanuts, lime juice, fish sauce, 2 teaspoons fried shallot oil, jalapeño, and sugar. Gently toss to combine, being careful not to break up the citrus. Taste and adjust the seasoning, adding more fish sauce, lime juice, sugar, or oil, as needed.

Transfer the salad to a large, shallow serving bowl and top with the coconut flakes, followed by the fried shallots. Serve immediately.

Malvasia

MELON AND PROSCIUTTO WITH RADISHES, AVOCADO, AND MINT

Makes 6 servings

Producers to Look For

Burja Estate
Castello di Luzzano
I Clivi
Poggiosecco

Malvasia, also known as malvazija (MAHL-va-zee-ah), depending which part of Europe you're in, is a grape that many people are unfamiliar with. Its habitat runs throughout Italy, Slovenia, Greece, Spain, and Portugal, with far-flung examples from California and South America. Ever drunk Malmsey Madeira? It's made from malvasia. It's a particularly sweet version of the grape, but also one of the great examples. There's a time and place for a honeyed, deeply caramelized dessert wine; this is not it. We're hoping to turn you on to dry malvasia, with its tropical fruits, beeswax, and chamomile profile. It's got acidity, but not too much, and an unexpected weightiness that makes it feel a bit more serious than you might expect. We've suggested malvasia from around Europe in hopes that you might taste a couple of different bottles side by side to see the differences in style. Many producers make orange, or skin-contact, malvasia. They'll be too tannic and savory for this recipe, so avoid them and grab a bottle of white.

This is a dish that's all about few, but very good, ingredients. Make this at the height of melon season, when the cantaloupes are dripping with their intoxicating juices and their flesh is both perfectly orange and slightly yielding. Choose a ripe avocado and watermelon radishes and really fruity olive oil. Have your butcher shave your prosciutto paper-thin. And please don't skimp on the freshly ground pepper and flaky salt. What you'll find with this pairing is that the salty-sweet combination of the melon and ham beautifully complements the perfumed aromatics of a dry malvasia.

½ ripe cantaloupe
4 ounces prosciutto, sliced paper-thin
1 ripe avocado
1 watermelon radish, or 6 red or Easter Egg
    radishes, thinly sliced
1 bunch fresh mint, leaves picked
¼ cup aromatic extra-virgin olive oil
    (use a good one for this)
Flaky sea salt
Freshly ground black pepper

Halve the cantaloupe and scoop out the seeds. Cut the melon lengthwise into quarters and trim off the rinds. Using a mandoline, or working carefully with a chef's knife, slice each quarter lengthwise into ⅛-inch-thick pliable ribbons. Arrange the ribbons on a large platter in an even layer, folding and rolling them in a beautiful tangle. Fold and nestle the prosciutto slices around the melon ribbons.

Halve the avocado, remove the pit, and cut the flesh lengthwise into quarters. Cut each quarter crosswise into very thin slices without cutting through the peel. Now scoop the slices from the peels. Dot the avocado around the salad, in groupings of 4 to 6 slices that are slightly fanned out.

Tuck the radish slices into the salad here and there. Tear the mint leaves if they are large, but keep the small ones whole, and scatter them over the top. Drizzle the salad with the oil, sprinkle with salt and several grinds of pepper, and serve.

Gewürztraminer

TOMATO CHAAT

Makes 4 to 6 servings

Producers to Look For

Domaine Bechtold
Domaine Bott-Geyl
Domaine Trapet
Ochota Barrels
Ovum
Teutonic Wine Company

In the world of sweet wine, gewürztraminer certainly stands close to the center of the crowd. Even one whiff of gewürz and her heady, intoxicating aromas of honey, rose petals, baking spices, and lychee will have you thinking that you're about to drink something sweet. But there's plenty of dry gewürztraminer in the world, and they work in perfect unison with spiced, and spicy, foods. The heaviest concentration of the grape is in Alsace, tucked up in France's northeast corner near Germany, and it's made in both dry and famously sweet styles. Here, dry gewürz has a weight and richness to it, making it a true full-bodied white wine, with just enough acidity to keep it from being flabby. The Italian alpine region of Alto Adige has a large quantity of gewürztraminer, generally leaner and more minerally than in Alsace. Germany, Australia, and the United States also produce various styles of the wine. We recommend looking for a bottle on the drier side, but still high in aromatics. Part of the magic of this chaat-and-wine duo is the spices in each and how they play off each other synchronistically.

There is nothing better than a just-picked tomato—warm from the sun, perfumed by tomato leaf, and so juicy it runs down your arm if you bite into it like it's an apple. Sure, you can make a simple tomato-and-mayo sandwich, or preserve them for wintertime sauce making. Or you can make a tomato salad. You've had panzanella, Italy's ingenious use for stale bread that's tossed with tomatoes and onions, and caprese, layers of tomato, mozzarella, and basil leaves doused in good olive oil. Those are certainly fabled dishes in the lore of the tomato. Our version of a tomato salad is a different take, inspired by Indian chaat, and relying on the tomato leaf aromatics and a kick of heat to pair with spicy, bold gewürztraminer. Only make this dish when tomatoes are in season—you'll want the reddest, beefiest, juiciest slicing tomatoes or the prettiest heirloom varieties you can find. They are the star of this salad. Everything that sits on top of the tomatoes are condiments that add spice, heat, crunch, and salt. There's yogurt for a creamy, cooling effect, and a big handful of cilantro and mint for freshness. Don't miss the opportunity to make this chaat—it's one of our most beloved recipes.

continued

Green Chutney

1½ cups packed fresh cilantro leaves
    and thin stems

¾ cup packed fresh mint leaves

1 serrano chile, seeded and coarsely
    chopped

2 (quarter-size) slices fresh ginger

Juice of ½ lime

3 tablespoons water

½ teaspoon kosher salt

½ teaspoon sugar

2 teaspoons cumin seeds

1½ teaspoons fennel seeds

¼ teaspoon Indian red chile powder, or
    ancho chile powder, or ⅛ teaspoon
    cayenne pepper

⅓ cup sweet corn kernels, cut from the cob

⅓ cup finely diced cucumber

⅓ cup finely diced red onion

2 to 2½ pounds heirloom or beefsteak
    tomatoes

Flaky sea salt

⅓ cup plain yogurt, thinned with
    1 tablespoon milk

⅓ cup puffed rice (see Note)

⅓ cup sev (optional; see Note)

Handful of cilantro leaves

Handful of mint leaves

To make the chutney: Put the cilantro, mint, serrano, ginger, lime juice, water, salt, and sugar in a blender or food processor and pulse to a coarse paste, scraping down the sides as needed. (The chutney will keep, covered, in the refrigerator for up to 3 days.)

Place a small skillet over medium heat and add the cumin seeds and fennel seeds. Toast the spices, shaking the pan often, until lightly browned and aromatic, 3 to 5 minutes. Transfer the toasted spices to a spice grinder or mortar and pestle and process to a powder. Combine the spice powder and chile powder in a small bowl.

In a medium bowl, combine the corn, cucumber, and red onion.

Cut the tomatoes into ⅜-inch-thick slices and arrange them, partially overlapping, on a large serving platter. Sprinkle each slice generously with salt, followed by the spice blend. Drizzle with the thinned yogurt, then the chutney. Sprinkle the corn mixture evenly over the top, then the puffed rice. Next, sprinkle on the sev and finish with a scattering of cilantro and mint leaves. Serve immediately.

Note

Puffed rice and sev (crispy chickpea noodle strands) are crunchy toppings common to Indian chaat. We love what sev adds to this salad, but it can really only be purchased at Indian grocers or online, which is why it is an optional topping. However, puffed rice can be found at your regular supermarket. Just be sure to get an unsweetened variety, usually stocked in the cereal aisle, or possibly in the natural foods section of the store.

Chenin Blanc

LITTLE LOUIE WEDGE

Makes 4 to 6 servings

Producers to Look For

Domaine aux Moines
Domaine de Bellivière
Domaine de Juchepie
Domaine du Closel-
Château des Vaults
Le Grange Tiphaine

Chenin blanc is one of the Loire Valley's most revered varieties, and it's high on the list of favorite grapes of sommeliers and everyday wine drinkers alike. Stylistically, the grape can make racy, high-acid wines, but it can also make wines of great richness and body, with a nutty, almost oily texture. Flavors range from stone fruits with a hint of smokiness to all-out overly ripe apples dipped in honey. We like the former with our Louie, so that the acid in the wine doesn't fight the acidity of the dressing and tomatoes. Look for chenin from regions such as Savennières, Jasnières, and Montlouis, or those labeled *Anjou Blanc* to hit that perfect balance between the salad and your bottle. They'll have both the richness and the acidity needed to match Louie. Be aware that some chenin blancs are semi- or fully sweet, so check in with your shopkeeper to make sure you're grabbing something that's dry.

On a hot day, nothing sounds quite as delicious for dinner as a crisp, refreshing salad and a cold glass of white wine. This is our take on the ages-old Louie, historically made with crab or shrimp, iceberg lettuce, tomatoes, hard-boiled eggs, and a sweet, mayonnaise-based dressing in the Thousand Island family. Instead of iceberg, we use Little Gem lettuces, which look like mini-heads of romaine. They're wonderfully dainty and tender. They have a short growing season in the late spring through midsummer, so if you can't find them, one large head of regular romaine cut into wedges will work just fine. Here they're topped with sweet corn and crispy, salty bacon, as well as cherry tomatoes and avocado, and finished with petite bay shrimp. What you end up with is a crunchy, toothsome, juicy-rich texture that gets together with a green goddess–inspired dressing, and summer dinner is served.

Creamy Green Buttermilk Dressing

¾ cup sour cream
¼ cup buttermilk
2 tablespoons Champagne vinegar
    or white wine vinegar
⅔ cup lightly packed fresh flat-leaf parsley
    leaves and thin stems
⅔ cup lightly packed fresh tarragon leaves
3 green onions, white and light green parts,
    coarsely chopped
1 small clove garlic, smashed
1 teaspoon kosher salt, or to taste
½ teaspoon freshly ground black pepper,
    or to taste

Salad

Kosher salt
2 ears yellow sweet corn, shucked
6 strips thick-cut bacon, cut crosswise into
    ½-inch pieces
4 to 6 heads Little Gem lettuce
1 pint cherry tomatoes, halved
1 large avocado, diced
12 ounces cooked bay shrimp

To make the dressing: Combine the sour cream, buttermilk, vinegar, parsley, tarragon, green onions, garlic, salt, and pepper in a blender and blend until smooth. Taste and adjust the seasoning. Transfer the dressing to a jar with a lid

continued

and refrigerate until cold and thickened, about 1 hour. (The dressing will keep, covered, in the refrigerator for up to 4 days.)

To make the salad: Bring a large pot of water to a boil and season it generously with salt. Add the corn and cook until it's bright yellow and just cooked through, about 3 minutes. Drain and set aside to cool. When cool enough to handle, cut the cobs in half crosswise (to make removing the kernels less messy), then cut the kernels from the cobs. Spread the corn on a large plate and refrigerate until chilled.

Meanwhile, warm a large skillet over medium heat and add the bacon. Cook until crispy and browned at the edges but still a little chewy in the center, about 5 minutes. Drain the bacon on a paper towel–lined plate.

Cut each head of lettuce in half lengthwise through the core and trim off the core ends. Arrange two halves on each chilled plate and drizzle generously with the dressing. Scatter the corn over each salad, dividing it evenly, then add the cherry tomatoes, avocado, and bacon. Finish with the shrimp and serve.

Sauvignon Blanc

OUR IDEAL GREEN SALAD

Makes 4 to 6 servings

Producers to Look For

Alexandre Bain
Bow & Arrow
Julien Pineau
Marc Deschamps
Weingut Maria + Sepp
Muster

We really, really like the idea of grabbing what we classify as an "easy" bottle of wine on the way home from work and making the simplest dinner possible to go with it. The idea being that neither the wine nor the food should require much thought, but that you can still end up with a delicious dinner and a wine you're happy to drink. Sauvignon blanc has become everyday wine for most people. It's generally not terribly complex, it's refreshing, and pairs well with lots of different foods, including notoriously tricky vinaigrette. While the acidity in some wines fights the acidity in a salad dressing, French-style sauvignon blanc has fewer of the typical "green" notes found in most New World wines. Some modern New Zealand and American sauv blancs can display flavors such as cut grass and sharp citrus, but their French and French-inspired counterparts are more minerally with softer yellow fruit, a great foil for vinegar. Fantastic examples can also be found in Austria and South Africa.

This is our ideal green salad: just a few fresh ingredients mixed in a bowl with olive oil and vinegar, and it can be served in less than ten minutes. Add some leftover grilled salmon or rotisserie chicken and you have a light meal, or serve it alongside any of the recipes in this book. Because it's so straightforward, use care with each ingredient and choose the best-quality extra-virgin olive oil and vinegar. Pluck the brightest herbs and shave the vegetables as thinly as possible to complement the texture of the delicate lettuce leaves, which we like to keep whole for a more exciting presentation.

1 large head butter lettuce
½ small fennel bulb, tops trimmed and fronds reserved
5 radishes, tops trimmed, leaving 1 inch of stems attached
¼ cup mixed herbs, such as dill fronds, tarragon leaves, and 1-inch-snipped chives, or a combination
¼ cup extra-virgin olive oil, or to taste
3 tablespoons Champagne or white wine vinegar, or to taste
Kosher salt
Freshly ground black pepper

Cut the core from the head of lettuce and separate the leaves. Wash and pat them dry between kitchen towels and place them in a very large bowl.

Using a mandoline, cut the fennel bulb lengthwise so thinly that the slices are bendy and translucent. Slice the radishes in the same way, from root to stem end. Add the sliced fennel and a small handful of fennel fronds, radishes, and herbs to the bowl. Drizzle in the oil and vinegar and sprinkle with a big pinch of salt and several grinds of pepper. Gently toss. Taste and add more vinegar, oil, salt, or pepper, as needed, and serve.

Jurançon Sec

ROOTS RÉMOULADE WITH SMOKED TROUT

Makes 4 to 6 servings

Producers to Look For

Camin Larredya
Domaine Bru-Baché
Domaine Castera
Domaine de Souch

When we talk about some of our favorite unsung white wines, we immediately talk about Southwest France. No fancy name for this region, just Sud-Ouest, bordered by Bordeaux in the west, the Languedoc-Roussillon in the east, and the Pyrenees to the south. It's wild and off the beaten path, and home to an incredibly diverse array of varieties that take a little influence from Bordeaux, but otherwise march to the beat of their own drummer. Jurançon is nearly in the southwest corner of the country and is known predominantly for three white grapes—gros manseng, petit manseng, and petit courbu—which make wines of depth and weight, without being high in alcohol. Traditionally known for its honeyed, tropical, sweet wines made from the mansengs, Jurançon also makes compelling dry wines labeled as Jurançon Sec. Notes of beeswax, almond skins, and scrub brush are common here, but always with a serious backbone of mineral freshness, which is just the thing for a wintry rémoulade.

Rémoulade is the name of a famous French condiment akin to mayonnaise, spiced with mustard and herbs and served alongside meat and fish or tossed with celery root for a céleri rémoulade salad. In our version, we've used crème fraîche for a brighter, more decadent base, and whipped it with whole-grain mustard, lemon juice, and delicate chervil. Celery root, which mirrors the traditional rémoulade, gives this salad a wonderful crunch and green note, and we added other white winter vegetables for texture and flavor. Be sure to use true whole-grain mustard, not stone-ground, so that the mustard seeds add another layer of crunch as they pop between your teeth.

1¼ cups crème fraîche

3 tablespoons whole-grain mustard

3 tablespoons fresh lemon juice

¾ teaspoon sea salt, or to taste

Freshly ground black pepper

1½ pounds mixed white-fleshed root vegetables, such as celery root, parsnips, white carrots, kohlrabi, and black radish

4 ounces smoked trout

½ cup fresh chervil leaves or ¼ cup chopped fresh flat-leaf parsley

1 cup nasturtium, miner's lettuce, mâche, purslane, or watercress

In a large bowl, whisk the crème fraîche, mustard, lemon juice, salt, and several grinds of pepper and set aside.

Peel the root vegetables and cut them into matchsticks, either by hand using a chef's knife, or in a food processor fitted with the julienne attachment. Toss the grated roots in the crème fraîche mixture to coat well. Cover and refrigerate for at least 30 minutes and up to 1 day to develop the flavor.

Flake the fish into bite-size chunks and gently toss with the chervil into the salad. Taste and adjust the seasoning. Transfer the salad to a large, shallow serving bowl. Scatter the nasturtium over the top and serve.

Corsican or Canary Islands Rosé

FIG FATTOUSH WITH GRILLED HALLOUMI

Makes 4 to 6 servings, or 8 to 10 as part of a larger meal

Our infatuation with Middle Eastern cuisines made for a very interesting discussion about how wine pairs with spice-route flavors. The smoky, savory, and heady aromas of food from Syria, Lebanon, Israel, Turkey, and their neighbors are often thought to pair best with a cold beer, anise-based spirits, or tea. But we are too curious (and wine-minded) to sit with tradition, and we thought the complexity of wine would not only stand up to but complement the bold tartness of pomegranate molasses and sumac. Eschewing the easy options—Provençal rosé or a simple white wine—we looked to the unusual island wines from Corsica and the Canaries for their mystique and downright wildness. Both tend to have a scrub brush, herbal quality, accompanied by gentle pink fruits and a kiss of sea-salt air. The Canaries, made up of seven major islands and several smaller ones, are known for their old vines that grow out of volcanic black sand. It's extremely hot and arid on these islands off the coast of North Africa, but also mountainous, which means that wines from the high-altitude vineyards still have plenty of acidity and lip-smacking freshness. Corsica sits southeast of mainland France, not far from Italy, and is formed from limestone and granite, lending minerality and saltiness to its wines. It's a mountainous island, with grapes that are quite reminiscent of those grown in neighboring Tuscany.

This salad is our wink at fattoush, the ubiquitous dish of the Levant that's generally made with staples such as cucumbers, tomatoes, peppers, feta, and stale flatbread. We toss fresh, soft figs in a tangy pomegranate molasses vinaigrette, then grill pita breads and salty slabs of halloumi cheese until nicely charred and tear them by hand for a rustic feel. It all gets mixed with tender spinach leaves and makes for a complex salad, rich in sweet and tart flavors that play off the savory notes of the aforementioned island wines. If you squint your eyes just a bit, take a bite of fattoush and a sip of rosé; you can almost imagine yourself in a windswept vineyard on Corsica, or perhaps the Canaries. Note that we definitely recommend seeking out fresh figs when in season, but high-quality dried figs, those that are still soft when squeezed gently between your fingers, will be delicious in this salad as well.

½ cup extra-virgin olive oil, plus more for brushing

2 tablespoons sherry vinegar

1 tablespoon pomegranate molasses

1 clove garlic, minced

1 teaspoon sea salt, or to taste

1 teaspoon sumac

Freshly ground black pepper

1 pound fresh figs, or 8 ounces dried figs, halved if small or quartered if large

3 (8-inch) pita breads

1 pound halloumi cheese, cut into ¾-inch-thick slabs

5 ounces baby spinach

1 cup packed mint leaves

Prepare a fire in a charcoal or gas grill, or preheat a grill pan over high heat until smoking. For charcoal, when the coals are ready, distribute them and preheat the grate. Wait until they've reached medium-high heat, or when you can hold your palm about 3 inches above the grill grate for 3 to 5 seconds. If using a gas grill, preheat on high, covered, for about 15 minutes, then adjust the heat as needed throughout cooking.

In an extra-large bowl, whisk the oil, vinegar, pomegranate molasses, garlic, salt, ½ teaspoon of the sumac, and several grinds of pepper to emulsify. Taste and adjust the seasoning. Add the figs to the bowl and toss briefly to coat. Set aside to marinate the figs while preparing the rest of the salad, or for up to 1 hour.

Brush both sides of the pita breads and the cheese slices with a light coating of oil. First, grill the pita until crisp but still a little soft in the center, with deep grill marks on both sides, turning occasionally to prevent burning, 2 to 4 minutes. Remove the pitas from the grill and sprinkle with the remaining ½ teaspoon sumac. Set aside until cool enough to handle, then tear the pita into jagged, bite-size pieces.

Meanwhile, grill the cheese until it has deep grill marks on both sides and feels softened in the center, 5 to 7 minutes.

Add the pita to the bowl of figs and vinaigrette and toss. Add the spinach and mint leaves and toss again to coat everything well. Tear the grilled cheese into small chunks over the salad. Top with several grinds of pepper and serve immediately.

Le Grand Aïoli
Provençal Wines

· Shallot Pissaldiere
· Olive Oil Poached Tuna
  w/ Herbes de Provence
· Aïoli by hand
· Crudités for Early Summer

Provençal Wines

Producers to Look For

Chàteau Pradeaux   Domaine de Sulauze

Chàteau Sainte Anne   Domaine les Fouques

Chàteau Simone   Domaine Tempier

Commanderie de Peyrassol

Wine has been made in Southern France's Provence region for more than 2,500 years, and the traditions and feelings about wine culture there are fierce. More than half of the production is rosé, made from grenache, syrah, cinsault, and mourvèdre, and save for a few pricey, age-worthy bottles, most Provençal pinks are the quintessential summertime wine for just about anything you're eating. There is delicious white wine made from bourboulenc (BOUR-bu-lenk), clairette, and ugni blanc (oo-NEE blahnk) to be had in Provence, specifically in the small region of Cassis. Given the warm temperatures along the Mediterranean, the whites there have characteristic beeswax, yellow apple, and herbes de Provence flavors, with lower acidity than some of their counterparts farther north. They're absolutely classic pairings with seafood, such as bouillabaisse, Provence's famed seaside stew. While they don't get as much of the spotlight as rosé, the red wines made here are second to none. Between Bandol, where wines are based on the inky mourvèdre variety, and Palette, the tiny region that mostly belongs to just one winery, some extremely serious, ageable reds can be found in the South of France. With their wild, rustic notes and deep, dark fruit profile, you might not imagine the region's reds being a great pairing with poached albacore tuna, but they do work exceptionally well together. While we might not suggest the gamiest, darkest Bandol you can find, a young red from Coteaux d'Aix-en-Provence or just Provence AOP is the right way to go, especially with a little chill on it.

Aioli, that famous oil and garlic sauce that hails from Provence, is so important in Southern French culture that it gets its own fête. Le Grand Aioli is indeed grand. In its purest form, aioli is just olive oil and garlic. Like many other modern cooks, we add egg for richness and to help secure the emulsion, and lemon juice to balance the rich flavor. A mild, fruity olive oil will taste better than a robust one, which would make the aioli bitter. Garlic is most delicate in the spring and summer, so don't be shocked by the amount called for in this recipe. Using garlic poached in olive oil further diminishes its potency and turns it into something altogether luxurious. But the addition of fresh garlic adds a kick of heat that makes our aioli that much more true to its roots. The sauce is traditionally, and most deliciously, made in a marble mortar with a wooden pestle. Whisking the oil into the garlic in a bowl is certainly an alternative, but it's never quite the same. The action of pounding and grinding the garlic in the mortar, and then slowly stirring in the oil with the pestle, releases flavors and textures beyond expectation.

Le Grand Aioli table is a showcase for delicately poached fish, boiled new potatoes, vibrant crudités, soft-cooked eggs, and vessels of garlicky, velvety aioli meant to be slathered over everything. This is a quintessential early summer feast to celebrate everything new: first-of-the-season garlic, baby vegetables, and fresh wines. Our menu is completed with another Provençal staple, pissaladière, to serve as your guests arrive. But what makes it really great for warm-weather parties is that every single dish is served at room temperature, so you can prepare it all ahead, and then just enjoy the feast.

LE GRAND AIOLI

Roasted Shallot Pissaldière (page 42)

Olive Oil–Poached Tuna with Herbes
de Provence (page 112)

Aioli by Hand (page 113)

Crudités for Early Summer
(page 114)

OLIVE OIL–POACHED TUNA WITH HERBES DE PROVENCE

Makes 8 to 10 servings

4 (12-ounce) tuna loins, such as albacore, tombo, or ahi

2 teaspoons sea salt

Freshly ground black pepper

1 large lemon, thinly sliced into rings

½ cup pitted Niçoise olives

30 cloves garlic, preferably first-of-the-season fresh garlic (see Note)

3 thyme sprigs

3 marjoram or oregano sprigs

1 rosemary sprig

1 teaspoon culinary lavender buds

About 4 cups mild, fruity extra-virgin olive oil

About 30 minutes before cooking, remove the tuna loins from the refrigerator and season them with the salt and several grinds of pepper.

Put half of the lemon slices in the bottom of a pot that will fit the tuna loins in a single, snug layer. Add the olives, garlic, thyme, marjoram, rosemary, and lavender and pour in the oil. Place the pot over medium-low heat and slowly warm the oil until it registers 160°F to 175°F on a deep-fry thermometer.

Carefully lower the tuna loins into the warm oil, moving the other ingredients to the edges of the pan so that the tuna is completely covered by the oil. Add the remaining lemon slices to the pan to displace the oil and cover the tuna. Slow-poach the tuna until an instant-read thermometer inserted into the center of each loin registers 110°F to 115°F for medium-rare doneness, this can take as little as 8 minutes and up to 20 minutes, depending on the type of tuna. Check the internal temperature often and be careful not to overcook the fish, as it will become fully cooked at just 120°F.

Lift the tuna loins from the oil, allowing excess to drain back into the pot, and transfer them to a serving platter. Set a fine-mesh strainer over a medium bowl and carefully pour the poaching oil through the strainer into the bowl. Quickly cool the oil by nesting the bowl in a larger bowl filled with ice water. Or place it, uncovered, in the refrigerator until cooled to room temperature, 30 to 45 minutes. Reserve 2 cups of the oil to make aioli (facing page).

Pick out the lemons, olives, and herbs from the strainer and scatter them around the tuna. Reserve the garlic to make the aioli. Arrange the lemon slices around the tuna. Set the platter aside to cool to room temperature before serving. (The whole platter will keep, covered, in the refrigerator for up to 2 days, but set it out for 1 hour to come back to room temperature before serving.)

Cut slices of the tuna at the table and serve each portion with some of the olives and lemons.

Note
If using mature garlic, be sure to discard any green sprouts in the center of the cloves, which will add a too-pungent flavor.

AIOLI BY HAND

Makes 8 to 10 servings (about 3 cups)

4 raw cloves garlic, preferably first-of-the-season fresh garlic (see Note, facing page)

Poached garlic from Olive Oil–Poached Tuna with Herbes de Provence (facing page), at room temperature, plus 2 cups poaching oil, at room temperature

2 teaspoons sea salt

4 large egg yolks, at room temperature

Juice of 1 lemon, at room temperature

½ to 2 teaspoons water

Make the aioli in two batches in a sturdy stone mortar with a wooden pestle, or in one batch in a large bowl with a whisk.

To make the aioli using a mortar and pestle, sprinkle half of the raw and poached garlic with 1 teaspoon of the salt and pound it to a smooth paste. Add 2 of the egg yolks and stir vigorously with the pestle until they are thoroughly mixed with the garlic paste. Begin to add 1 cup of the oil, drop by drop in a very small trickle to the side of the mortar, while stirring constantly with the pestle. As the mixture begins to thicken, the oil can be added in a more steady, thin stream. Be sure to continue stirring briskly with the pestle the whole time when the oil is being added. Once the aioli becomes quite thick, begin intermittently stirring in a little of the lemon juice to thin it, then continue drizzling in the oil while stirring. Once all the oil is added, taste and adjust the seasoning, stirring in up to half of the lemon juice and up to 2 teaspoons water, if needed, to thin it slightly. Transfer the aioli to a small bowl, and repeat to make a second batch using the remaining half of the ingredients.

To make the aioli in a bowl with a whisk, mince the raw garlic on a cutting board and sprinkle it with a pinch of the salt. Tilt the blade of your knife and drag it over the garlic, scraping and smashing the garlic across the surface of the board. Pile the garlic, add another pinch of salt, and scrape it across the board again. Continue piling and scraping the garlic until you have added all the salt and it is a smooth paste. Next, mash the poached garlic with the edge of the knife (they should mash easily without salt). Put the raw and poached garlic in a large bowl and whisk in the egg yolks. Begin to add the oil in a small trickle to the side of the bowl while whisking constantly. Once the aioli is thickened, begin adding the oil in a thin stream, and add a splash of the lemon juice intermittently with the oil. Once all the oil and lemon juice is added, whisk in up to 2 teaspoons water, if needed, to thin it slightly. Taste and adjust the seasoning.

The aioli can be served directly from the mortar, or in a serving bowl to pass at the table.

Store, covered, in the refrigerator for up to 2 days.

CRUDITÉS FOR
EARLY SUMMER

Makes 8 to 10 servings

1 pound small new potatoes

1 bay leaf

Kosher salt

1 bunch baby carrots, trimmed to leave
    1 inch of stem intact

1 pound green beans, trimmed

1 head purple, orange ("cheddar"), or white
    cauliflower, trimmed, cored, and cut
    into florets

1 large fennel bulb, tops trimmed, fronds
    reserved, and bulb thinly sliced
    lengthwise through the core

1 bunch French breakfast radishes with
    fresh-looking green tops attached

1 pound snap peas

5 soft-cooked eggs (see Note, page 74)

Flaky sea salt

Freshly ground black pepper

Put the potatoes and bay leaf in a large saucepan and add enough cold water to cover the potatoes by 1 inch. Season generously with kosher salt. Place the pan over high heat and bring to a boil. Decrease the heat to maintain a simmer and cook until the potatoes are tender when pierced with a fork, 5 to 10 minutes, depending on their size. Drain the potatoes in a colander and discard the bay leaf. Set the potatoes aside to cool to room temperature.

Meanwhile, bring a large pot of water to a boil and season it generously with kosher salt. Prepare a large bowl of ice water and season that generously with salt too.

Drop the carrots into the boiling water and cook until crisp-tender, 3 to 4 minutes. Lift the carrots from the water using a large spider or skimmer and transfer them to the ice water to stop cooking. Once cooled, remove the carrots from the ice bath and pat them dry. Repeat to blanch the green beans and cauliflower.

Store, covered with damp paper towels in a sealed container, in the refrigerator for up to 2 days.

Attractively arrange all the carrots, green beans, cauliflower, fennel, radishes, and snap peas on a large serving platter. Tear the eggs in half and nestle them among the vegetables. Season the yolks with flaky salt and pepper. Add small sprigs of fennel fronds here and there and serve.

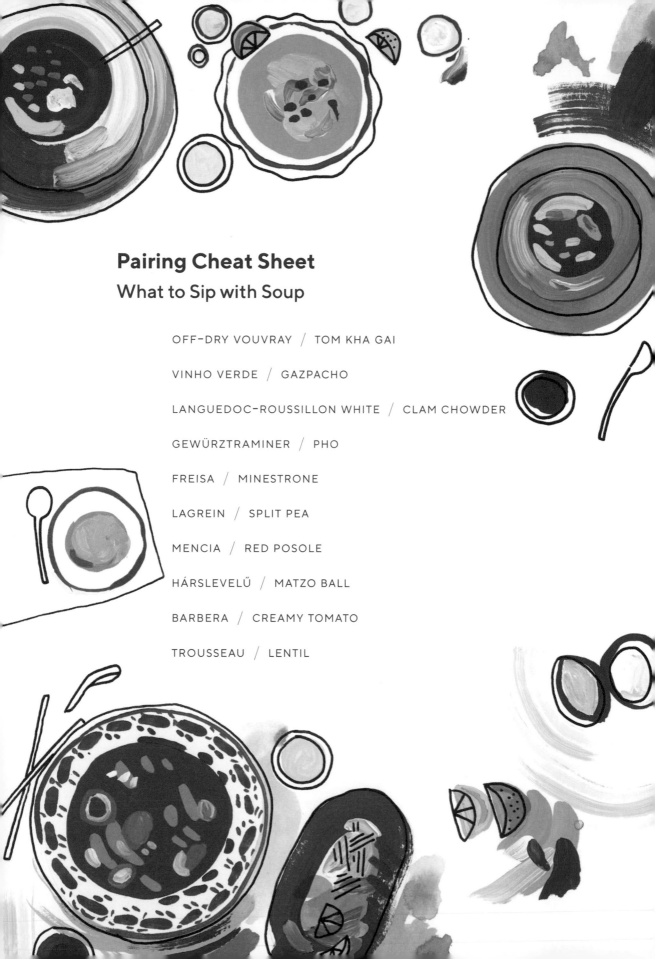

Pairing Cheat Sheet
What to Sip with Soup

OFF-DRY VOUVRAY / TOM KHA GAI

VINHO VERDE / GAZPACHO

LANGUEDOC-ROUSSILLON WHITE / CLAM CHOWDER

GEWÜRZTRAMINER / PHO

FREISA / MINESTRONE

LAGREIN / SPLIT PEA

MENCIA / RED POSOLE

HÁRSLEVELŰ / MATZO BALL

BARBERA / CREAMY TOMATO

TROUSSEAU / LENTIL

The Big Veg

Prosecco

SPRING FLING

Makes 3 servings as a main course, or 4 to 6 as a side

Producers to Look For

Ca' dei Zago
Casa Coste Piane
Costadilà
Le Vigne di Alice
Zanotto

Prosecco is a delightful companion to vegetables, in a way that many wines aren't. It's chock-full of apple, white flower, and biscuit notes, and sometimes has just the faintest touch of sweetness. It's pretty easy drinking, and even though it's a go-to for mimosas and other sparkling cocktails, good prosecco brings out the inherent sweetness and tames the vegetal notes in green vegetables. There are two distinct styles of prosecco, but both are based on the glera grape. The first is the regular, clear fizz that most of us are familiar with. Rather than the bubbles being a result of a second fermentation that happens in the bottle (like Champagne), the wine goes into a large steel tank and either undergoes its second fermentation there, or has carbon dioxide pumped into it, and then it's bottled. This is known as the charmat method and is responsible for the majority of prosecco we consume. The second style is called *col fondo* and means the fermentation finishes in the bottle and any sediment stays in the bottle. Rather than the wine fermenting in a tank, it goes right into bottle while it's still fermenting. The remaining yeast eats the rest of the sugar in the unfinished wine and off-gasses CO_2 that gets trapped in the bottle. The result is a bubbly prosecco that's cloudy, totally dry, and much more interesting than its clear counterpart. Either style will taste delicious with our celebration of spring vegetables.

This is definitely a dish you'll want to cook after an inspiring trip to the farmers' market. A good wander around the market, looking at what the farmers have to offer, is the perfect way to gather inspiration for your cooking and, since this recipe is based on the best of spring's bounty, don't hold back in grabbing whatever looks the most delicious. You can substitute any of the ingredients we have listed with whatever's available. No fava beans? Add shelled English peas. Can't find baby turnips? Skip them and use radishes and their tops instead. We give you full creative license with this one. The point is that you'll be able to cook up a brilliantly green pan of spring things coated in a rich miso sauce and topped with crunchy breadcrumbs.

1 pound fava beans in their pods
6 tablespoons unsalted butter
¼ cup white miso paste
⅓ cup coarse breadcrumbs (homemade or panko)
1 bunch hakurei turnips (Japanese baby turnips), including tops

1 bunch asparagus
1 cup snap peas or snow peas
1 bunch spring onions or scallions
¼ cup minced green garlic or 2 cloves garlic, minced
Juice of ½ lemon
Freshly ground black pepper

Fill a small saucepan with about 2 inches of water and bring it to a boil over high heat. Prepare a bowl of ice water and set it near the stove. Snap the stem ends off the fava beans and peel away the stringy seams on either side of the pods. Pull open the pods and remove the beans inside. They have a light green, waxy outer shell that needs to be removed. To do this, drop the beans in the boiling water for 30 seconds, then drain and immediately plunge them into the ice water for a few minutes to stop the cooking. When cool enough to handle, tear the outer shell with your fingernail and pinch out the bright green beans inside. Discard the shells.

Mash 2 tablespoons of the butter and the miso paste together in a small bowl.

Melt 1 tablespoon butter in a medium skillet over medium heat. Add the breadcrumbs and cook, stirring, until toasted and crunchy, 2 to 3 minutes. Set the toasted breadcrumbs aside.

Prepare the vegetables, keeping them separated since they will be added to the pan at different times. Cut the tops from the turnips, keeping about 1 inch of stem attached to the bulbs. Quarter the bulbs lengthwise, then cut the tops crosswise into 2-inch-wide strips. Snap the ends from the asparagus and peel them if the bottoms are thick and woody. Cut the asparagus on a severe bias into 1½-inch segments. Trim and remove the strings from the peas, then cut them in half on a severe bias. Trim the spring onions, removing the root end and any wilted or discolored tops. Thinly slice the white and light green parts and cut any tender dark green tops into 1-inch segments.

Heat a large skillet over medium heat. Add 2 tablespoons butter, swirling to melt, then add the turnip bulbs. Cook, stirring occasionally, until lightly browned and just tender, 10 to 12 minutes. Transfer the turnips from the pan to a bowl using a slotted spoon; set aside.

Melt the remaining 1 tablespoon butter in the hot skillet. Add the asparagus, peas, spring onions, and garlic and cook, stirring occasionally, until the vegetables are slightly softened, about 5 minutes. Stir in the turnip tops, cover the pan, and cook until they are wilted and the other vegetables are tender, 3 to 5 minutes. Remove the lid and return the turnip bulbs to the pan. Decrease the heat to medium-low and add the fava beans, miso butter, lemon juice, and several grinds of pepper, stirring and tossing until everything is nicely coated, about 1 minute. Taste and adjust the seasoning.

Serve the vegetables in warm bowls, topped with a generous sprinkling of toasted breadcrumbs.

Sparkling Vouvray

NEON COCONUT CURRY WITH PANEER (OR TOFU) AND GREENS

Makes 4 to 6 servings

Producers to Look For

Catherine & Pierre Breton

Domaine du Clos Naudin

Domaine Vincent Carême

François Pinon

Vouvray sits in the heart of the Loire Valley and is singular in the region because wineries make sparkling, still, and dessert wines all from one grape: chenin blanc. More than half of the area's production is sparkling wine, labeled either *méthode traditionelle*, *pétillant*, or *mousseux*, and it can be anywhere from bone dry to honeysuckle sweet. Chenin blanc from Vouvray tends to have fall fruit aromas—quince, Bartlett pear, and green apple—but also a very pretty toasted-nut quality. We find that with something slightly spicy and rich, like our vibrant curry, the fruitiness of the wine we're drinking makes all the difference between the flavors melding or clashing. And the bubbles keep the palate fresh between each bite.

If you're like us, you generally leave curry-making to your favorite Indian restaurant, because who has time to make curry from scratch? It might seem like a lot of work, but this recipe actually comes together in just thirty minutes, making it an ideal healthy weeknight meal. Turmeric adds an intense savory flavor and puts the "neon" in the neon curry. Fresh is best, but powdered will do. Choose vibrant greens, like mustards, which add plenty of nutrients, color, and lusciousness, while snow peas offer a snappy crunch. Once you gather your ingredients and make a quick curry paste, you're off and running. Stir in some creamy coconut milk and paneer cheese, or tofu, if you prefer, and let it bubble away while you set the table and pop the Vouvray.

4 serrano chiles, sliced

4 cloves garlic

1 (1½-inch) piece fresh ginger, peeled and sliced

1 (2-inch) piece fresh turmeric root, peeled and sliced (see Note)

2 tablespoons coconut oil

½ large yellow onion, finely chopped

6 curry leaves

6 green cardamom pods, cracked

1½ teaspoons brown mustard seeds

1 teaspoon coriander seeds, ground

1 teaspoon cumin seeds, ground

1 (13.5-ounce) can coconut milk

1½ cups water

2 teaspoons kosher salt, or to taste

1 bunch hardy greens, such as mustard, collard, or kale, stemmed and coarsely chopped

4 ounces snow peas, trimmed

8 ounces paneer cheese or firm tofu, cubed

1 lime, ½ juiced and ½ cut into wedges

Steamed brown basmati rice, to serve

Cilantro sprigs, to serve

Mint leaves, to serve

Using a mortar and pestle, pound and grind half of the chiles, the garlic, and ginger to a coarse paste. Add the turmeric and continue pounding and grinding to a relatively fine paste.

Warm the oil in a large saucepan over medium heat. Add the onion and cook, stirring occasionally, until softened and translucent, 3 to 4 minutes. Add the curry paste and cook until fragrant, about 2 minutes. Add the curry leaves, cardamom pods, mustard seeds, coriander, and cumin and cook, stirring, for another 2 minutes. Stir in the coconut milk, water, and salt and bring to a simmer.

Add the greens and stir to coat them in the sauce. Cover and cook until the greens are just wilted, 3 to 4 minutes. Add the snow peas and cook until crisp-tender, 3 to 4 minutes. Stir in the paneer or tofu and return the curry to a simmer. Remove the pot from the heat and squeeze in the lime juice. Taste and adjust the seasoning.

Serve the curry over rice in warm shallow bowls, with the lime wedges, cilantro, mint, and remaining sliced chiles at the table.

Store, covered, in the refrigerator for up to 3 days. Reheat before serving.

Note
Fresh turmeric root can now be found at many grocery stores and specialty markets, usually next to the ginger. If you can't find it, omit the turmeric from the curry paste and add 2 teaspoons ground turmeric with the dried spices.

Verdejo

STUFFED PEPPERS WITH SWEET CORN, HERBY RICE, AND POSSIBLY TOO MUCH CHEESE

Makes 6 servings as a main course, or 12 as a side

Producers to Look For

Barco del Corneto
Bodegas Vega de Tera
Isaac Cantalapiedra
MicroBio

While Spain is most often thought of for red wines, it makes exceptional white wines in the north, including in the region of Rueda, where verdejo (vehr-DAY-ho) is grown. While a lot of Rueda's verdejo is mass-produced, dosed with sulfur, and made with commercial yeasts that impart flavors like grapefruit gummy candies and overt grassy notes, there is a real treasure to be found in conscious farming and winemaking. Rueda has soils based predominantly on limestone, and the producers we recommend here are able to clearly translate the mineral component of the soil and leave out all of the artificial flavors that verdejo has become known for. Left to its own devices, verdejo has fragrant stone fruit and mineral notes, as well as a wild herb characteristic that is incredibly beautiful. It's the quintessential summery white and a winner sidled up next to stuffed sweet peppers.

We fill our summer peppers with cheesy rice and corn, and we're not sorry about it. Playing off the herbal notes in verdejo, we load the rice with all things green: cilantro, tomatillos, green onions, lime zest, and pumpkin seeds. Roasted corn kernels and a whole lot of tangy cheese are added, and everything comes together as the peppers finish roasting to tenderness. This recipe is at once comforting for a weeknight dinner and great for those long weekends when the sun sets at 9 PM and you're ready for a cold glass of verdejo.

Pickled Red Onions

1 red onion, very thinly sliced into rings
1 cup hot tap water
½ cup white wine vinegar
1 tablespoon sugar
1½ teaspoons kosher salt

6 large bell peppers, in a variety of colors
2 ears sweet corn, shucked
12 ounces tomatillos, husks removed
2 tablespoons extra-virgin olive oil, plus more for drizzling
2 teaspoons and a pinch of kosher salt, plus more to taste

¼ cup medium-grain white rice
¼ cup water
⅓ cup very finely chopped fresh cilantro, plus leaves for garnish
¼ cup pumpkin seeds
2 green onions, thinly sliced
1 large clove garlic, minced
Zest of 1 lime
1½ teaspoons fresh lime juice
1 pound Monterey Jack or Colby Jack cheese, or a combination, grated
8 ounces cotija cheese, crumbled
2 tablespoons sour cream

continued

To make the pickled onions: At least 1 hour before serving, pack the onion rings into a glass jar with a tight-fitting lid. Pour in the hot water, followed by the vinegar, sugar, and salt. Seal the jar tightly with the lid and shake to mix it all together. Set aside at room temperature until pickled, about 1 hour. (The pickled onions will keep in the refrigerator for up to 1 month.)

Preheat the broiler with a rack positioned about 6 inches from the heating element. Line a large rimmed baking sheet with aluminum foil.

Halve the bell peppers lengthwise and scoop out the seeds and white pith. Arrange the peppers on the prepared baking sheet with their cut sides down, along with the corn and tomatillos. Coat the vegetables on all sides with the oil and season them with 2 teaspoons of the salt. Broil until all the vegetables are lightly charred on one side and the tomatillos collapse, 10 to 12 minutes. Remove the tomatillos from the pan and transfer them to a cutting board to cool slightly. Turn the corn and peppers and continue broiling until both are tender and nicely charred on all sides, 10 to 15 minutes more. Transfer the corn to the cutting board to cool, keeping the peppers on the baking sheet.

Switch the oven to bake at 400°F.

Meanwhile, combine the rice, water, and pinch of salt in a small saucepan and bring to a boil over medium-high heat.

Decrease the heat to low, cover, and cook until the rice absorbs the water, about 10 minutes. Remove the pan from the heat and set aside, covered, for 5 minutes. Uncover and fluff the rice with a fork.

In a large bowl, toss the rice with the chopped cilantro, pumpkin seeds, green onions, garlic, lime zest, and lime juice until the rice is evenly coated and green. Stir in the Jack cheese, about half of the cotija cheese, and the sour cream. When cool enough to handle, coarsely chop the tomatillos and cut the corn kernels from the cobs. Stir the tomatillos and corn into the filling mixture. Taste and adjust the seasoning, adding salt, if needed.

Stuff the peppers with the filling, dividing it evenly. Sprinkle the remaining half of the cotija cheese over the filling and drizzle a little more oil over the top. Roast until the filling is hot and melty and the cotija on top is browned in spots, 16 to 18 minutes.

Serve the peppers hot and gooey, with a pile of the pickled red onions on each plate and cilantro leaves scattered over the top.

Store leftover peppers, covered, in the refrigerator for up to 2 days. Reheat in a 350°F oven for 15 to 20 minutes.

Furmint

CARROT-ZUCCHINI LATKES

Makes 4 to 6 servings (12 latkes)

Producers to Look For

Apátsági Pince
Bott Pince
Fekete Pince
Samuel Tinon

Furmint is Hungary's famed white grape that's made into the wine most of us know as Tokaji Aszú (TOE-kai-AH-zoo)—sweet and honeyed, and the perfect sip with a hunk of cheese and a handful of nuts after dinner. But furmint also makes glorious medium-bodied, dry wines without the high-acid zinginess that can make the back of your jaw tingle. They are dynamic and beautiful, and burst with flavors of wild grasses, ripe pears, a subtle smokiness, and, best of all, Middle Eastern spices. And that's where the wine-and-food romance happens here. Think sweet vegetables, the savory spice of cumin, and crunchy-crispy latke bites paired with the complexity of dry furmint.

Latkes have a special place in Dana's heart, as she grew up eating them every year at Hanukkah. Her family recipe of grated potatoes and onions, a couple of eggs, and a sprinkling of matzo meal is fairly standard as far as latkes are concerned. And they're delicious, but relegated to winter status, so why not have pan-fried vegetable pancakes in the dead of summer when zucchini are growing like weeds and carrots are fresh out of the dirt? Packed with green herbs and topped with a dollop of bright turmeric-and-cumin-spiked yogurt, these are the grown-up, warm-weather cousin of the potato latke of Dana's childhood. We love these latkes just as they are, but you can certainly dress them up with some sliced smoked salmon or sunny-side-up eggs for a weekend brunch.

1 pound carrots, tops trimmed

1 pound zucchini, ends trimmed

1 tablespoon plus ¼ teaspoon kosher salt, or to taste

¾ cup plain Greek yogurt

1 teaspoon ground cumin

1 teaspoon ground turmeric

½ cup thinly sliced green onions, plus more for garnish

2 tablespoons chopped fresh cilantro

2 tablespoons torn dill fronds

2 tablespoons thinly sliced fresh mint

Freshly ground black pepper

2 large eggs

⅓ cup all-purpose flour, plus more as needed

Extra-virgin olive oil, for frying

Flaky sea salt

Grate the carrots and zucchini using the shredding attachment in a food processor, or on the large holes of a box grater. Put the shredded vegetables in a colander and sprinkle with 2 teaspoons of the salt. Toss to coat and set aside until much of their water has been released, about 10 minutes.

Meanwhile, in a small bowl, whisk the yogurt, cumin, turmeric, and ¼ teaspoon salt. Taste and adjust the seasoning. Set the sauce aside for the flavor and yellow color to develop while you make the latkes.

Preheat the oven to 200°F. Line a baking sheet with paper towels and set it near the stove.

continued

Wring out the vegetables in a clean kitchen towel (that you don't mind staining orange) or a double layer of cheesecloth, or squeeze small handfuls at a time to extract as much moisture as possible, and put them in a large bowl. Add the green onions, cilantro, dill, mint, remaining 1 teaspoon salt, and several grinds of pepper. Mix it all together with your hands, breaking up the compressed vegetables. Add the eggs and flour and mix with your hands until everything is evenly distributed. When you squeeze a small handful of the mixture, it should just hold together; if not, add more flour, 1 tablespoon at a time.

Warm a large, heavy skillet over medium-high heat. Pour in enough oil to heavily coat the bottom of the pan. When the oil is shimmering-hot, press ⅓ cup of the latke mixture between your palms to make a 3-inch-wide, flat pancake with frilly edges. Add it to the skillet. Repeat to make 2 or 3 more and add them to the skillet without crowding the pan.

Cook the latkes until the edges and bottoms are deeply browned and crisp, 3 to 5 minutes. If the oil starts smoking or they seem to be browning too quickly, decrease the heat to medium. Flip the latkes and continue frying on the other side until deeply browned, another 3 to 5 minutes. Transfer the latkes to the prepared baking sheet as they are done and sprinkle them with flaky salt. Place the cooked latkes in the oven to stay warm as you fry the remaining mixture in batches of 3 or 4, adding more oil to the pan if it becomes dry, for a total of 12 latkes.

Arrange the latkes on a platter or individual plates and sprinkle with more green onions. Serve a dollop of the yellow yogurt sauce on each one, with the extra on the side.

Carignan

RATATOUILLE GRATIN

Makes 6 servings as a side dish, or 4 as a main course

Producers to Look For

Bodegas el Viejo
Almacén de Sauzal
Domaine Matassa
Domaine Maxime Magnon
Domaine Olivier Pithon
Martha Stoumen Wines

Carignan is a rustic yet beautiful grape originating in Southern France's Languedoc-Roussillon region. For many years it was simply a blending grape, used to bulk up grenache-based wines—a workhorse, if you will. Like zinfandel, carignan can grow to old-vine status in a way that varieties like pinot noir and cabernet sauvignon could only dream of. That matters because old vines produce fewer bunches of grapes, but what they do produce are extremely complex, loaded with flavors of the soil, rich in fruitiness, and more delicious than a vine that produces generous bunches of grapes. And this is what makes carignan really special. Aside from France, the grape is found abundantly in California and Spain, as well as in smaller quantities all over the world. Expect intense fruit flavors, such as red bush berries, spiced jerky, and anise. Carignan, especially when from old vines, isn't very tannic and generally has a nice touch of acidity.

There are many thoughts about which types of food and wine should go together. Case in point, vegetable dishes are often thought best served with white wines. But ratatouille turns that notion upside down. An unctuous, meltingly tender gratin of midsummer vegetables should be eaten with nothing other than a red wine that started life as grapes baking in the sun along the Mediterranean coast. You can serve this as a summery side dish, or over polenta as a main course that will be loved by both omnivores and vegetarians. As we've mentioned before, please use really good olive oil, as it adds flavor to the broth that the vegetables create. Our ratatouille is perfumed by fresh summer herbs, and is finished with a blanket of finely grated Parmigiano that creates a toasty brown crust. And that savory crust is the perfect foil to both the impossibly tender vegetables and the fruity spice of carignan.

12 ounces eggplant, cut into 2 by 1-inch wedges

12 ounces summer squash, such as zucchini, pattypan, and yellow squash, trimmed and cut into 2 by 1-inch wedges

12 ounces sweet peppers, cut into ½-inch strips

1 heaping pint (10 to 12 ounces) cherry tomatoes

6 cloves garlic, smashed

12 fresh basil leaves

1 tablespoon fresh thyme leaves

¼ cup extra-virgin olive oil

2 teaspoons kosher salt, or to taste

½ teaspoon piment d'Espelette or freshly ground black pepper

2 cups finely grated (not shredded) Parmigiano-Reggiano cheese

Preheat the oven to 400°F with a rack positioned in the upper third.

In a large bowl, combine the eggplant, squash, sweet peppers, cherry tomatoes, garlic, basil, and thyme. Drizzle with the oil and add the salt and piment d'Espelette. Toss to coat and distribute everything well. Dump the vegetables into a 2-quart baking dish in a heaping layer (they'll cook down) and cover tightly with aluminum foil. Place the baking dish on a large rimmed baking sheet and bake until the vegetables give up some of their juices, about 30 minutes. Uncover and continue cooking until the vegetables are very tender, about 25 minutes more.

Remove the pan from the oven and preheat the broiler. Taste the ratatouille and add more salt if you think it needs some. Sprinkle the top with the cheese in a thick layer. Place the pan under the broiler until the cheese is deep golden brown and crusty, 5 to 7 minutes. Let the gratin cool for 5 minutes.

Serve hot or just above room temperature, in shallow bowls with the juices from the bottom of the pan spooned around each portion.

Store, covered, in the refrigerator for up to 2 days. Reheat in a 350°F oven for 15 to 20 minutes.

Chianti Classico

SPAGHETTI SQUASH PARMIGIANO

Makes 6 servings

Tuscany is Italy's hotbed for sangiovese, with other red and white grape varieties included in the mix. And the beating heart of Tuscan wine is Chianti Classico. As with many regions throughout Europe, it's been a difficult place to make wine due to the bureaucracy of the consortium (the governing body of the region). In the 1970s, Chianti Classico was often made from a large percentage of sangiovese, along with the addition of white grapes to make cheap, easy-drinking wines. At the time, a handful of producers resisted the consortium's white-grape-inclusion laws and, in the process, created the first "Super Tuscan" wines. Some of these wines were made from all sangiovese, some were blends of red Bordeaux varieties, but the point is that these rebel winemakers no longer wanted white grapes to be included in Chianti Classico. It was a revolution. Wineries began producing wines outside of the bounds of governance, which meant that they couldn't use the words *Chianti Classico* on their labels, and they didn't care one bit. To make matters more challenging, beginning in 1996, the consortium decided Chianti Classico wines were no longer allowed to use white grapes. So those who had left the consortium to focus on red wines made from red grapes could have gone back to the consortium, but nearly none of them did. To this day, some of the best wines from Chianti Classico do not have the designation anywhere on their label. Instead, they bear the words *Toscana IGP*. Our recommendations include wines with and without the Chianti Classico label, but all come from within the bounds of the region, and are nearly, if not 100 percent, all sangiovese.

Turkey and Swiss, Canadian bacon and pineapple, and root beer and vanilla ice cream have long been enjoyed together for a reason: they're really delicious combinations. And so it goes with sangiovese and red sauce. But that red sauce can blanket a nutty, roasted spaghetti squash, get a melty mozzarella finish, and be just as comforting and satisfying as a bowl of pasta.

We're Marcella Hazan devotees. Considered the foremost authority on Italian cooking, Marcella wrote many must-have compendiums introducing Americans to real Italian food. Her tomato butter sauce is undoubtedly one of her most famous recipes and includes just three ingredients: tomato, onion, and butter. We started there but added toasted garlic, red pepper flakes, and fresh basil for extra flavor. Spaghetti squash appears in the fall and can be easily confused for certain types of football-shaped melons. Its interior bakes into wonderfully textural strands that look like deep golden noodles, and makes the perfect bed for your new favorite red sauce.

4 to 5 pounds spaghetti squash

4 to 5 tablespoons extra-virgin olive oil, plus more for drizzling

Kosher salt

Freshly ground black pepper

4 large cloves garlic, smashed

½ teaspoon red pepper flakes

1 (28-ounce) can whole tomatoes

½ sweet yellow onion

¼ cup unsalted butter

10 to 12 fresh basil leaves

1½ cups freshly grated Parmigiano-Reggiano cheese

8 ounces fresh mozzarella cheese, sliced or torn

Preheat the oven to 400°F.

Halve the spaghetti squash lengthwise using a long, sturdy knife and scoop out and discard the seeds. Rub with 3 to 4 tablespoons of the oil, mostly the cut sides, but lightly slick the skin sides, too, and season them well with salt and pepper. Place the squash cut-side down on a large rimmed baking sheet and roast until tender when pierced with a fork and lightly browned, anywhere from 35 to 50 minutes (depending on size). Remove the squash from the oven and set aside briefly to cool.

Meanwhile, warm the remaining 1 tablespoon oil with the garlic in a medium saucepan over medium heat. When the garlic begins to sizzle, decrease the heat to medium-low and gently cook until the garlic is toasted and light golden, 3 to 5 minutes. Add the red pepper flakes and cook for 1 minute more. Add the tomatoes, onion half, butter, 5 of the basil leaves, and 1 teaspoon salt. Bring the sauce to a boil over medium-high heat. Decrease the heat to maintain a steady simmer and cook, stirring occasionally, until the sauce is slightly thickened and the butter separates into glistening droplets on the surface, about 45 minutes. Remove and discard the onion.

Heat the broiler with an oven rack positioned 5 or 6 inches from the top heating element.

When the squash is just cool enough to handle, use a fork to gently scrape the flesh into long, spaghetti-like strands. Sprinkle the squash with ½ cup of the Parmigiano-Reggiano cheese and gently toss it in. Loosely pile the squash in a large casserole dish or divide it evenly among 6 smaller gratin dishes for individual servings.

Spoon the sauce over the squash, covering the surface. Scatter the mozzarella cheese over the sauce. Sprinkle the remaining 1 cup Parmigiano-Reggiano cheese over the top and drizzle generously with oil. Broil until the cheese is melted and browned in spots, 3 to 5 minutes. Tear the remaining basil leaves over the top and serve.

Store, covered, in the refrigerator for up to 2 days. Reheat in a 350°F oven for about 30 minutes.

Cabernet Franc

WILD MUSHROOMS AND BAKED EGGS, OR BREAKFAST OF CHAMPIGNONS

Makes 4 servings

Producers to Look For

Bernard Baudry
Domaine Benoit Courault
Domaine du Mortier
Domaine les Roches
Eminence Road Farm Winery
Methode Sauvage

Cabernet franc can be a gutsy, spicy, full-bodied, low-acidity wine when grown in a warm climate like those in Tuscany, California, and Washington state. But when it's grown in a cool climate, such as the Loire Valley or upstate New York, it drinks brighter with pretty red fruit, roasted pepper, and wet stone notes. In Bordeaux it's a blending variety, adding a savory depth to cabernet sauvignon and merlot. When we think about cabernet franc, we almost always gravitate toward the singular Loire Valley wines from Chinon, Bourgueil, Anjou, and Saumur. Sitting at the epicenter of great wine in Northern France, these are the finest examples of cabernet franc in the world, and thus the producers we've suggested you try (plus bonus wines from New York and California). Look for wallet-friendly, slurpable examples labeled *Anjou* or *Saumur*. For just a little more money, you can drink some very fine wines from the villages of Chinon and Bourgueil that will be more savory and complex, but will still cost a fraction of what a bottle of Bordeaux or Burgundy would.

This recipe isn't in the brunch chapter because we really like eggs for dinner, and you should, too. You can sauté up any number of vegetables, fry an egg, add some fresh herbs, and a satisfying dinner is served. As an added bonus, red wine has a lovely way with eggs, balancing the richness of a soft-cooked yolk. Here, we've taken a beautiful assortment of wild mushrooms and some toothsome barley cooked with aromatics, tossed everything together, and baked it with eggs on top until the yolks are runny. Finished with a handful of crunchy breadcrumbs and a glass of cabernet franc, this is our kind of dinner. And you could certainly serve this for breakfast, because if you're drinking cab franc before noon, you're a champion in our eyes.

1¼ cups pearled barley

½ yellow onion

1 bay leaf

Kosher salt

2 slices rye bread, torn into pieces

5 tablespoons extra-virgin olive oil

12 ounces wild mushrooms, such as maitake, matsutake, black trumpet, and/or chanterelle (any mushrooms, really), trimmed and very coarsely torn or chopped

1 large shallot, sliced

2 cloves garlic, minced

2 teaspoons caraway seeds, crushed

¾ cup dry red wine

2 teaspoons fresh thyme leaves

4 large eggs, at room temperature

Freshly ground black pepper

2 tablespoons minced fresh chives

Put the barley, onion half, bay leaf, and 2 teaspoons salt in a medium saucepan and add enough water to cover by 2 inches. Bring to a boil over high heat, then decrease the heat to maintain a gentle simmer. Cover and cook until the barley is tender but still chewy, 25 to 40 minutes. Reserve about 1 cup of the cooking liquid, then drain. Discard the onion and bay leaf. Set the barley and reserved cooking liquid aside.

Meanwhile, preheat the oven to 425°F.

Pulse the torn bread in a food processor to coarse crumbs (it's nice when some pieces are a little larger and some are finer). Transfer the crumbs to a rimmed baking sheet, drizzle with 1 tablespoon of the oil, sprinkle with a pinch of salt, and toss to coat evenly. Spread the breadcrumbs in an even layer and bake until crunchy and lightly browned, 10 to 12 minutes, stirring once about halfway through. Set aside to cool. Keep the oven on.

Heat 2 tablespoons of oil in a 10-inch ovenproof skillet over medium-high heat. Add about half of the mushrooms and half of the shallot and cook, stirring occasionally, until tender and nicely browned, 3 to 5 minutes. Transfer the mixture to a bowl.

To the hot pan, add the remaining 2 tablespoons oil and repeat to cook the remaining mushrooms and shallot. About 1 minute before this batch is done, stir in the garlic and caraway.

Return the first batch of cooked mushrooms to the pan and pour in the wine, scraping up any browned bits from the bottom. Season with a big pinch of salt and bring the wine to a simmer. Stir in the cooked barley, ¾ cup of the cooking liquid, and the thyme and continue cooking until the mixture is bubbling and slightly thickened, 2 to 3 minutes. Taste and adjust the seasoning.

Decrease the heat to medium-low and make 4 shallow wells in the mushroom-barley mixture. Crack 1 egg into each well. Season the eggs with salt and pepper. Transfer the pan to the oven and bake until the whites have set but the yolks are still runny (the eggs should jiggle when the pan is agitated), 6 to 10 minutes. Sprinkle with the breadcrumbs and then the chives. Serve family-style at the table.

Southern Rhône Red

POMEGRANATE-ROASTED CARROTS WITH LENTILS, LABNEH, AND CARROT-TOP ZHOUG

Makes 4 to 6 servings

Producers to Look For

Domaine de la Ferme Saint-Martin

Domaine de l'Amandier

Domaine de Piaugier

Domaine du Joncier

Domaine L'Oratoire St. Martin

The spices of the Middle East are wonderful mates for a good bottle. Think of the assertiveness of cumin and coriander, the warmth of cardamom and cloves, and the lip-smacking zip of fresh chiles as perfect foils to juicy red wine, such as a Southern Rhône grenache blend. And here we mean the glugable, fresh grenache that's brimming with juicy berries and floral notes, and made in either stainless-steel or cement vessels. Look for lower-alcohol wines, which pair nicely with a bit of heat. This dish is ideal for most Southern Rhone reds and certainly for one from the Côtes du Rhône Villages. These wines can be made of about twenty permitted grape varieties. At least 50 percent of the blend has to be grenache, and syrah and mourvèdre must comprise at least 20 percent. But between the three of them they have to total 80 percent of the blend. The point is that grenache is the dominant grape in these blends, and the focal point of this pairing.

Zhoug, the spicy green condiment popular in Yemen and Israel, gets a twist here, made with earthy carrot tops instead of parsley. Zhoug can be quite hot, so we dialed back the chiles to complement the wine's acidity—add more if you want the heat. Look for colorful farmers' market carrots with bushy green tops. They take a roll in tangy pomegranate molasses before roasting in a hot oven, giving way to caramelized, crispy tips and perfectly tender flesh. Partnered with garlicky lentils, labneh (the thick Levantine spread), and a just-spicy Middle Eastern green sauce, you'll have a vegetarian dinner that will make even the pickiest meat eater happy.

Lentils

1½ cups green lentils du Puy

½ yellow onion, halved again

2 ribs celery, quartered

1 large carrot, quartered

2 cloves garlic, 1 smashed and 1 minced

3 tablespoons extra-virgin olive oil

Kosher salt

Freshly ground black pepper

Carrots

2 pounds rainbow carrots (reserve tops)

2 tablespoons extra-virgin olive oil

2 tablespoons pomegranate molasses

1 teaspoon kosher salt

Freshly ground black pepper

Zhoug

1 teaspoon coriander seeds

1 teaspoon cumin seeds

½ teaspoon cardamom seeds
    (from about 6 whole green pods)

½ teaspoon whole cloves

½ teaspoon kosher salt, or to taste

2 serrano chiles, seeded and sliced

2 cloves garlic, peeled

1½ cups cilantro sprigs, leaves and stems
    separated, stems chopped

1½ cups carrot top leaves (stems discarded)

½ cup extra-virgin olive oil

1 tablespoon fresh lime juice

Heaping ½ cup labneh (see Note)

⅓ cup pomegranate seeds

continued

To make the lentils: Place the lentils, onion quarters, celery, carrot, and smashed garlic clove in a medium saucepan and add enough water to cover the lentils by 2 inches. Add 1 tablespoon of the oil and 1 teaspoon salt. Bring to a boil over medium-high heat, then decrease the heat to maintain a gentle simmer and cook until the lentils are tender but still hold their shape, 20 to 25 minutes. Drain, reserving about ½ cup of the cooking liquid. Return the lentils to the pan and immediately stir in the minced garlic clove and remaining 2 tablespoons oil while they are hot. Season with salt and pepper and set aside to cool. (If needed, add a splash of the cooking liquid to loosen the lentils just before serving.)

To make the carrots: Preheat the oven to 450°F. Scrub the carrots and decide whether to peel them; it's nice to leave the peels on if they are thin and not too gnarly. Halve lengthwise any carrots that are more than 1 inch in diameter, leaving the dainty ones whole. In a large bowl, toss the carrots with the oil, 1 tablespoon of the pomegranate molasses, the salt, and several grinds of pepper until evenly coated. Spread the carrots and any excess marinade on a large rimmed baking sheet and roast until they are very tender, deeply browned, the skins are wilted, the tips are a little chewy, and they're almost candylike (the smaller ones even more so), 25 to 30 minutes, turning once when the bottoms are nicely browned. Remove the pan from the oven and immediately drizzle the hot carrots with the remaining 1 tablespoon pomegranate molasses, tossing to coat. Set aside to cool slightly.

To make the zhoug: Toast the coriander, cumin, cardamom, and cloves in a small, dry skillet over medium heat until fragrant and a shade darker in color, about 2 minutes. Transfer the spices to a mortar, along with the salt, and pound and grind with a pestle to a coarse powder. Add the chile slices, garlic, and cilantro stems and pound and grind to a coarse paste. Add the cilantro leaves and carrot top leaves a handful at a time, pounding and grinding until all are added and the mixture is a coarse but cohesive green paste. Stir in the oil and lime juice, taste, and adjust the seasoning. The zhoug will keep, covered, in the refrigerator for up to 2 days. (Alternatively, you can grind the spices in a spice or coffee grinder, and then transfer everything to a food processor to pulverize into a sauce. We just prefer the texture and flavor you get with the mortar and pestle.)

Smear the labneh on a serving platter to cover, or divide it among individual plates. Top with the lentils and then the roasted carrots. Drizzle generously with the zhoug, sprinkle with the pomegranate seeds, and serve.

Note

No labneh at your market? It's just strained yogurt, so it's pretty simple to make it at home. Line a fine-mesh strainer with two layers of cheesecloth and set it over a bowl. Add 1 cup of Greek yogurt (preferably full-fat, but low-fat will work), cover loosely with the overhanging cheesecloth, and refrigerate until thickened, at least 8 hours and up to 24 hours. You should end up with a heaping ½ cup of labneh, with the excess whey collected in the bowl. If you want to make more to have on hand for other uses, just start with more yogurt. Labneh should keep in your refrigerator up to the expiration date printed on the tub of yogurt you use.

Zinfandel

ROOTS TAGINE WITH CAULIFLOWER "COUSCOUS"

Makes 6 servings

Zinfandel made its mark in American viticulture in California in the 1850s, making it one of the oldest grape varieties on our continent. With its ability to produce grapes for upward of one hundred years, zinfandel is as close to "old vine" as we get in the United States. Interestingly, zinfandel, identified by some as the same grape as Southern Italy's primitivo or Croatia's tribidrag (TREE-bee-drahg), and thought by others to be a descendent of something suitcased from Austria by way of Hungary, is one of America's greatest grapes. She's an old stalwart: gnarly, crooked vines that rise out of California's soil like knobby witch fingers, vines growing grapes loaded with sugar and ripe fruit, and the ability to hang in the heat of the day and the cool of the night.

And what about white zin, your mother's old favorite wine, her answer to your grandma's cream sherry? You can thank the seventies for that classy contribution to American wine history. Consumer demand for more white wines during that time had Sutter Home and others producing "white" wines made from red grapes. One fermentation stubbornly stuck and stopped converting sugar to alcohol, which led to a semisweet, pretty pink wine that was enthusiastically guzzled by the masses. A trend of the bygone eighties, perhaps, but nearly 10 percent of wine sales in the United States can still be credited to white zinfandel. And some fantastic small wineries are now back on the bandwagon, making delicious versions of the stuff.

Zinfandel also went through a dark period in its more recent history, when dense, rich, high-alcohol red versions were predominant. We're excited to see a return to restraint, and to bright, dynamic wines perfectly made for food. Zin's inherent flavors include explosive, brambly red fruits and ample spices like star anise and black pepper. With a spiced North African tagine, full of prunes, salty olives, and earthy roots, you end up with a magical pairing that brings out the depth of the stew and the juiciness of the wine. Keep your eyes peeled for zinfandels in the range of 13.5 to 14.5% alcohol by volume (ABV)—that (relatively) lower alcohol will help accentuate the food's flavors.

continued

Tagine

3 pounds root vegetables, such as a mix
 of sweet potatoes, carrots, parsnips,
 turnips, rutabagas, and celeriac
3 tablespoons extra-virgin olive oil
1 small yellow onion, chopped
3 cloves garlic, smashed
2 teaspoons ground coriander
2 teaspoons ground cumin
½ teaspoon ground allspice
½ teaspoon ground cardamom
½ teaspoon ground cinnamon
2 tablespoons tomato paste
3 cups low-sodium vegetable broth
20 pitted prunes, halved
½ cup oil-cured black olives,
 pitted and halved
2 teaspoons kosher salt

"Couscous"

1 head cauliflower
2 teaspoons extra-virgin olive oil
1 teaspoon ground turmeric
1 teaspoon kosher salt

Tahini Sauce

½ cup stirred tahini
3 tablespoons fresh lemon juice
½ teaspoon kosher salt, or to taste
About ½ cup water

Herb Salad

½ cup fresh cilantro leaves
½ cup fresh flat-leaf parsley leaves
½ cup torn fresh mint leaves
½ cup slivered almonds, toasted for about
 5 minutes (see Note, page 29)
1 teaspoon fresh lemon juice
1 teaspoon extra-virgin olive oil
Pinch of sea salt

To make the tagine: Peel the root vegetables and cut them into large chunks, wedges, or half-moons, all about 1½ inches in thickness or width. A mix of shapes is fun, but they all need to be about the same general size to cook evenly.

In a large tagine or Dutch oven, warm the oil over medium heat. Add the onion and garlic and cook until softened and just beginning to brown, about 5 minutes. Stir in the coriander, cumin, allspice, cardamom, cinnamon, and tomato paste and cook until the spices are toasted and very aromatic and the tomato paste is deep red, 2 to 3 minutes. Pour in the broth and add the root vegetables, prunes, olives, and salt, stirring to combine. Bring it to a boil, then decrease the heat to maintain a gentle simmer. Cover with the lid (keep it partially ajar if using a Dutch oven) and cook, stirring occasionally, until the vegetables are very tender but not quite falling apart, 25 to 35 minutes. Taste and adjust the seasoning. Remove the tagine from heat and let stand for about 10 minutes to allow the sauce to thicken and the flavors to marry. (The tagine will keep, covered, in the refrigerator for up to 3 days. Reheat over medium-low heat before serving.)

To make the "couscous": Quarter the cauliflower and trim away the core and any leaves. Cut or tear the cauliflower into large florets and place them in a food processor. (If you don't have a food processor, you can grate the cauliflower quarters on the large holes of a box grater instead.) Avoid filling the food processor more than three-quarters full, so process in two batches if needed. Pulse the food processor, scraping down the sides as needed, until the cauliflower is in couscous-size granules. (The cauliflower will keep, covered in the refrigerator for up to 3 days.)

Warm the oil in a 12-inch skillet over medium heat. Stir the turmeric and salt into the oil, then add the cauliflower. Cook until the "couscous" is tender but still has a bite and the turmeric is evenly distributed, 3 to 5 minutes. (It's delicious warm or at room temperature.)

To make the tahini sauce: In a medium bowl, whisk the tahini, lemon juice, and salt to a thick paste. Whisk in the water, using just enough to get it to a pourable, saucy consistency. Taste and adjust the seasoning. Cover and set aside, or chill for up to 1 week.

To make the herb salad (just before serving): In a small bowl, gently toss together the cilantro, parsley, mint, and almonds. Drizzle with the lemon juice and oil, sprinkle with salt, and toss again.

Divide the "couscous" into individual bowls and top with a few big spoonfuls of the tagine. Drizzle with the tahini sauce, top each with a handful of the herb salad, and serve.

GEORGIAN SUPRA

Khinkali (page 143)

Roasted Vegetables in Walnut Sauce
(page 145)

Beets with their Greens and
Dried Cherries (page 146)

A Plate of Pickled Vegetables,
Radishes, and Herbs

Cured Meats and Smoked Fish

Khachapuri or other
Eastern European Bread

Ajika and Tkemali

Georgian Wines

Producers to Look For

Aleksi Tsikhelashvili	Mariam Iosebidze
Didimi	Nika Winery
Iago's Wine	Nikoloz Antadze
Mandili	Pheasant's Tears

The Republic of Georgia, nestled in the Caucasus between Russia, Azerbaijan, Armenia, and Turkey, is arguably the birthplace of wine. At eight thousand years old, its history is extremely deep, intertwined not only in the food culture, but in art, philosophy, and religion. Even the written language is believed to have been created as a representation of the twisting, fruit-bearing grape vine. To say that wine is a way of life in Georgia is a massive understatement. Georgia is home to more than five hundred native varieties—grapes most of us have never heard of and can't pronounce. Nearly as important as the beverage itself is the vessel it's made in: the hand-shaped *qvevri* (KWEV-ri), made of clay and buried underground, predating the Roman amphora. Most Georgian wine is made in qvevri, and with a very high percentage of grape-skin contact, producing orange-amber whites and deeply brooding reds. The word *natural* in the context of Georgian wine is almost unnecessary because the traditional methods of grape growing and winemaking are alive and well today and involve absolutely no additives. For many, these represent the OG natural wines. It is almost impossible to characterize what these wines taste like, as they're singular in their aromatics and textures. Every bottle is unique, exploding with soulfulness and curiosity, proving that what's old is new again. White grapes such as rkatsiteli, mtsvane, tsolikouri, and kisi are grown in abundance, as is the red grape saperavi.

Dana attended her first Georgian feast a couple of years ago, and suffice it to say, it was a life-changing experience. The table was set with traditional clay drinking cups, bowls and plates full of typical Georgian foods were passed among friends and strangers alike, and wine flowed freely, as if it could never run out. She was left with a deep desire to learn as much as she could about Georgian culture and wine, and that one meal was the inspiration for this menu. The *supra*, as it's called, is not just a feast, but a celebration of life. It's a spiritual event lead by a *tamada*, or toastmaster, who spends the evening—yes, the entire evening—raising a drinking horn to everything from the food on the table to the children playing outside to the social struggles that guests at the table may be dealing with. A traditional supra is hours long, as food comes in waves, wine is constantly poured, toasts are proclaimed, and enchanting polyphonic music fills the air. It is unlike any other dinner party in the world.

The word *supra* means "tablecloth" and refers to the notion that the table should be filled from end to end with platters of handmade Georgian soup dumplings, called *khinkali*; smoked fish and skewered meats; roasted vegetables with *satsivi*, a spiced, tangy walnut sauce; and accoutrements, including pickles, piles of fresh herbs, and condiments such as spicy *ajika*, a red chile paste, and *tkemali*, made from sour green plums. (Both condiments can be found in jarred form at Eastern European markets throughout the United States.) Georgian food is rooted in vegetable cookery, with meat often playing a lesser role. For our most recent supra, we made these classic dishes, as well as a roasted beet and dried cherry salad, playing off familiar flavors of the Caucasus but reimagined to something just slightly more modern.

KHINKALI (GEORGIAN SOUP DUMPLINGS)

Makes 8 to 10 servings
(26 dumplings)

Dough

4½ cups all-purpose flour
½ teaspoon kosher salt
1¼ cups cold water

Filling

2 cups loosely packed fresh cilantro,
 including thin stems
1 yellow onion, coarsely chopped
2 cloves garlic, smashed
2½ teaspoons kosher salt
1 teaspoon sweet paprika
1 teaspoon ground coriander
½ teaspoon ground cumin
½ teaspoon freshly ground black pepper
½ teaspoon freshly ground white pepper
Pinch of cayenne pepper
1 pound 80 to 85 percent lean ground beef

1 bay leaf
¼ cup butter, melted
Tkemali sauce, for serving

To make the dough: In a large bowl, mix 3½ cups of the flour and the salt. Make a well in the center and pour in the water. Use a fork to stir the flour and water together to form a shaggy dough. Dust a clean work surface with the remaining 1 cup flour and dump the dough out onto it. Knead the dough together to form a smooth ball. Continue kneading, working in as much of the flour as needed, until you have a firm, smooth dough that is no longer sticky, 10 to 15 minutes. Wrap the dough tightly in plastic wrap and set aside at room temperature while you make the meat filling, at least 10 minutes and up to 1 hour. (The dough can be made up to

2 days in advance and kept chilled; bring it to room temperature before using.)

To make the filling: In a food processor, combine the cilantro, onion, garlic, salt, paprika, coriander, cumin, black pepper, white pepper, and cayenne. Process to a relatively smooth, wet puree.

Put the ground beef in a large bowl and pour in the cilantro-onion puree. Using your hands, mix the meat and puree, massaging and kneading to form a smooth, emulsified mixture. Set the filling aside while you roll out the dough.

On a generously floured work surface, use a floured rolling pin to roll out the dough into a large circle with ⅛ inch thickness. Using a 3-inch biscuit cutter or the rim of a drinking glass, cut rounds from the dough. Gather the scraps of dough, pat them into a smooth ball, reroll it out to ⅛ inch thickness, and cut more rounds. You should be able to get 26. Roll out each dough round to a 4½-inch circle. Dust the rounds with more flour and stack them between sheets of parchment or wax paper as they are made.

Place 2 level tablespoons of the filling in the center of each dough round. To seal the dumplings, make as many accordion pleats as you can, gathering a little dough at a time and folding it behind the previous one, working in a clockwise direction and gently stretching the dough

continued

until the filling is completely enclosed like a little purse. Hold the dumpling in one hand and pinch the pleats together at the center, forming a knot at the top. Pinch off the excess dough above the knot. Repeat to fill and close the remaining dough and filling. (The uncooked dumplings can be wrapped tightly in plastic and frozen for up to 1 month. Proceed with the recipe without defrosting, but increase the boiling time to about 15 minutes.)

Bring a large pot of water to a boil, add the bay leaf, and season it generously with salt. Make a whirlpool in the center of the boiling water using a large spoon, then add half of the dumplings. Gently stir to keep the whirlpool going until the water returns to a simmer to prevent the dumplings from sticking to the bottom. Once the dumplings float, about 2 minutes, decrease the heat to maintain a gentle simmer and continue cooking until the dough is tender and the meat is cooked through, about 3 minutes. Using a slotted spoon or skimmer, carefully lift the cooked khinkali from the water and transfer them to a serving platter.

Drizzle the khinkali with 2 tablespoons of the melted butter and sprinkle with more freshly ground pepper. Serve the khinkali while hot, with tkemali sauce. Repeat to cook and serve the remaining half of the dumplings.

ROASTED VEGETABLES IN WALNUT SAUCE

Makes 8 to 10 servings

Walnut Sauce

8 ounces raw walnuts
3 cloves garlic, smashed
1½ teaspoons kosher salt, or to taste
1 teaspoon ground coriander
1 teaspoon ground fenugreek
⅛ teaspoon cayenne pepper
1 tablespoon white wine vinegar
¾ to 1 cup water

Vegetables

1 small eggplant, cut into
    1 by 3-inch strips
8 ounces baby zucchini, halved, or larger
    zucchini, quartered and cut into
    3-inch strips
8 ounces cauliflower, cut into large florets
8 ounces red and yellow bell peppers, cut
    into ½-inch strips
8 ounces Romano beans or wax beans,
    trimmed
1 large sweet yellow onion, such as Walla
    Walla, peeled and cut into 1-inch
    wedges, leaving the root end intact
¼ cup extra-virgin olive oil
Kosher salt
Freshly ground black pepper

½ cup fresh cilantro leaves
¼ cup pomegranate seeds

To make the sauce: Put the walnuts and garlic in a food processor and process until they are very finely chopped and almost pasty (but not quite). Transfer the nut mixture to a medium bowl and stir in the salt, coriander, fenugreek, and cayenne. Add the vinegar and ¾ cup of the water and vigorously stir for about 20 seconds. You're looking for a consistency similar to Romesco sauce or a saucy nut butter; if it seems too thick to be considered a sauce, stir in the remaining ¼ cup water. Taste and adjust the seasoning. Set the sauce aside at room temperature for at least 1 hour and up to 2 hours for the flavors to meld, or cover and refrigerate for up to 3 days.

To roast the vegetables: Preheat the oven to 500°F.

In a very large bowl, combine the eggplant, zucchini, cauliflower, bell peppers, beans, and onion wedges. Drizzle them with the oil and sprinkle with a few big pinches of salt and several grinds of pepper. Spread about half of the vegetables on a large rimmed baking sheet and roast until tender and browned in spots, 15 to 20 minutes. (Roasting half the vegetables one tray at a time will allow them to brown nicely in the oven. Don't attempt to roast two trays at a time or pack all of the vegetables onto one tray because they will steam rather than caramelize.) Repeat to roast the remaining vegetables. Cool the vegetables to room temperature before serving.

Spread the walnut sauce to cover a large serving platter. Pile on the roasted vegetables and scatter the cilantro leaves over the top. Sprinkle with the pomegranate seeds and serve at room temperature.

BEETS WITH THEIR GREENS AND DRIED CHERRIES

Makes 8 to 10 servings as part of a feast, or 4 servings for a smaller menu

1½ pounds red beets with fresh-looking greens, preferably baby beets (or the smallest you can find)

4½ tablespoons extra-virgin olive oil

Kosher salt

Freshly ground black pepper

1 large shallot, thinly sliced

⅔ cup dried cherries

¼ cup red wine vinegar

½ cup fresh dill fronds or tarragon leaves, or a combination

Preheat the oven to 425°F.

Cut the tops from the beets, leaving 1 inch of stems still connected to the roots; set the tops aside. Peel the roots and cut them lengthwise through the stems, in halves if using baby beets, or into wedges for larger beets. In a large bowl, toss the roots with 1½ tablespoons of the oil and season them generously with salt and pepper. Spread them in a single layer on a large rimmed baking sheet with the cut sides down and roast until caramelized, wrinkly, and tender when pierced with a fork, about 30 minutes.

Meanwhile, put the shallot in a small bowl and add enough cold water to cover and a big pinch of salt. Put the cherries in another small bowl and add enough hot water to cover them. Set both aside until the beets are done roasting, or about 20 minutes.

Transfer the hot roasted beets to a large bowl. Drain the cherries and shallots and add them to the bowl, along with the vinegar, and toss to coat. Add the remaining 3 tablespoons oil and toss again. Season with several grinds of pepper and more salt, if needed. Set aside to cool to room temperature, about 20 minutes, or for up to 2 hours.

Trim the thick, fibrous stems from the beet greens and cut the leaves and tender stems crosswise into ½-inch shreds. You should have 5 to 6 cups. Wash the greens well and spin them dry, or pat dry with paper towels.

Put the beet greens in a large bowl and pile the beets on top. Strew the herbs over the beets and serve.

Pairing Cheat Sheet
Want to Drink but Don't Want to Cook

WHITE BURGUNDY / LAY'S POTATO CHIPS

VERDEJO / TINNED FISH ON CRACKERS

PINOT GRIGIO / CURED MEAT AND CHEESE

BEAUJOLAIS / FRIED EGGS AND BACON

MONTEPULCIANO D'ABRUZZO / FROZEN PIZZA

ERBALUCE / BOXED MAC AND CHEESE

SYLVANER / INSTANT RAMEN

ROSÉ / QUESADILLA WITH SALSA

POULSARD / HAM AND BUTTER SANDWICH

LITERALLY ANY WINE YOU HAVE / POPCORN (FOR DINNER)

Picnics and Other Reasons to Eat Outside

Txakoli

SALT-AND-PEPPER FRIED CHICKEN WITH GENERAL TSO'S DIPPING SAUCE

Makes 4 to 6 servings

Producers to Look For

Agerre
Bengoetxe
Doniene Gorrondona
Uriondo

Admit it: sometimes you really crave the flavor of General Tso's chicken. You want that sticky-sweet, chile-coated, mess-of-fried-chicken goodness that only your neighborhood Chinese restaurant can deliver. But then there's your other favorite: the crispy, crunchy, salt-and-pepper-flecked fried squid. How do you choose? With this recipe, you don't have to. This is our take on two of the most loved Chinese-American classics, rolled into one tantalizing fried chicken recipe to pack in your picnic basket. To be sure it stays über-crunchy, even when served cold, we took our time perfecting the coating, and then we added a serious dose of both white and black pepper for zingy heat. Leaving the chicken on the bone ensures the meat will be moist and picnic ready—no silverware needed—with that sweet-and-sour General Tso's sauce spun into a tangy dip.

And since you're taking General Tso out for a picnic, you should plan to pack one of the best outdoor-friendly summertime wines: txakoli. Hailing from Spain's coastal Basque country, it's slightly effervescent and made from the hondarrabi zuri (own-dah-RAHB-ee tsoo-REE) grape. (That just rolls off the tongue, doesn't it?) It's a straight-up summer guzzler, and best served really cold. Because it has a touch of fizz, txakoli, or txakolina as it's sometimes called, is fantastic with fried food, and even more fantastic with said fried food on a blanket under a shady tree. It's light and low-alcohol, and the Basques drink it as if it were water. For a great party trick, pour it from up high above your shoulder into a glass you hold down low, by your outer hip. You'll get your wine a little bit fizzier this way, and also provide some entertainment for your picnic buddies. And no one will care if you spill a little in the grass.

3 egg whites
⅓ cup dark soy sauce
⅓ cup vodka
⅓ cup Shaoxing wine
1½ cups plus ⅓ cup cornstarch
1 teaspoon baking soda
3½ to 4 pounds bone-in chicken pieces,
    such as 2 breasts (each halved),
    2 thighs, 2 legs, and 2 wings
1½ cups all-purpose flour
2 teaspoons freshly ground black pepper
2 teaspoons freshly ground white pepper
1½ teaspoons baking powder
1½ teaspoons kosher salt

1½ quarts peanut or canola oil
12 small dried red Chinese or árbol chiles
Flaky sea salt

General Tso's Dipping Sauce

3 tablespoons dark soy sauce
3 tablespoons hoisin sauce
2 tablespoons minced garlic
2 tablespoons minced ginger
2 tablespoons Shaoxing wine
2 tablespoons unseasoned rice vinegar
1 tablespoon plus 1 teaspoon sugar
1 teaspoon toasted sesame oil

continued

In a large bowl, beat the egg whites until slightly foamy. Whisk in the soy sauce, vodka, and wine. Transfer half of this marinade mixture to a small bowl, cover, and set aside. To the large bowl of egg white mixture, add ⅓ cup of the cornstarch and the baking soda and whisk to combine. Add the chicken pieces, turning to coat all sides. Cover and set aside for at least 1 hour and up to 2 hours to marinate and come to room temperature, or refrigerate the chicken and extra marinade for up to 12 hours.

In another large bowl, whisk the remaining 1½ cups cornstarch with the flour, black and white peppers, baking powder, and salt. Drizzle the reserved marinade mixture (in the small bowl) over the dry ingredients and whisk to form moist, shaggy clumps. Using your fingers, rub any larger clumps to break them up into smaller bits that are evenly distributed.

Have a large baking sheet nearby. One at a time, remove a piece of chicken from the marinade, allowing excess to drip back into the bowl, and put it in the bowl of coating mixture. Press the coating into the chicken so it adheres well on all sides. Transfer the chicken to the baking sheet and repeat to coat the remaining chicken pieces. Let stand for about 30 minutes.

Line another large rimmed baking sheet with paper towels and set a cooling rack on top. Heat the oil in a large wok or Dutch oven to 350°F.

First, fry the chiles in the oil until puffed, deep reddish-brown, and crisp, 1½ to 2 minutes. Transfer the fried chiles to the cooling rack.

Carefully lower half of the chicken pieces into the oil. Fry the chicken, moving it around and turning occasionally for even cooking, and adjusting the heat to maintain the temperature between 275°F and 300°F. Cook until the crust is very crispy and deep golden and an instant-read thermometer inserted in the thickest pieces registers 160°F, about 10 minutes for wings and legs and 12 to 15 minutes for breast and thigh pieces. Transfer the fried chicken to the cooling rack and immediately sprinkle with flaky salt. Repeat to fry the remaining pieces.

The fried chicken can be packed for a picnic while still warm, but be sure to transport it in a wide baking dish or platter, and keep it uncovered to prevent steam from making the crust soggy. To serve cold, let the chicken cool completely on the rack, then refrigerate for up to 1 day before packing for the picnic. Scatter the fried chiles around the chicken as you're packing it up.

To make the sauce: Put the soy sauce, hoisin sauce, garlic, ginger, wine, vinegar, sugar, and sesame oil in a jar with a tight-fitting lid and shake vigorously to combine and dissolve the sugar. Taste and adjust the seasoning. It should be quite salty, with the sweet-and-sour flavors in balance. The sauce will keep, covered, in the refrigerator for up to 1 week.

Serve the chicken warm or cold, with the fried chiles crumbled over the crust to add more heat, if desired, and the General Tso's sauce for dipping.

Gemischter Satz

SPRING GREEN PICNIC ROLLS

Makes 6 servings

Gemischter satz (ghem-ISH-ter szatz): it's a mouthful. But we can't emphasize its deliciousness enough—it's a wine definitely worth seeking out. It has the illustrious designation of being grown in the only wine region that's completely within the borders of one of Europe's great cities—Vienna. That's right, it's city wine, and it has a deep history in Austria, despite being unknown anywhere else. In fact, vines have been planted in and around Vienna since the end of the Middle Ages. By law, Gemischter satz must be a blend of a minimum of three and up to twenty white grape varieties, such as grüner veltiner, weissburgunder, and welschriesling, that are co-planted and co-fermented. The region has three distinct soil types that each favor specific varietals, so every winery has its own specific blend that makes up its Gemischter satz. It's one of summer's quintessential wines: aromatics that jump from the glass, easy drinking and quenching, and a great pairing with green vegetables and savory vinaigrettes.

These "spring" rolls might be the ultimate lunch to go: healthier than a burrito, neater than a sandwich, and absolutely spot-on for an outdoor meal. Vibrant chard leaves are rolled around a stuffing of quinoa, tangy feta, roasted shiitakes, and first-of-the-season raab, all tied together with a zippy green garlic vinaigrette. Throw these in your picnic basket with a blanket and a Frisbee and a glugable bottle of Vienna's finest wine for an impromptu adventure.

Green Garlic Vinaigrette

¼ cup fresh lemon juice
2 teaspoons honey
2 teaspoons Dijon mustard
1½ teaspoons kosher salt
Freshly ground black pepper
⅔ cup extra-virgin olive oil
¼ cup finely chopped green garlic

Rolls

12 extra-large Swiss chard leaves (see Note)
12 ounces shiitake mushrooms, large ones quartered and small ones halved
8 ounces raab (1 bunch), such as broccoli, arugula, or kale raab, tough ends discarded and tender stems, flowers, and leaves very coarsely chopped
2 tablespoons extra-virgin olive oil
1¼ teaspoons kosher salt, plus more for seasoning cooking water
Freshly ground black pepper
⅔ cup quinoa, rinsed and drained
1 cup water
⅓ cup crumbled feta cheese
⅓ cup sliced almonds, toasted for about 5 minutes (see Note, page 29)

continued

Preheat the oven to 450°F.

To make the vinaigrette: In a medium bowl, whisk the lemon juice, honey, mustard, salt, and several grinds of pepper. Slowly drizzle in the oil while whisking constantly to emulsify the dressing. Whisk in the green garlic. Transfer the vinaigrette to a jar with a lid and refrigerate for up to 5 days.

To make the rolls: Trim the thick stems from the chard leaves. Coarsely chop the stems and set the leaves aside.

In a large bowl, using your hands, toss the mushrooms, raab, and chard stems in the oil. Season with 1 teaspoon of the salt and several grinds of pepper and spread the vegetables on a large rimmed baking sheet. Roast until the vegetables are tender and lightly browned and the raab leaves are crispy, about 15 minutes. Set aside.

Put the quinoa in a small saucepan and add the water and remaining ¼ teaspoon salt. Bring it to a boil over high heat. Decrease the heat to maintain a gentle simmer, cover, and cook until the water is absorbed, about 15 minutes. Remove the pan from the heat and set aside, still covered, for 5 minutes. Uncover and fluff the quinoa with a fork. Toss with the roasted mushrooms, raab, and chard stems. Drizzle in ⅓ cup of the vinaigrette and toss the hot quinoa and vegetables to coat them evenly. Spread the quinoa mixture on a large baking sheet to cool, then toss in the cheese and almonds.

Meanwhile, bring a large pot of water to a boil over high heat and season it generously with salt. Add the chard leaves and cook until just tender, about 45 seconds. Carefully remove the leaves from the water and lay them out flat on a countertop. Pat them dry with a kitchen towel. With the stem sides up, spoon a pile of the quinoa onto each leaf, placing it about 2 inches from the tip of the leaf, dividing it evenly. For each roll, fold the tip of the leaf over the quinoa, and then fold in the sides of the leaf. Roll them up like burritos and allow them to cool completely.

Once cooled, wrap the rolls individually in plastic wrap, or nestle them together in a single layer in a container with a lid. Serve at room temperature with the remaining vinaigrette on the side for dipping.

Store, covered, in the refrigerator for up to 2 days.

Note
If you can only find medium to large chard leaves, use two leaves and overlap them to make the rolls.

Greek White

WHOLE GRILLED FISH WITH HERBY FENNEL RELISH

Makes 6 servings

Producers to Look For

Domaine Karanika
Hatzidakis Winery
Methymnaeos
Sant'Or Winery
Scalvos Wines
Stilianou Winery

We haven't had enough exposure to Greek wines, and it's a real tragedy. Some of Europe's oldest vineyards and winemaking traditions lie in Greece. Those who've had the unfortunate experience of drinking retsina (ret-ZEE-nah) in the seventies or eighties probably never want to go anywhere near wines from Greece again. We can't say we blame them. That pine-laced, insipid white left a bad taste in many people's mouths, literally. You'll be happy to know that Greek wines have grown up a lot in the past few decades (yes, even retsina is more enjoyable now), and you should be drinking them with crazy abandon. If you know anything about the islands, you know they're a haven for seafood, fruity olive oil, wild oregano, and sunny beaches kissed by the salty waters of the Ionian and Aegean seas. And grapes! There are whites that are easy drinking, fruity, and lively, as well as those that are richer and more robust. Try malagousia (mala-GOO-zee-yah), moscofilero (mos-co-FEE-leh-ro), or robola (row-BOW-la) for an opposites-attract, floral, apricot-y complement. Assyrtiko (ah-SEER-tee-ko) or athiri (ah-THEE-ree) will bring more yellow apple and pear qualities, with a briny note that's made for fish. You're likely to find them as single varietals as well as blends. All of these grapes make crisp, beautiful wines that completely represent the islands they're grown on. While some Greek labels may be difficult to read, you will be handsomely rewarded with what's in the bottle.

Our whole grilled fish is a dreamy summer dinner, packed with fresh herbs evocative of the Greek isles. If you're looking for a milder flavor, choose branzino or trout. If you like a more assertively flavored fish, mackerel or sardines really stand up to the smokiness of the grill. But whatever whole fish is freshest at your market that day will be best, and be sure to use really good extra-virgin olive oil since it plays such a big role in the dish. The relish is full of aromatic tarragon, oregano, and parsley and studded with bits of grilled fennel that offer a wonderful counterpoint to the smoky charred fish skin. Serve simply with steamed or roasted potatoes.

⅓ cup fresh tarragon leaves, plus 12 sprigs
¼ cup fresh oregano leaves, plus 12 sprigs
¼ cup fresh flat-leaf parsley leaves, plus 6 sprigs
1 tablespoon capers, drained
1 large clove garlic
⅔ cup extra-virgin olive oil, plus more for brushing
2 tablespoons fresh lemon juice, plus 1 lemon, halved lengthwise and sliced into half-moons

Sea salt
Freshly ground black pepper
6 small whole fish, such as sardines, mackerel, trout, or branzino, cleaned and scaled
1 fennel bulb, cut lengthwise through the core into ⅓-inch-thick slices

continued

Prepare a fire in a charcoal or gas grill (preferably charcoal). For charcoal, when the coals are ready, distribute them and preheat the grate. Wait until they've reached medium-high heat, or when you can hold your palm about 3 inches above the grill grate for 3 to 5 seconds. If using a gas grill, preheat on high, covered, for about 15 minutes, and adjust the burners as needed throughout cooking.

Meanwhile, pile the picked herb leaves and capers on a cutting board and chop them all together. Transfer the herbs to a medium bowl. Finely mince the garlic and add it to the bowl, along with the oil, lemon juice, a couple big pinches of salt, and several grinds of pepper. Set aside.

Lightly brush the skins of the fish and interior cavities with just enough oil to lightly coat. Season the fish generously with salt and pepper, inside and out. Stuff 2 tarragon sprigs, 2 oregano sprigs, and 1 parsley sprig into each cavity, along with the lemon slices, dividing them evenly.

Brush the fennel slices on both sides with a light coating of oil and season them with salt and pepper.

Just before grilling, grease the grill grates well. If there is enough room on the grill for both the fish and the fennel slices, grill them simultaneously. If not, arrange the fennel slices on the hottest part of the grill and cook until nicely charred with grill marks but not mushy, 2 to 4 minutes per side. Transfer the fennel to a cutting board. Chop the fennel into ¼-inch pieces and stir them into the relish. Taste and adjust the seasoning.

Place the fish on the grill and cook until the skin is nicely charred on both sides and the flesh is cooked through, 5 to 8 minutes per side. If flare-ups happen, try moving the fish to another area of the grill, and turn them as needed to prevent blackening. Transfer the grilled fish to a serving platter.

Serve the fish hot, with a spoonful of the relish dolloped over each and the rest passed at the table.

Carricante

FLATBREAD ALLA NORMA

Makes 6 servings

Producers to Look For

Benanti
Calabretta
I Custodi delle vigne dell'Etna
Salvo Foti/I Vigneri
Vino Quantico

Pasta alla Norma might well be one of Sicily's most famed dishes, hailing from the eastern side of the island with nearby Mount Etna looming in the distance. It's home to the longest and hottest summers in all of Italy, making it the perfect growing region for tomatoes, eggplant, and basil, Norma's star ingredients. In midsummer, it's fun to take these ingredients outside to top tangy whole-wheat flatbreads hot off the grill. We celebrate the idea of "what grows together, goes together" for this recipe, and serve it with a citrus-laced carricante, also from Eastern Sicily. While the island is very much known for its red wines, carricante makes some of the best whites in all of Italy, and that's saying a lot. Noted for their saline and petrol notes, wines made from carricante can also be a touch punchy and bright. These are wines from the seaside, where the vines are constantly swept with ocean air, keeping the vineyards cool and imparting a salty taste.

Consider this a Sicilian party where your dinner guests can get involved. The flatbread dough is extremely easy to put together, and is inspired by one from our friends Martha Holmberg and Joshua McFadden in their book *Six Seasons*. It rolls out in a cinch, and takes only a couple minutes to grill—no summer baking required. So while someone is charged with rolling out flatbreads, others can prep the veggies and manage the grill, and a wine-fueled assembly line will have your flatbreads topped and on the patio table in no time.

Dough

1 cup unbleached all-purpose flour, plus more for dusting
1 cup whole-wheat flour
2 teaspoons kosher salt
½ teaspoon sugar
½ teaspoon baking powder
1 cup plain yogurt (not Greek)

Toppings

1 heaping pint (10 to 12 ounces) cherry tomatoes
1 (10 to 12-ounce) eggplant
6 ounces red cipollini onions, halved, or red onion, cut into wedges
1 (6-ounce) wedge ricotta salata cheese
¼ cup extra-virgin olive oil, plus more brushing and drizzling
Kosher salt
Freshly ground black pepper
2 tablespoons fresh lemon juice
2 teaspoons colatura or fish sauce (see Note)
2 cloves garlic, finely grated or smashed in a garlic press
Flaky sea salt, for topping
Red pepper flakes, for topping
Handful of fresh mint leaves, torn
Handful of fresh basil leaves, torn

Soak six 8-inch wood grilling skewers for 1 hour.

To make the dough: In a large bowl, whisk both flours, the salt, sugar, and baking powder. Add the yogurt and fold it in with a rubber spatula just until blended. Dump the dough onto a work surface dusted generously with all-purpose flour. Knead the dough gently until smooth, about 30 seconds, then cut it into 6 equal portions. Using a well-floured rolling pin, roll each portion of dough into an imperfect oval, about ⅛ inch thick. Add more flour to the surface or the pin as needed, as the dough will be rather sticky. On a large baking sheet, stack the dough between sheets of parchment paper and cover loosely with plastic wrap while you prepare the toppings and preheat the grill, or for up to 1 hour.

To prepare the toppings: Meanwhile, divide the tomatoes among the soaked skewers. Brush the tomatoes, whole eggplant, onions, and cheese with a light coating of oil. Season the vegetables with kosher salt and pepper.

Prepare a fire in a charcoal or gas grill. For charcoal, when the coals are ready, distribute them and preheat the grate. Wait until they've reached medium-high heat, or when you can hold your palm about 3 inches above the grill grate for 3 to 5 seconds. If using a gas grill, preheat on high, covered, for about 15 minutes, then adjust the burners as needed throughout cooking.

Place the tomato skewers, eggplant, onions, and cheese on the grill and cook, turning occasionally, until everything is nicely charred; the cherry tomatoes have burst, 3 to 5 minutes; the onions are very tender, 8 to 10 minutes; the ricotta salata has deep grill marks on every side (top, bottom, cut edges, and end), 10 to 12 minutes; and the eggplant feels completely soft inside, about 20 minutes.

Remove the toppings from the grill as they are done and collect them on a large rimmed baking sheet. Put the eggplant in a large bowl and cover it with plastic wrap to steam the skin free from the flesh, about 5 minutes.

Add additional coals to the fire, if needed. Brush the grill grates clean and grease them with oil.

Grill the flatbreads, two or three at a time, until puffy and nicely charred in spots, 1 to 2 minutes per side.

While the flatbreads are grilling, peel and discard the eggplant skin and coarsely chop the flesh. Put it in a food processor with the ¼ cup oil, lemon juice, colatura or fish sauce, and garlic and process until smooth and creamy. Taste and adjust the seasoning.

To assemble the flatbreads, top each with a generous smear of the eggplant spread, dividing it evenly. Pull apart the onion layers and divide them among the flatbreads, along with the tomatoes. Using a vegetable peeler, shave strips of the grilled cheese over each one. Sprinkle with flaky salt and red pepper flakes and scatter with the mint and basil leaves. Cut the flatbreads into triangle-shaped slices, drizzle with a little more oil, and serve warm.

Note
Colatura is Italian fish sauce made from fermented anchovies, and it's nearly identical to fish sauce from Southeast Asia. The Italian version tends to be much more expensive, so we often use high-quality Asian fish sauce in its place and no one can tell the difference. We like Red Boat brand from Vietnam.

Full-Bodied Rosé

DEVILED HAM HAND PIES

Makes 8 servings

Producers to Look For

Alfredo Maestro
Fausse Piste
Iberieli
Le Sot de L'Ange
Minimus Wines
Torre dei Beati

Gone are the days of sweet, sticky "blush" in a box on the bottom shelf of the fridge. Rosé now comes in every shade of pink, from pale salmon to almost-but-not-quite red, and is made in every corner of the world from hundreds of different grape varieties. Nearly all rosés are made from red grapes that are lightly crushed and left with their skins to bleed as much color as the winemaker chooses. The pink-tinged juice is then pulled off the red skins and allowed to ferment and age until bottling. Generally speaking, lighter rosés will have more mineral and savory notes, while darker rosés will be fruitier and more robust. When thinking of salty, meaty, rich flavors—hey there, ham and cream cheese—we recommend a rosé with a bit of personality. Richer rosés are made in Italy from grapes such as sangiovese, in Argentina from malbec, and in Spain from tempranillo. In France's Southern Rhône, the Tavel appellation makes only rosé, predominantly from grenache and cinsault. The Greeks make vivid, full-bodied rosés, as do the Georgians—look for examples made from the saperavi (SAH-pear-ah-vee) grape.

Our ideal picnic scenario includes a glass of rosé in one hand and a pocket-size savory pie in the other. Here, humble deviled ham salad, studded with bright green peas and green onions, is reinvented when enveloped in a crispy cream-cheese crust. Baked until flaky and golden, these hand pies are the ideal accompaniment to a full-bodied rosé because no one flavor outdoes the other. The smoky, salty ham tastes wonderfully meaty next to the fruity notes of red cherries, cranberries, and raspberries that you'll find in these wines. And all that fruit means you'll have a lively wine that will keep your palate feeling fresh between each buttery bite.

Dough

1½ cups all-purpose flour
9 tablespoons cold unsalted butter, cubed
6 ounces cold cream cheese, cubed
¾ teaspoon kosher salt

Filling

4 ounces cream cheese, at room
    temperature
¼ cup mayonnaise
2 teaspoons stone-ground mustard
½ teaspoon sweet paprika
Freshly ground black pepper
8 ounces cooked ham, cut into ¼-inch cubes
½ cup fresh or frozen peas (no need to
    defrost if frozen)
2 green onions, white and light green parts
    thinly sliced

All-purpose flour, for dusting
1 large egg, lightly beaten

To make the dough: In a food processor, pulse the flour, butter, cream cheese, and salt until the dough is moistened and just comes together in a big clump. Divide the dough into 8 equal portions and roll each into a ball. Flatten each ball into a small disk and wrap them individually in plastic wrap. Refrigerate until cold and firm, about 1 hour. (The dough can be made up to 2 days in advance and kept refrigerated.)

To make the filling: In a medium bowl, mash and stir the cream cheese, mayonnaise, mustard, paprika, and pepper. Add the ham, peas, and green onions and stir until it's all well combined. (The filling can also be made up to 2 days in advance, covered, and kept refrigerated.)

Preheat the oven to 450°F. Line two large rimmed baking sheets with parchment paper.

On a lightly floured work surface, use a floured rolling pin to roll out each dough ball to a 6½- to 7-inch round. Divide the filling evenly among the rounds, spreading about ¼ cup over one side in a half-moon shape, leaving a ½-inch border. Lightly brush the border edges with some of the beaten egg, then fold the empty half of dough over the filling to enclose it, creating half-moon pies. Pinch the edges together, then crimp them with the tines of a fork to seal. (The unbaked hand pies can be individually wrapped tightly in plastic wrap and frozen for up to 1 month.)

Space out the hand pies on the prepared baking sheets. Brush them lightly with egg and pierce the tops with a paring knife for two ½-inch vents. Bake until golden brown and crisp, 15 to 20 minutes, rotating the pans in the oven after about 10 minutes. Transfer the hand pies to a rack to cool for 5 minutes. Serve warm or at room temperature.

Store, covered, in the refrigerator for up to 2 days, or wrapped tightly in plastic wrap and placed in a zip-top bag in the freezer for up to 3 months. Reheat in a 350°F oven for about 10 minutes if refrigerated, or 20 minutes if frozen.

Rossese

BIG BOULE SANDWICH WITH ROAST BEEF, PICKLED BEETS, AND GORGONZOLA

Makes 6 servings

Producers to Look For

Azienda Agricola Pisano Danila
Punta Crena
Terre Bianche
Testalonga

The cliff-side towns of Genoa and Savona are some of the most dramatic in Italy, so it makes sense that not too far inland you'll find a wine that's equally as special. Rossese is the red grape of Liguria, way up on Italy's northwestern coast, and can be light enough to be confused for a dark rosé. It grows in limestone-heavy soils and ranges from heady and floral to herbal and quenching. Rossese can be peppery, fruity, and full of lip-smacking acidity—just the foil for creamy blue cheese and meaty roast beef. Look for straight rossese, which will be lighter in color, or the famed Rossese di Dolceacqua, which will have just a bit more weight and body to it. Either way, pop your bottle in the fridge for a pre-lunch chill.

The sandwich is arguably the most ubiquitous food, with its easy-to-eat, anything-goes, found-around-the-world, super-portable package. And while you may not think you need to be told how to make a sandwich, this one's got a few twists to make it exciting enough for a picnic at the beach or a pit stop on a road trip. This recipe is as much a way to highlight a freshly baked bread as it is an excuse to make a family-style lunch to take outside. We started with a fresh boule, the recognizable French bread that looks like a slightly flattened circular loaf, and treated it a bit like a jack-o'-lantern, cutting off its top and scooping out its insides. Folds of tender roast beef and frilly frisée are layered with quick-pickled beets for their much-needed crunch. Beets have a good friend in blue cheese, and together they make for a tangy, creamy one-two punch of flavor. As if the surprise of an impressively big sandwich for six isn't enough for your pals, the fact that you've packed a slightly chilled bottle of light red will take your picnic to the next level.

Quick-Pickled Beets

10 ounces red beets, peeled and cut into ⅛-inch-thick slices
1 large shallot, thinly sliced
1¼ cups red wine vinegar
1 cup water
2 tablespoons honey
1 tablespoon whole allspice
1 tablespoon kosher salt

6 ounces Gorgonzola dolce cheese, at room temperature
½ cup buttermilk
¼ cup minced fresh chives
Freshly ground black pepper
1 (2-pound) boule (rustic round French bread)
1 pound sliced roast beef
4 cups packed coarsely chopped frisée or whole baby arugula leaves
½ cup packed fresh flat-leaf parsley leaves

To make the pickled beets: Pack the beets and shallot into a quart-size glass canning jar or other heatproof vessel. Combine the vinegar, water, honey, allspice, and salt in a medium saucepan and bring to a boil over medium-high heat, stirring until the honey and salt are dissolved. Boil for about 2 minutes. Pour the boiling-hot brine into the jar to completely cover the beets and shallot. Cover and set aside to allow the brine to slowly cool to room temperature as it pickles the vegetables, about 4 hours. When completely cooled, either use the pickles immediately or refrigerate them for up to 1 month.

In a small bowl, mash and mix the cheese with the buttermilk, chives, and several grinds of pepper to a chunky, thick spread.

Using a serrated knife, cut the top off the loaf of bread. Dig out the inside of both the top and bottom, getting into the edges, leaving an evenly excavated ½-inch-thick bread shell (use the bread scraps for another use, like croutons or breadcrumbs).

Coat the inside top, bottom, and edges of the bread shell with the cheese spread. Beginning with half of the roast beef, add to the loaf, folding the slices and completely covering the bottom of the bread. Next add a layer of pickled beets, using up half of them. Scatter half of the shallot over the beets. Top with 2 cups of the frisée and ¼ cup of the parsley leaves. Repeat to form another layer. Add the top of the bread and gently press down on the fillings so that they are completely encased in the loaf. Wrap the sandwich in parchment or butcher paper. It will keep at room temperature for up to 4 hours.

To serve, place six 6-inch wooden skewers around the sandwich, from the top all the way through to the bottom crust, which will help hold the individual sandwiches together once they are cut. Slice the sandwich into 6 wedges.

Glou-Glou

GLOU-GLOU THAI BBQ

Makes 4 to 6 servings

Producers to Look For

Château d'Oupia
Holden Wine Company
Jauma Wine
Louis-Antoine Luyt
Bodega Vinifícate
Wind Gap Wines

Glou-glou is the French expression for the most fantastic way to describe a wine: Drinkable. Chuggable. Slammable. It's for wines that are so delicious we can't get enough of them. These aren't serious wines. They're not meant to be aged or pondered over, just meant to be poured and drunk. They are the backbone of our summer drinking (aside from rosé and white, of course), and we encourage you to find glou-glou red wines that you want to have stocked and ready to drink all summer. In general, glou-glou is made using carbonic or semi-carbonic maceration, which leads to a softer, easy-drinking, and juicy red wine. During carbonic maceration, whole clusters of red grapes are put in a closed bin or tank. The clusters at the bottom of the tank are crushed under the weight of the rest of the fruit and release their juice, which starts fermentation in this closed environment. The carbon dioxide that's released during the fermentation then begins to penetrate the whole grapes toward the top of the tank, causing them to ferment inside of their skins and burst open. Historically, carbonic maceration has been linked to gamay in Beaujolais; however, winemakers now employ the technique all over the world with all sorts of grapes. Our suggestions for producers cover a wide range from around the globe, and while they don't all use carbonic maceration, they all make at least one seriously glou-glou wine. We like drinking them slightly (or fully) chilled.

The zippy tartness of the tamarind in the Thai-inspired barbecue sauce plays seamlessly with the fruitiness of glou-glou wines. If you've cooked ribs before, you may be used to a low-and-slow approach, which means hours of maintaining your grill temperature. Ours get a simple, flavorful marinade and are finished on the grill before your first bottle of wine will be drained. Plan to eat this entire meal with your hands, get messy, and put fingerprints all over your wine glasses.

Fried Garlic and Garlic Oil

12 cloves garlic, minced
½ cup vegetable oil

3 to 4 pounds baby back pork ribs
3 tablespoons fish sauce
3 tablespoons soy sauce

Tamarind Dipping Sauce

½ cup seedless tamarind pulp (see Note)
2½ cups water
½ cup light brown sugar
1½ tablespoons finely ground mild red chile powder, such as gochugaru, Kashmiri, ancho, guajillo, or New Mexican

1½ tablespoons kosher salt
1½ teaspoons soy sauce

2 to 3 pounds seasonal vegetables, such as gai lan or broccoli, bok choy or yu choy, Japanese baby turnips with tops attached, Asian eggplants cut into thick slices, long beans, and halved peppers
Kosher salt
4 cups steamed sticky rice or short-grain rice

continued

To make the Fried Garlic and Garlic Oil: Combine the garlic and oil in a small saucepan and place it over medium heat. Once the garlic begins to sizzle, decrease the heat to medium-low and gently fry the garlic, stirring often, until golden and crisp, 15 to 20 minutes. Drain the garlic through a fine-mesh sieve set over a small bowl to collect the infused oil. Use immediately, or store the fried garlic and garlic oil at room temperature in separate sealed containers for up to 1 month.

Place the ribs on a large rimmed baking sheet and pat them dry. In a small bowl, whisk the fish sauce, soy sauce, and 3 tablespoons of the garlic oil. Brush this mixture all over the ribs and set aside to marinate for at least 1 hour and up to 2 days. (Cover with plastic wrap and refrigerate the ribs if marinating for more than 2 hours.)

To make the dipping sauce: Combine the tamarind pulp with the water in a small saucepan and place it over medium heat. Bring the water to a simmer and cook, mashing the tamarind with a potato masher or a large fork until it mostly breaks down, 2 to 3 minutes. Remove the pan from the heat, cover, and set aside for about 15 minutes to soften. Pour the tamarind mixture through a fine-mesh sieve set over a medium bowl, pushing and scraping it through to extract as much of the tamarind water as possible. Discard the solids left in the sieve.

Combine the tamarind water, brown sugar, chile powder, salt, and soy sauce and bring to a simmer in a small saucepan over medium heat. Maintain a good simmer, stirring occasionally, until the sauce is slightly thickened but not syrupy, about 10 minutes. Remove the pan from the heat and stir in 1½ tablespoons of the fried garlic and 1½ tablespoons of the garlic oil. Cool the sauce to room temperature before serving. It will keep in a sealed container in the refrigerator for about 1 week.

Prepare a fire in a charcoal or gas grill. For charcoal, when the coals are ready, distribute them and preheat the grate. Wait until they've reached medium heat, or when you can hold your palm about 3 inches above the grill grate for 5 to 7 seconds. If using a gas grill, preheat on high, covered, for about 15 minutes, then turn the burners to medium.

Place the ribs on the grill directly over the heat, meaty-sides down. Cook for a total of 25 to 30 minutes, turning every 5 minutes or so. After the first turn, begin basting with some of the tamarind sauce, and continue basting each time you turn them over. The ribs are done when the meat is tender but not falling apart and the outside is nicely charred in spots. Remove the ribs from the grill and loosely tent them with aluminum foil; set aside to rest while you grill the vegetables. Brush the grill grates clean.

Toss the prepared vegetables in enough of the reserved garlic oil to lightly coat them, and season generously with salt. Grill the vegetables, turning occasionally, until just tender and nicely charred in spots, 5 to 10 minutes depending on the vegetable.

To serve, cut the ribs between each bone, and arrange them on a serving board, with the grilled vegetables, steamed rice, and remaining sauce on the side.

Note
Look for seedless tamarind pulp removed from the pod and compressed into a sticky, dense block in an Asian market or grocery store with a good selection of international foods.

Oregon Pinot Noir

CAMPFIRE CASSOULET

Makes 4 servings, or 6 as part of a larger meal

If you're like Andrea, the best part of camping isn't the cold dip in the lake or the glass of whiskey by the fire. It's not even waking up to the sound of tweeting birds or the smell of pine needles underfoot. Nope. The best part of camping is the campfire cooking. Planning the menu, packing the ingredients, and then roughing it with a good cast-iron skillet and a worn-in wooden spoon is one of life's great pleasures. After a long day of playing in the woods, there's nothing nicer than sitting down to a proper meal. Forget those freeze-dried packet entrées or Top Ramen eaten out of the pot it was cooked in. Here's our recipe for a simple yet incredibly comforting and delicious cassoulet that takes about an hour and a half to cook—the perfect amount of time for a game of horseshoes while you watch dinner bubble away over the fire. It's loaded with chunks of smoky pork sausage and bacon and white beans directly from the can, and finished with a shower of garlicky breadcrumbs.

And maybe it's our outdoorsy Oregon roots that have us craving pinot noir when we're camping, but this pairing is almost too easy. It's partly environment that makes these wines a shoo-in for campfire cooking: the aromatics of pinot perfectly complement the dusty tree-scented air of nature. But the stewy smokiness of the cassoulet begs for a truly pretty wine, something that pinot noir is known for. Our favorite Oregon pinots are lighter- to medium-bodied and well balanced between earthy fruit, tingly acidity, and an almost ethereal texture. They're not big fruit bombs, they shy away from oakiness, and they really taste like the place they come from. Oregon is arguably one of the greatest regions in the world for grapes, so we tend to feel spoiled with our access to great wine. We are proud to call all of these winemakers friends and greatly admire how they represent the very best of our beautiful state. Before leaving for the camping trip, pack a piece of string (to tie the herbs together later).

Breadcrumbs

1 tablespoon extra-virgin olive oil
½ cup coarse breadcrumbs (homemade or panko)
1 clove garlic, minced
2 tablespoons minced fresh flat-leaf parsley
¼ teaspoon kosher salt

Cassoulet

8 ounces slab bacon, cut into ½ by ½ by 2-inch rectangles (also known as lardons)

12 ounces smoked pork sausages, such as kielbasa, cut on a bias into thick slices
1 yellow onion, diced
1 large carrot, halved and sliced
2 large ribs celery, sliced
4 cloves garlic, minced
4 flat-leaf parsley sprigs
2 thyme sprigs
1 bay leaf
2 (14-ounce) cans white beans
1 (14-ounce) can diced tomatoes with juices
¼ teaspoon freshly ground black pepper
1 cup chicken broth

continued

To make the breadcrumbs: Warm the oil in a medium skillet set over medium heat. Add the breadcrumbs and garlic and cook, stirring, until the breadcrumbs are toasted and crunchy, 2 to 3 minutes. Remove the pan from the heat and stir in the parsley and salt. Set the toasted breadcrumbs aside to cool completely, then transfer them to a zip-top bag to pack for the trip.

To make the cassoulet at the campsite: Build a campfire for cooking. As the fire burns down and turns to coals, use a stick to bank some of the coals toward one end of the fire pit, to create a hot side and a warm side. Place a grate over the fire.

Heat a 10- to 12-inch cast-iron skillet on the grate directly over the fire. Add the bacon and cook, stirring often, until some of the fat is rendered, 2 to 4 minutes. Add the sausages and cook until both meats are nicely browned, 4 to 8 minutes. If at any point they seem to be cooking too quickly, move the skillet to the cooler side of the fire.

Add the onion, carrot, celery, and garlic to the skillet and cook until tender and lightly browned, stirring rarely, 8 to 10 minutes. Gather the parsley, thyme, and bay leaf into a bundle and tie securely with the string you packed. Stir in the beans and their liquid, the tomatoes with their juices, and pepper, then bury the herb bundle in the middle of the pan. Pour in the broth and bring to a simmer. Cook, uncovered, without disturbing until the liquid has thickened but the mixture is still a little stewy and the top looks a bit dry and crusty, 30 to 50 minutes, depending on the size of your pan and the heat of the fire. If at any point a steady simmer is lost, stoke the fire and pile the coals to keep the heat concentrated. Add more kindling, if needed.

Remove the skillet from the fire and allow it to cool for about 5 minutes. Sprinkle the breadcrumbs in an even layer over the top and serve.

Northern Rhône Syrah

TOMAHAWK STEAKS WITH GRILLED RADICCHIO AND CHERRY TAPENADE

Makes 6 servings

When someone says "tomahawk steaks," we think "serious dinner." And when we think about big, bone-in steaks grilled outside in the height of summer, we think about syrah. Grown all over the world, and made into rich, deep reds full of forest berry, olive, and smoky notes, syrah is one of the very best wines you can treat yourself to, especially when it comes from France's Northern Rhône Valley. According to law, the only permitted red grape in the Northern Rhône is syrah. The region has eight appellations, three of which focus exclusively on white wines, two of which make only syrah, and three that make both syrah and white wines. Look to the appellations of St. Joseph and Crozes-Hermitage for delicious but less expensive syrahs. Bottles from Côte-Rôtie, Hermitage, and Cornas will cost you the most, and generally need five to ten years of age to be drinking nicely. While the Southern Rhône has the power and heat of wines from Châteauneuf-du-Pape, Gigondas, and the general Côtes du Rhône area, the Northern Rhône produces syrahs that are prolific in their mineral and smoked meat notes. They have acidity and can age for many years, and the vineyards are mostly incredibly steep and extremely difficult to farm. Soils range from schist to clay to granite, and greatly contribute to the way that syrah from here tastes. Do not be mistaken: you'll still enjoy a bigger red in these wines, but they also have a finesse and elegance to them that can't be found in syrah grown elsewhere. They really do deserve the prices they command. The way we figure it, if you're going to spend a little extra money on a great steak, you might as well throw down for a special bottle of wine.

We've tied some of syrah's unmistakable flavors into this recipe, with dark-red-almost-black cherries, balsamic vinegar, and grill smoke being major players. You'll be using cherries in three ways: in a black olive tapenade with a hint of rosemary as a condiment for the steak; in a smooth, vibrant pink balsamic vinaigrette; and fresh halves tossed with grilled radicchio and thick-cut red onion rings. The lush fruit of the wine can handle the assertiveness of the radicchio, and the tapenade coaxes out every enticingly aromatic found in these syrahs. Ask your butcher for tomahawk steaks, which are sometimes called "cowboy chops." You can also use bone-in rib eyes if a big caveman cut isn't available.

continued

Pre-Salted Steaks

2 (2-inch-thick) tomahawk steaks
    (sometimes labeled "cowboy chops")
    or 4 pounds bone-in rib eyes
1 tablespoon sea salt

Cherry-Olive Tapenade

6 ounces (about 18) sweet red cherries,
    pitted and finely chopped
½ cup Kalamata olives, pitted and finely
    chopped
2 tablespoons extra-virgin olive oil
1 anchovy, minced
1 clove garlic, minced
1½ teaspoons minced fresh rosemary
Freshly ground black pepper
Sea salt

Cherry Vinaigrette

6 ounces (about 18) sweet red cherries,
    pitted
½ cup extra-virgin olive oil
1½ tablespoons balsamic vinegar
1 small clove garlic, smashed
½ teaspoon sea salt, or to taste
Freshly ground black pepper

2 large (1 pound total) heads red chicories,
    such as radicchio, Treviso, or a
    combination
2 red onions
Extra-virgin olive oil, for brushing
Sea salt
Freshly ground black pepper
Several fresh rosemary sprigs, for resting
    the steak (optional)
6 ounces (about 18) sweet red cherries,
    pitted and halved

To pre-salt the steaks: At least 1 hour and up to 24 hours before grilling, season each of the steaks with 1½ teaspoons of the salt, coating all sides. Cover and refrigerate the steaks, if cooking later, or set them aside at room temperature if they will be cooked within 2 hours.

To make the tapenade: In a small bowl, combine the cherries, olives, oil, anchovy, garlic, rosemary, and several grinds of pepper. Taste and add salt, as needed. Set aside at room temperature for at least 1 hour and up to 4 hours for the flavors to meld. The tapenade will keep in a covered container in the refrigerator for up to 3 days.

To make the vinaigrette: Put the cherries, oil, vinegar, garlic, salt, and several grinds of pepper in a blender and blend until smooth. Taste and adjust the seasoning. The dressing will keep in a covered container in the refrigerator for up to 3 days.

Prepare a fire in a charcoal or gas grill (preferably charcoal). For charcoal, when the coals are ready, bank them on one side of the grill for an indirect heat zone. Preheat the grate for high-heat grilling, or when you can hold your palm about 3 inches above the grill grate over the coals for less than 3 seconds. If using a gas grill, preheat on high, covered, for about 15 minutes, then turn half of the burners off.

Discard any wilted outer leaves from the chicories. Halve each head through the core, then cut each half into four quarters, so that each wedge is held together by a small piece of the core. Halve and peel the red onions, and trim their cores of any crusty bits but keep the halves intact. Cut each onion half into four quarters, through the core to keep the wedges together, as you did with the radicchio. Brush the radicchio and onion wedges with a light coating of oil and season them with salt.

Pat the steaks dry and brush them lightly with oil, then season each with another pinch of salt and several grinds of pepper on all sides. To impart extra flavor to the steaks, line a platter with a bed of rosemary sprigs to rest them on after grilling.

Place the steaks on the grill grate, directly over the coals, and grill until nicely charred with a deep brown crust, 5 to 10 minutes per side. When flare-ups happen, try moving the steaks to another area of the grill, and turn them as needed to prevent blackening. Once a crust forms, move the steaks to the side of the grill without coals, and continue cooking with the grill lid closed until an instant-read thermometer inserted in the middle of a steak registers 140°F to 145°F for medium doneness (ideal for this cut), turning every 6 minutes or so, 12 to 25 minutes total, depending on the thickness of the steaks and whether you are using a charcoal (which cooks the steaks more quickly) or a gas grill. Transfer the steaks to the prepared platter and rest, loosely tented with aluminum foil, for about 10 minutes before slicing.

Meanwhile, place the onions cut-side down on the grill over the direct flame until deeply charred on each of the cut sides, about 5 minutes, then move them to the cooler side to continue cooking through, about 5 minutes more. Place the radicchio over the direct flame and cook until nicely charred and wilted throughout, about 5 minutes.

Combine the grilled radicchio and onions in a large bowl as they are removed from the grill. Toss with a liberal dose of the cherry vinaigrette to coat quite well, as the warm vegetables will soak it up. Add the halved cherries and toss again. Transfer the warm salad to a serving platter and drizzle with a few more spoonfuls of the vinaigrette.

Slice the steaks on a cutting board, then return them to the serving platter. Sprinkle the cut sides with more sea salt. Scatter some of the tapenade over the top, and pass the rest at the table.

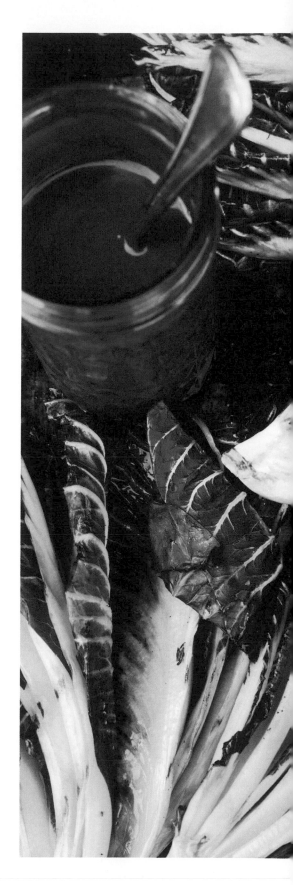

Spanish Wines

Producers to Look For

Daniel Ramos
Daterra Viticultores
Dominio del Urogallo
Envínate

Goyo Garcia Viadero
Mandrágora Vinos de Pueblo
Ulibarri Winery

We admit to going through a Spanish Wine Dry Spell, when we didn't drink much from the country except for txakoli. It lasted a long time because most of the wines we tasted were made in a modern style—big, oaky, high-alcohol—and mostly from Rioja, Ribera del Duero, and Toro. They didn't hold any appeal to us. But thanks to the hard work of several national wine importers, the past few years have ushered in a new school of wines that, quite frankly, have changed the way we think about wine from the Iberian Peninsula. Gone are the days of over-the-top, hangover-inducing reds and candied-grapefruit whites. Those wines still exist, but they're nearly crowded out by fantastic options from the Basque country, Catalonia, the Canary Islands, Extremadura, and Galicia. What's more, although paella is rooted in Spain's southeastern city of Valencia, we've found that this abundance of interesting and off-the-beaten path wines beautifully complement the dish.

Our recipe for paella de la corona is a nod to our friends Scott and Emily Ketterman of Crown Paella. They make such a good version that we would confidently say it rivals the best we've tasted in Valencia. The goal with paella is to make it as thin as you possibly can, so buy the biggest pan that will fit on your grill. According to Scott, the masters in Valencia say that the perfect paella is only two-grains-of-rice deep, so as to cook all of the ingredients evenly and create the magical *socarrat*, the crust that forms on the bottom of the pan.

Cooking a giant paella over a live fire with friends looking on is now one of our favorite things to do in the summertime. It's dinner theater where everyone oohs and aahs every time another ingredient is added to the pan. We start the party with a big tableful of tapas, or *pintxos* (PEEN-chos) as they are called in the Basque region, and pull out the *porron*, the glass wine pitcher with a thin spout designed to get the wine to your lips without using a glass. It's a traditional way to drink wine throughout Spain. Pop the cork on a bottle, pour the wine into the porron, tip your head back, and hope for the best. The key is to raise the porron away from your mouth as the wine hits your tongue, all without spilling it down your chin or on your shirt. We suggest starting with a white wine.

Pintxos Gilda—green olives skewered with pickled white anchovies and mild, spindly pickled guindilla peppers—are ubiquitous in pintxos bars throughout San Sebastián. Another common offering is pimientos de padrón, which are (usually) mild green peppers that are sautéed in olive oil until they blister and wilt. We've offered a lot of options in this menu, because Spanish tapas are so simple to put together, and it's fun to have a substantial array on the table, as they do in Spain. But don't feel like you have to do it all; just pick and choose a few. Tinned fish and seafood—such as Spanish sardines, mackerel, octopus, mussels, and cockles— are some of our favorite wine snacks. When the paella is ready to serve, clear the table and have your guests gather around while you grab a pal to help you parade the pan to the table (the procession of the paella is important!). Be sure to scoop some of the prized socarrat onto everyone's plate, and keep passing the porron.

PAELLA
AND PORRONS

Jamón and Peas (page 28)

Pintxos Gilda (page 178)

Blistered Padrón Peppers (page 178)

Fig Fattoush with Grilled Halloumi
(page 106)

Paella de la Corona (page 178)

Tapas Board of Spanish Charcuterie,
Tinned Fish and Seafood, and Cheeses with
Membrillo Paste and Marcona Almonds

PINTXOS GILDA

Makes 8 to 10 servings

20 boquerones (pickled white anchovies)
20 whole pitted green Spanish olives
20 pickled guindilla peppers (from one
    4.5-ounce jar; also called piparras)

To assemble each gilda, wrap a
boquerone around an olive, and thread
it on a cocktail pick so that each end
of the anchovy is skewered. Thread a
pepper at an angle onto the pick. Repeat
to make 20 skewers. Arrange them on
a serving plate and serve immediately,
or cover and refrigerate for up to
1 day. Bring the skewers back to room
temperature before serving.

BLISTERED PADRÓN PEPPERS

Makes 8 to 10 servings

2 tablespoons extra-virgin olive oil,
    plus more for drizzling
1 pound padrón peppers
Fine sea salt
Flaky sea salt

Warm 1 tablespoon of the oil in a large
skillet over medium-high heat. When
it just begins to smoke, add half of the
peppers and a big pinch of fine sea
salt and cook until the peppers collapse
and blacken in spots, about 5 minutes.
Transfer the peppers to a serving plate.
Drizzle the blistered peppers with more
oil and sprinkle with flaky sea salt.
Serve hot. Repeat to cook the remaining
peppers in the rest of the oil, garnish,
and serve.

PAELLA DE LA CORONA

Makes 8 to 10 servings

Sofrito

2 tablespoons extra-virgin olive oil
1 green bell pepper, diced
1 yellow onion, diced
2 cloves garlic, slivered
1 cup tomato puree, such as Pomì
Sea salt

Paella

3 tablespoons extra-virgin olive oil,
    plus more for drizzling
1½ pounds boneless rabbit, or chicken
    thighs, cut into 2-inch chunks
Sea salt
1½ pounds unpeeled jumbo shrimp
    (preferably head-on), deveined by
    cutting a slit through the back of
    the shell with kitchen shears
1 pound Romano beans or wax beans,
    trimmed and cut into 2-inch pieces
1 (4.5-ounce) dry-cured Spanish chorizo,
    thinly sliced
1 tablespoon smoked Spanish paprika
2 quarts low-sodium chicken broth
2 teaspoons saffron threads
3½ cups Bomba rice
1½ cups whole pitted green Spanish olives
1½ pounds mussels, scrubbed and
    debearded
1 (9.9-ounce jar) piquillo peppers,
    quartered lengthwise
12 squash blossoms (optional)
Lemon wedges, for serving

To make the sofrito: Warm the oil in
a medium skillet over medium heat.
Add the bell pepper, onion, and garlic
and cook, stirring occasionally, until
everything is tender and the onion is
translucent, 5 to 7 minutes. Stir in the
tomato puree and a big pinch of salt and
bring to a simmer. Decrease the heat
to maintain a gentle simmer and cook,
stirring frequently, until most of the

liquid is reduced and the sofrito is very thick, about 30 minutes. (The sofrito can be made in advance and stored in the refrigerator, covered, for up to 5 days.)

To make the paella: Prepare a fire in a charcoal or gas grill (preferably charcoal). For charcoal, when the coals are ready, distribute them in an area the size of the bottom of the paella pan. Add about 20 more charcoal briquets, dotted on top of the coals, which will ignite and keep the fire going long enough to cook the paella. If at any point the fire dies down, add more briquets. If using a gas grill, preheat on high, covered, for about 15 minutes, and adjust the heat as needed throughout cooking.

Place a 17- to 22-inch paella pan on the grill grate, directly over the coals. If at any point during cooking the paella you notice hot spots in certain areas of the pan, rotate it occasionally for even cooking.

Add the oil to the pan and heat it until smoking. Add the rabbit or chicken, season with a big pinch of salt, and cook, stirring with a flat-edged wooden spoon or a wok spatula, until it is lightly browned, 6 to 8 minutes. Push the meat to the edges of the pan and add the shrimp and beans to the center. Season with another pinch of salt and cook until they are lightly colored, about 3 minutes. Add the chorizo and cook until it's sizzling, about 1 minute. Push the meat back to the center of the pan and sprinkle in the paprika. Cook until the paprika is aromatic, about 1 minute. Stir in the sofrito and cook until a thin layer caramelizes on the bottom of the pan, about 3 minutes.

Pour in the broth, sprinkle in the saffron and 1 tablespoon salt, and bring to a simmer. Sprinkle (or rain) the rice evenly into the simmering broth. Make sure the rice is completely covered and in a relatively even layer, and then avoid stirring or moving the rice for the rest of the cooking process.

Dot the olives evenly around the paella. Arrange the mussels in the pan in concentric rings, nestling the hinge sides into the liquid. Next, arrange the piquillo peppers and squash blossoms (if using) around the paella in a ring pattern.

Continue cooking the paella, without disturbing except to rotate the pan occasionally, until the rice has absorbed all of the liquid and smells slightly toasted because a *socarrat*—a caramelized crusty layer—has formed on the bottom of the pan, 30 to 45 minutes. To check if your paella has a socarrat, drive a small metal spoon through the rice to the base of the pan to feel for a crusty, slightly sticky bottom.

Once the socarrat has formed, remove the paella pan from the grill, cover it with aluminum foil, and allow it to rest for at least 5 minutes and up to 15 minutes.

Serve the paella in the center of the table, straight from the pan, with more oil drizzled generously over the top and lemon wedges on the side.

Pairing Cheat Sheet
Pasta-Pairing Primer

KERNER / CARBONARA

TEROLDEGO / LASAGNA

VALPOLICELLA / BOLOGNESE

PIGATO / TRENETTE AL PESTO

SOAVE / LINGUINE ALLE VONGOLE

BARBARESCO / BUCATINI ALL'AMATRICIANA

FRIULIAN ORANGE WINE / PENNE ARRABIATA

GRECO DI TUFO / CACIO E PEPE

NERO D'AVOLA / SPAGHETTI ALLA NORMA

TREBBIANO / TORTELLINI EN BRODO

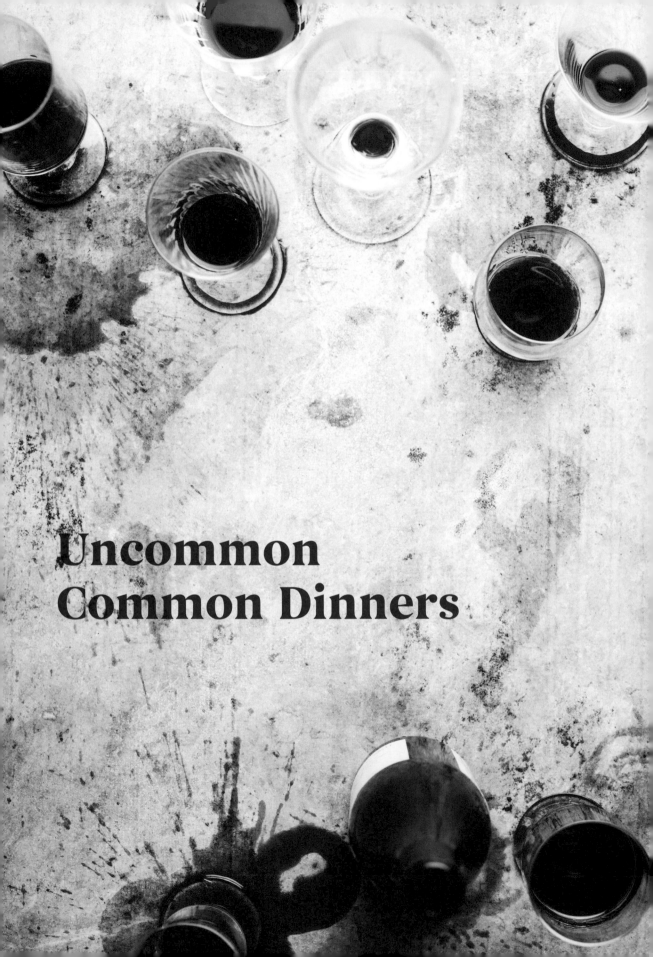

Uncommon
Common Dinners

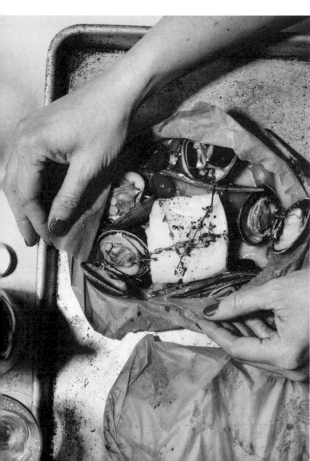

Grüner Veltliner

FORBIDDEN RICE BOWLS WITH SLOW-ROASTED SALMON AND THOSE SWEET-AND-SOUR CUCUMBERS EVERYONE LOVES

Makes 6 servings

Producers to Look For

Christian Tschida
Martin & Anna Arndorfer
Michael Gindl
Milan Nestarec
Veyder-Malberg

Grüner veltliner (GROO-ner VELT-lee-ner) is among the best grapes of Austria and accounts for the plantings in more than 30 percent of the country's vineyards. Grüner, as it's often called, is also found in neighboring countries, such as the Czech Republic. At its simplest, grüner is stony and can smell of white pepper, green grass, and lime zest. At its best, grüner takes on a beautiful complexity where the fruit appears riper and richer (think pink grapefruit and white nectarines), and it has a waxy mouthfeel. It's nearly always a high-acid wine with a refreshing tartness, which makes it fantastic with foods that have any richness, such as salmon and avocado. Some Austrian grüners will be labeled with the words *Steinfeder*, *Federspiel*, or *Smaragd*, indicating levels of ripeness and alcohol. We don't often see Steinfeder-level wines in the United States, but they are considered the easiest drinking at less than 11% alcohol. Far more common are the Federspiel-level bottlings for everyday drinking and the Smaragd-level wines, which certainly are the richest and most powerful. You'll surely find Austrian grüner, but do seek out versions from other Central and Eastern European countries.

This recipe is one of those magical wine and food moments. Separately, this wine and this rice bowl are tasty, but together they make each other ten times better. We wanted to jazz up the now-ubiquitous rice bowl with a floral and fragrant alternative, so we chose black rice (also marketed as Forbidden Rice), which cooks up with a snappy bite and a gorgeous hue. The salmon gets a quick soy marinade before the skins are baked to a crispy bacon texture. The fish is slow-roasted, and it's all finished with that classic cucumber salad with sweetened rice vinegar dressing and creamy chunks of avocado.

2 cups black rice (also labeled as Forbidden Rice)

2½ cups water

2½ teaspoons sea salt

6 (4- to 5-ounce) skin-on wild salmon fillets, scaled (see Note)

1 tablespoon dry white wine

1½ teaspoons honey

1½ teaspoons soy sauce

¼ teaspoon toasted sesame oil, plus more for drizzling

⅓ cup unseasoned rice vinegar

1 tablespoon sugar

½ teaspoon freshly ground black pepper

1 English cucumber, quartered lengthwise and cut crosswise into ¼-inch-thick triangles

¼ red onion, thinly sliced crosswise and soaked in cold water for 10 minutes and drained

1 avocado, diced

¼ cup black or toasted white sesame seeds, or a combination

1 sheet toasted nori, cut with scissors into matchsticks

Preheat the oven to 450°F. Line a rimmed baking sheet with parchment paper.

Put the rice in a medium saucepan and add the water and 1½ teaspoons of the salt. Bring to a boil over high heat. Decrease the heat to low, cover, and cook until the water is absorbed, about 30 minutes. Set aside, still covered, for at least 5 minutes to finish steaming. The rice will keep warm like this for up to 30 minutes before serving.

Meanwhile, remove the salmon skins from each fillet (if it wasn't done by your fishmonger) and scrape off any remaining bits of flesh. The goal is to have paper-thin, flesh-free skins that will get crispy in the oven.

In a medium bowl, whisk the wine, honey, soy sauce, and sesame oil to make a marinade. Dredge the skins in the marinade, allowing the excess to drip off. Spread the salmon skins on the prepared baking sheet, stretching them completely flat, with the scale side facing up. Add the salmon fillets to the marinade and turn each to coat all sides. Set the fillets aside to marinate for 20 to 30 minutes.

While the fillets marinate, bake the skins until they are crispy and deeply browned in spots and feel generally dehydrated, which will take anywhere from 5 to 10 minutes. They can get quite dark, but if it seems like they are starting to burn but still feel a little soft in the center, take them out; they will continue to crisp up as they cool, and even a little chewiness is okay. Peel the skins off the parchment paper and set them aside to cool and crisp. Discard the parchment paper.

Decrease the oven temperature to 250°F and put a fresh piece of parchment paper on the baking sheet.

After marinating, transfer the salmon fillets from the marinade to the baking sheet and roast until they reach about 120°F in the center for medium done-ness, 8 to 12 minutes.

In a medium bowl, whisk the vinegar, sugar, pepper, and remaining 1 teaspoon salt to dissolve. Add the cucumber and onion and toss to coat. Add the avocado and toss gently, taking care not to mash it up.

Fluff the rice and divide it among shallow bowls. Place a salmon fillet in each bowl and top with the cucumber-avocado salad, plus some of the dressing from the bottom of the bowl. Crumble or tear a crispy salmon skin over each serving. Sprinkle each generously with sesame seeds, drizzle with a little toasted sesame oil, top with a pile of nori strips, and serve.

Note
If you aren't comfortable skinning salmon fillets yourself, ask your fishmonger to do it, but keep the skins.

Croatian White

COD AND CLAMS EN PAPILLOTE

Makes 4 servings

Producers to Look For

Bura-Mrgudić Winery
Carić Vina
Enjingi
Šipun
Zlatan Otok

Croatia has to be one of the most beautiful countries in the world. Its entire western border stares out at the aquamarine waters of the Adriatic Sea, dotted with more than one thousand islands. The northwest part of the country, known as Istria, butts up to Slovenia and is a literal stone's throw from Italy. The northeast presses into Slovenia and Hungary, and the entire south, Dalmatia, spoons Bosnia-Herzegovina. It could not be more diverse. Wine is made in every part of the country, with the north being dominated by continental-climate whites and the south by Mediterranean reds. It's as if the white grapes know their vineyards precariously overlook the ocean, and that the seafood bounty that comes from it feeds everyone along the coastline. You'll find Croatian whites to be extremely refreshing, aromatic with vibrant stone fruit and white flowers, all balanced by a good dose of sea air that is almost always noticeable in the glass. These wines are meant to be enjoyed with seafood. Look for varieties such as malvazija, grk (gerk), and graševina (GRAH-sheh-vee-nah).

There's something very fun about serving a delicate piece of white fish that has been cooked in a paper packet. Not only is it easy to put together and cleanup is a breeze, but who doesn't love to tear into that steaming pouch to peek at what's inside? Choose a quick-cooking piece of fish, such as cod, snapper, or sole—we went for cod here—surround it by vegetables that steam up nicely, a handful of briny clams, and herbs on their stems, and douse it all with good olive oil. Twist the parchment paper into a tight package that will trap the steam that cooks the fish. Slide those steamy packets onto plates and get them to the table swiftly so everyone can rip into them. The fish will be perfectly flaky, the veggies tender. The clams will have burst open, their juices making a delicious sauce that practically begs for a seaside white wine. And when it's all devoured, just slide the empty parchment into the compost, toss your plates in the dishwasher, and finish off your bottle of wine. This recipe can easily be scaled up or down to accommodate the number of hungry people you're cooking for.

2 tablespoons extra-virgin olive oil
10 ounces waxy potatoes, peeled and
    sliced ⅛ inch thick
Sea salt
Freshly ground black pepper
4 (4- to 6-ounce) skinless cod fillets
20 green beans, trimmed and halved
    lengthwise

12 cherry tomatoes, halved
24 small black olives, such as Niçoise
20 Manila clams, scrubbed
12 thyme sprigs
2 teaspoons minced garlic
1 lemon, cut into 4 wedges

continued

Preheat the oven to 450°F.

Cut four 12½ by 16-inch sheets of parchment paper. Fold one of the sheets of parchment paper in half crosswise and open it up like a book. On one side, close to the crease, drizzle about ½ teaspoon of the oil and lay down about one-fourth of the potato slices, slightly overlapping them like scales, to cover an area a little larger than the size of one of the fish fillets. Season the potatoes with salt and pepper. Season a fish fillet generously with salt and pepper and place it atop the potatoes. Disperse one-fourth of each of the remaining ingredients (except for the lemon) around the fish fillet: 10 halves of the green beans, 6 tomato halves, 6 olives, 5 clams, 3 thyme sprigs, and ½ teaspoon of the garlic sprinkled over everything. Drizzle with 1 teaspoon oil.

To close the parchment packet, fold the other half of parchment over the fish. Starting at the top, leaving enough space within the packet to allow air flow around the ingredients, begin making small, very tight overlapping folds, working your way along the outside edge of the parchment to the bottom. Twist the bottom end and fold it under the packet to seal tightly.

Repeat to make 3 more packets, and place them all on a large rimmed baking sheet. Place the packets in the oven for 10 minutes. If they are sealed tightly, they will balloon up as they cook from the steam trapped inside.

Place a hot packet and a lemon wedge on each of 4 plates. Cut or rip them open at the table.

Aligoté

THE NEW TUNA NOODLE

Makes 4 to 6 servings

Producers to Look For

Alice et Olivier DeMoor
Didier Montchovet
Domaine A. et P. de Villaine
Domaine Naudin-Ferrand
Olivier Morin

Aligoté is the white grape of Burgundy you've possibly never heard of. While it may not be as prolific as chardonnay, there are stunning examples to be had, and they're definitely worth finding. Burgundians love aligoté, and they keep it in their vineyards even though it doesn't fetch the prices that chardonnay can, because it's a more quaffable, lighter expression of Burgundy's terroir. It has a citrus brightness to it and a light floral quality, and it doesn't need to be aged to be delicious, unlike most white Burgundy. In general, aligoté will be labeled with the generic *Bourgogne Aligoté AOP*, although there is one specific town known for its perfect soils, Bouzeron, that gets to have its name on the bottle.

With its pay-attention-to-me acidity, aligoté is a no-brainer for our updated take on the fifties' classic tuna noodle casserole. We took the flavors we love about the dish and spun it into a sophisticated pasta, coated with a creamy sauce and finished with crispy fried capers. The toasted walnuts offer a lovely crunchy bite that make a wonderful match with aligoté, and the flourish of parsley and Parmigiano take this from the nostalgia of your childhood to your next dinner.

Sea salt
1 pound linguine
¼ cup extra-virgin olive oil
1 (3.5-ounce) jar capers, rinsed and
    patted dry
4 cloves garlic, minced
¼ teaspoon red pepper flakes
¼ cup dry white wine
2 (6- to 7-ounce) cans best-quality tuna in
    olive oil, drained
½ cup heavy cream
½ cup finely chopped fresh flat-leaf parsley
Freshly ground black pepper
1 cup freshly grated Parmigiano-Reggiano
    cheese
1 cup chopped walnuts, toasted for 5 to
    7 minutes (see Note, page 29)

Bring a large pot of heavily salted water to a boil over high heat and add the linguine. Cook it 2 minutes less than called for on the package directions, to keep it just slightly firmer than al dente. Drain, reserving 11/2 cups of the cooking liquid.

Warm the oil in a large skillet over medium-high heat. Add the capers (they will spatter) and fry until they crisp and burst open, 2 to 3 minutes. Remove the pan from the heat and use a slotted spoon to transfer the capers to a plate, reserving the oil in the pan.

Return the pan of oil to medium heat and add half of the garlic and all of the red pepper flakes. Cook until the garlic is golden, 1 to 2 minutes. Pour in the wine, bring to a simmer, and reduce by half, about 3 minutes. Add the tuna and cream and bring to a simmer, breaking up the tuna into chunks.

Add the drained pasta, the parsley, the remaining garlic, and several grinds of pepper and toss. Alternate adding the cheese and just enough of the pasta water to create a creamy sauce that coats the noodles. Stir in half of the walnuts.

Serve in warmed pasta bowls, topped with the remaining walnuts and the fried capers.

Tempranillo

SUMMER PIPERADE WITH FRIED EGGS

Makes 4 servings

Producers to Look For

Bodega Akutain
Alfredo Maestro
Correcaminos
Goyo Garcia Viadero
Maisulan

Tempranillo is a natural pairing for piperade, with its rustic fruitiness and tomato-leaf notes. It's an easy wine to find in shops and on wine lists, given that it's the most widely planted grape in Spain. But tempranillo has its challenges: there are less-than-enjoyable styles made at huge industrial wineries, and nowadays it's all too easy to find big-bodied versions from Rioja, Toro, and Ribera del Duero, all aged in American oak barrels, giving the wines toasty vanilla flavors and too much tannin—enough to erase the summery brightness of this piperade. But there are also the small-volume producers who make dynamic tempranillo that truly speaks to how and where it's grown. They're working with grapes grown all over the country, from vines planted in soils that range from sand to limestone, and are pushing the limits of what most consumers expect tempranillo to be.

The producers we suggest make a variety of wines that are mostly aged in stainless-steel or cement vats or older barrels, which lets the best of the grapes sing without the background noise of oak. And check out this added benefit: these types of tempranillo tend to be a steal because oak-aging, especially in new barrels, generally makes wines more expensive. You might be surprised at how fresh and vibrant tempranillo can be, especially if you're accustomed to more modern versions. Be adventurous and look to Castilla y León, Penedès, and Valdepeñas for their versions of tempranillo that offer very different characteristics from those of the more popular Rioja.

We love eggs for dinner. Most of us have them around the house as part of our staple groceries, and they quickly and easily add richness to a dish. Eggs on toast are perfect for breakfast. But eggs over a summery stew of farmers' market sweet peppers, onions, and fruity piment d'Espelette says *dinner* to us. Don't cut corners on the peppers here—get a mix of sweet yellow, orange, and red peppers at the height of summer. Choose a selection of sizes and shapes so the piperade has varying texture, and definitely pass on green peppers, which give the stew an astringent, vegetal flavor.

2 pounds mixed sweet peppers, such as bell, Italian, pimento, and Jimmy Nardello, cored, seeded, and cut into ⅓-inch-thick slices or rings
1 large sweet onion, such as Walla Walla, halved and sliced ¼ inch thick
½ cup extra-virgin olive oil
4 cloves garlic, smashed
1 tablespoon piment d'Espelette, or sweet paprika, plus more for sprinkling

Kosher salt
1¼ pounds juicy ripe tomatoes, cored and diced
2 teaspoons sherry vinegar
8 large farm-fresh eggs
2 tablespoons fresh lemon juice
Crusty bread, for serving

Put the sweet peppers, onion, ¼ cup of the oil, the garlic, piment d'Espelette, and a few big pinches of salt in a 12-inch skillet or a Dutch oven. Partially cover and cook over medium heat, stirring rarely, until the peppers are tender and the onion just becomes translucent, 15 to 20 minutes.

Stir in the tomatoes and continue cooking, still partially covered and stirring rarely, until the peppers are quite tender but not mushy, and the tomatoes give up their juice to make a jammy sauce, 15 to 20 minutes more. Remove the pan from the heat and stir in the vinegar. Taste and adjust the seasoning; the piperade should be sweet, but with a hint of bright acidity from the vinegar. Cover and set aside momentarily while you fry the eggs. (The piperade will keep, covered, in the refrigerator for up to 5 days.)

Warm an 8-inch nonstick skillet over medium-high heat, then add 2 tablespoons oil. When it's shimmering hot, crack in 4 of the eggs (they will spatter). The bottom of the whites will set almost on contact. When they do, sprinkle the eggs with salt and 1 tablespoon of the lemon juice and immediately cover the pan with a lid. Let the eggs cook for about 1 minute longer for molten yolks and crispy whites. Slide them out of the pan and onto a plate, and repeat to cook the remaining 4 eggs. Sprinkle the eggs with piment d'Espelette.

To serve, divide the piperade among 4 warm plates and top each with 2 of the fried eggs. Pass the bread at the table.

Beaujolais

SPATCHCOCK ROAST CHICKEN WITH SCHMALTZY POTATOES AND CABBAGE

Makes 4 to 6 servings

Producers to Look For

Clos de la Roilette

Domaine de la Grand 'Cour

Domaine des Terres Dorées

Jean Foillard

Julien Sunier

Beaujolais is home to one of the greatest grapes on Earth, gamay. This thin-skinned, fruity variety had a long history of making bubblegum-flavored, soft wines that were drunk by the gallons in the seventies and eighties. Now, though, it's easy to find gorgeous Beaujolais, still with a fruity foundation, but also with a certain seriousness and structure. The region sits just south of Burgundy in Eastern France, and while you can drink very inexpensive versions simply labeled *Beaujolais* or *Beaujolais-Villages*, we definitely think it's worth spending just a tiny bit more to enjoy gamay from one of the ten *crus*. In other parts of France, the word *cru* identifies a specific vineyard, but in Beaujolais, cru refers to an entire village or area. North to south, the crus are Juliénas, Saint-Amour, Chénas, Moulin-à-Vent, Fleurie, Chiroubles, Morgon, Régnié, Cote de Brouilly, and Brouilly. Cru Beaujolais has all of the things necessary for a simple chicken dinner. It's big on the fruit, but also on minerality, as the soils range from quartz to granite to clay, and whether more elegant or sturdy, the crus always make wines with an inherent smokiness and structure. If you're feeling adventurous, grab a bottle from any of these places. If you like a wine with a bit more gutsy fruit and structure, choose a Morgon or Moulin-à-Vent, but if you fancy something more elegant, go for a Fleurie or Brouilly. Honestly, you won't go wrong no matter which cru you choose.

Chicken and Beaujolais is hands down our favorite everyday dinner. As simple as roasting a chicken and pouring a glass of red wine can be, we've made it even simpler by putting it all on one baking sheet, popping it in the oven, and suggesting that you drink a glass of wine while everything cooks. A spatchcocked chicken sounds much more daunting than it is. Just cut the backbone from a whole chicken (or even easier, ask your butcher to do it for you) and press it flat. That's it. Think of it like a mock rotisserie: all of the fatty, luscious chicken drippings are soaked up by creamy potatoes and tender green cabbage. Everything is seasoned with a smoky spice rub that perfectly complements a great bottle of Beaujolais.

1 (4- to 4½-pound) chicken, patted dry

1 tablespoon plus 1 teaspoon kosher salt

¼ cup extra-virgin olive oil

2 cloves garlic, finely grated

1 tablespoon dried sage

1 tablespoon dry mustard

1 tablespoon onion powder

1 tablespoon smoked paprika

½ teaspoon freshly ground black pepper, plus more for sprinkling

1 (2-pound) green cabbage, halved, cored, and cut into 12 wedges

1½ pounds Yukon gold potatoes, cut into 1-inch chunks

1 yellow onion, cut into ¾-inch chunks

3 bay leaves, preferably fresh

continued

At least 1 hour and up to 3 days before roasting, set the chicken on a cutting board and, starting at the neck, use poultry shears or a chef's knife to cut out the backbone, snipping through the ribs on each side. Lay the bird breast-side down and press on each flank to flatten it. Season the chicken all over with 2½ teaspoons of the salt, cover, and refrigerate, breast-side up, for up to 3 days, or set it aside at room temperature if it will be roasted within 1 hour.

Preheat the oven to 450°F.

In a small bowl, mix the oil, garlic, sage, dry mustard, onion powder, paprika, and black pepper. Rub half of this mixture on the chicken, coating all sides and being sure to get under the folds of the wings and legs and in all crevasses. Tuck the wing tips behind the bird's shoulders.

Arrange the cabbage wedges in a single layer on a large rimmed baking sheet and season with ½ teaspoon salt. Toss the potatoes, onion, and bay leaves with the remaining half of the spice rub, remaining 1 teaspoon salt, and several grinds of pepper. Spread the potatoes and onion over and around the cabbage. Place the chicken, breast-side up, over the vegetables, put the pan in the oven, and immediately decrease the temperature to 375°F. Roast until an instant-read thermometer inserted in the thickest part of each breast registers 150°F, 45 to 55 minutes.

Transfer the chicken to a carving board to rest for about 10 minutes. Toss the roasted vegetables on the baking sheet to coat them in the chicken drippings and return the pan to the oven to continue cooking while the bird rests.

After 10 minutes, carve the chicken into 10 pieces: 2 drumsticks, 2 thighs, 2 wings, and 2 breasts each halved crosswise. Pile the roasted vegetables on a platter, arrange the chicken pieces on top, and serve.

Barbera

BORSCHT RISOTTO

Makes 6 servings

Producers to Look For

Cascina delle Rose
Cascina 'Tavijn
Ezio T.
Iuli
La Miraja

Piedmontese barbera instantly becomes this dish's best friend, with its high-toned red fruits and bright acidity to complement the comforting richness of the risotto. Barbera, one of the great grapes of Northern Italy, has become among the most recognizable and easy-to-find wines today, thanks to its inexpensiveness and proliferation in growing regions outside of Piedmont. This is a great pairing because barbera is just so drinkable. It offers what we most enjoy in a good bottle of wine: balance.

The marriage of these humble dishes may seem bizarre at first, but reimagine them this way: replace the boxed chicken broth from your everyday risotto recipe with homemade beef broth spiked with vibrant beets. Stir the rice to creamy perfection, toss in some toasted caraway seeds, and finish with a dash of vinegar for that borscht sourness. You'll have a bowl of gorgeous, ruby-red risotto, flecked with tender shreds of beef and finished with a dollop of sour cream. What's not to love?

Borscht

1 pound beef chuck, trimmed of excess fat and cut into 2-inch chunks
Kosher salt
Freshly ground black pepper
2 tablespoons extra-virgin olive oil
½ onion, cut into 2-inch chunks
1 large carrot, cut into 2-inch chunks
1 rib celery, cut into 2-inch segments
¼ cup dry red wine
12 ounces small red beets, tops trimmed, scrubbed, and peeled
1 quart beef broth
1 bay leaf
2 cups water

Risotto

2 tablespoons unsalted butter
⅓ cup finely diced yellow onion
1 teaspoon caraway seeds, coarsely crushed
2¼ cups arborio rice
1 cup dry red wine
Hot water, as needed
1½ teaspoons red wine vinegar
½ teaspoon kosher salt
Freshly ground black pepper

Sour cream, for serving
Dill fronds, for serving

To make the borscht: Season the beef with 1 teaspoon salt and several grinds of pepper. In a Dutch oven, warm the oil over medium-high heat. Sear the beef, working in batches if needed, until a deep crust forms on all sides, 8 to 10 minutes. Transfer the seared beef to a plate and set aside.

Add the onion, carrot, and celery to the rendered fat and cook until the vegetables start to take on some color, about 5 minutes. Pour in the wine and scrape up the bits from the bottom of the pan. Add the beef and any accumulated juices, the beets, beef broth, bay leaf, 1 teaspoon salt, and the water. Increase the heat and bring to a boil, then decrease the heat to maintain a gentle simmer, cover, and stew until the beets are fork-tender in the center and the beef shreds easily, 2 to 2½ hours.

continued

Transfer the beef and beets to a cutting board. When cool enough to handle, shred the beef using two forks and cut the beets into ¼-inch dice; set both aside. Strain the borscht broth into a saucepan, discarding the solids. Set aside to cool, skimming and discarding the fat as it rises to the surface; this will be your broth for cooking the risotto. (The beets, beef, and broth will keep, in separate covered containers, in the refrigerator for up to 4 days.)

To make the risotto: Set the saucepan of borscht broth over low heat. Melt the butter in a large, heavy skillet over medium heat. Add the onion and caraway seeds to the melted butter and cook until soft and fragrant, about 5 minutes. Add the rice, stirring to coat, and toast for about 2 minutes. Pour in the wine and simmer until it's absorbed, about 1 minute. Begin adding the warm broth in 2-cup increments, maintaining a gentle simmer and stirring often (not constantly!). Keep adding broth and simmering until the rice becomes plump and creamy but still has a chewy bite left to it, about 20 minutes. Begin adding hot water once all the broth has been used. The risotto should drink up about 6 cups of liquid total, while remaining a little loose and saucy. If it seems too thick, stir in one more splash of water just before serving. Stir in the shredded beef, diced beets, and vinegar and season with the salt and pepper.

Serve the risotto in warm shallow bowls, topped with a dollop of sour cream and a smattering of dill fronds.

Dolcetto

DELICATA CROSTATA WITH FENNEL SAUSAGE, RICOTTA, AND BUCKWHEAT HONEY

Makes 6 servings

Producers to Look For

Giuseppe Mascarello
Pecchenino
Roagna
San Fereolo
Simone Scaletta

Dolcetto is the quiet little sister of the Northern Italy wine family, often thought of as easy-drinking, not-so-serious wine. And while we can't totally argue with that description, there are some delicious, rustic bottlings that really go the distance with dishes such as this crostata. Dolcetto has softer tannins, a range of blue- and black-berried fruits, and good acidity, all of which pair really nicely with both a savory crostata and a weeknight dinner. If possible, ask your wine steward for an earthier-style dolcetto, as we found the funky layers of buckwheat in the crust and honey were truly elevated with a wine that wasn't too fruity.

You could think of a savory crostata as a grown-up pizza of sorts. The crust is easy to make yet unbelievably flaky; the filling can be any combination of cheese, veggies, and meat; and it all comes together in a quick bake and lunch, brunch, or dinner is served. This is our Italian version, pairing fennel-flecked pork sausage with sweet delicata squash, creamy ricotta, oregano, and assertive buckwheat honey.

Crust

¾ cup cold unsalted butter
1 cup all-purpose flour,
    plus more for dusting
½ cup buckwheat flour
¼ teaspoon kosher salt
⅓ cup ice-cold water

Filling

1 tablespoon extra-virgin olive oil
8 ounces mild Italian bulk sausage or links,
    casings removed
1 teaspoon fennel seeds, coarsely crushed
1 (12-ounce) delicata squash, halved,
    seeded, and thinly sliced
¾ teaspoon kosher salt
Freshly ground black pepper
1 pound whole-milk ricotta
1 tablespoon chopped fresh oregano
1 tablespoon buckwheat honey,
    plus more for drizzling

1 large egg, beaten
Flaky sea salt
Oregano leaves, for garnish

To make the crust: Cube the butter, put it in a small bowl, and stick it in the freezer until firm and really cold, about 10 minutes. In a food processor, pulse the chilled butter with both flours and the kosher salt until no butter chunks are larger than the size of a pea. Add the water and process just until the dough comes together in a shaggy mass.

Line a rimmed baking sheet with parchment paper. Transfer the dough to a lightly floured countertop and gather and pat it into a smooth ball. Using a floured rolling pin, roll it out to a 15-inch circle, rotating it occasionally to be sure it isn't sticking, and dusting with additional flour as needed. Roll the dough up loosely onto the rolling pin and unroll it onto the baking sheet. Loosely fold in any overhanging edges, cover with plastic wrap, and place the dough in the refrigerator until cold and firm, about 20 minutes.

Preheat the oven to 400°F.

To make the filling: Warm the oil in a large skillet over medium-high heat. Add the sausage and fennel seeds and cook until the meat is browned, about 5 minutes. Set the pan off the heat and stir in the squash, ½ teaspoon of the kosher salt, and a few grinds of pepper, coating it in the fat and bits of pork and spices.

In a medium bowl, stir the ricotta with the oregano, honey, and remaining ¼ teaspoon kosher salt.

Remove the chilled dough from the fridge. Spread the ricotta mixture in the center of the dough, leaving a 2-inch border. Scatter the squash-sausage mixture in an even layer over the ricotta. Fold the edges of dough over the filling, overlapping every 4 inches or so to create an evenly pleated crust. Brush the crust lightly with some of the beaten egg and sprinkle generously with flaky salt.

Bake the crostata until nicely browned and crisp, 40 to 45 minutes. Remove it from the oven and immediately drizzle generously with honey. Scatter oregano leaves over the filling and cut the crostata into wedges to serve.

Store, covered, in the refrigerator for up to 2 days. Reheat in a 350°F oven until crisp.

Aglianico

BUTTERNUT LAMB CHILI

Makes 6 to 8 servings

Producers to Look For

Azienda Agricola Musto
Carmelitano
Cantina Giardino
Ciro Picariello
Luigi Tecce

Here, Texas terrain meets Italian terroir. A humble dish like all-American chili needs a fruity, deep red wine with enough structure to stand up to lamb and warm spices. Perhaps nothing better fits that description than the rustic aglianico grape of Campania and Basilicata in Southern Italy. Most of Italy's "noble" grapes, like nebbiolo and barbera, are located in the northern reaches of the country. Even sangiovese, the king of Tuscany, is out of the far reaches of the south. Southern Italy used to be considered wild and off the radar and paid little attention to its wines, except for aglianico, which has been, and remains, the south's stalwart grape variety. It's full of brambly forest fruits and in the only DOCG noted for aglianico, called Taurasi, the wines are tannic and broad and age incredibly well. They have acidity to balance their meatiness, too, which is a necessity for pairing with food. If you pick up a bottle of Taurasi, we recommend decanting it for about an hour. A little air will do wonders for a tannic, muscular wine, opening it to open up so that you can enjoy it sooner.

This chili is our take on the meat-and-bean stew. We've swapped ground lamb for beef and added cubes of comforting butternut squash to soak up the chili spice.

2 teaspoons extra-virgin olive oil

1¼ pounds ground lamb

1 yellow onion, diced

2 large poblano chiles, seeded and chopped

2 cloves garlic, minced

3 tablespoons chili powder

2 teaspoons ground cumin

2 teaspoons dried oregano

1 cup dry red wine

1 (28-ounce) can whole peeled tomatoes

2 cups low-sodium beef broth

½ small butternut squash (about 1¼ pounds), peeled, seeded, and cut into ½-inch cubes

1 (14-ounce) can black beans, drained

1 (14-ounce) can pinto beans, drained

2 teaspoons kosher salt, or to taste

Freshly ground black pepper

Sour cream, for garnish

Toasted pumpkin seeds, for garnish

In a large heavy pot, warm the oil over medium-high heat. Add the lamb and break it up into small chunks. Stir in the onion, poblanos, and garlic and cook until the excess liquid evaporates, the lamb is browned, and the vegetables are soft, 10 to 15 minutes.

Drain off most of the fat and return the pan to the heat. Stir in the chili powder, cumin, and oregano and cook for about 30 seconds. Pour in the wine and scrape up any bits from the bottom of the pot. Simmer until it's reduced by about half, 2 to 3 minutes. Stir in the tomatoes and their juices, breaking them up a bit with a wooden spoon. Pour in the broth, then add the squash, all the beans, salt, and several grinds of pepper. Bring it to a boil, then decrease the heat to maintain a gentle simmer and cook until the squash is tender when pierced with a fork and the chili thickens slightly, about 25 minutes. For a thicker chili, leave the pot uncovered, or partially cover when it reaches your desired consistency. Taste and adjust the seasoning. Serve the chili topped with sour cream and pumpkin seeds.

Oloroso Sherry

CARAMELIZED ONION AND BREAD SOUP WITH BRÛLÉED BLUE CHEESE

Makes 4 to 6 servings

Producers to Look For

Bodegas Alba Viticultores
Bodegas César Florido
Bodegas Grant
Bodegas Gutiérrez Colosía
El Maestro Sierra

The universe of sherry has been somewhat shrouded in mystery for many, many years, although its place in the history of wine is as important as port, Champagne, and Bordeaux. Grown and produced only around Jerez de la Frontera, Sanlúcar de Barrameda, and El Puerto de Santa María in southwestern Spain's famed "Sherry Triangle," sherry is singular in its ability to express the place it comes from. The unique salty and oxidative flavors come from a combination of the chalky albariza soil, the warm sea breezes off the Atlantic Ocean, and *flor*, the special yeast veil that grows over certain styles of sherry. It is one of the world's great drinking wines, gaining popularity in recent years for its ability to pair with everything from a hunk of good cheese to Japanese food.

Oloroso is the older, oxidized sister of the sherry family. Unlike fresh fino and manzanilla sherries and briny amontillado, oloroso is all about notes of toasted nuts, tobacco, and salty caramel. After some time under flor the base sherry is fortified, bumping its alcohol above 17%, creating an environment where the yeast veil can't survive. The wine is left to age without flor, but with some space in the top of the barrel where it comes into contact with air. As time passes, the wine evaporates in small amounts, it concentrates, and it oxidizes ever so perfectly. While certainly a dry wine, the richness of oloroso sherry can give hints of dried fruit. We think it makes the perfect partner for sweet onions cooked into a luxurious soup, topped with hearty torn bread and umami-rich Stilton. Both are complex and delicious in the most complementary way. It's exactly what you want in a pairing.

4½ pounds mixed onions, such as 2 large yellow, 2 large red, and 2 large sweet onions, halved and thinly sliced from root to stem
2 tablespoons extra-virgin olive oil
2 tablespoons unsalted butter
¼ cup oloroso sherry
6 cups low-sodium chicken or vegetable broth (homemade would be great)
6 to 8 thyme sprigs
1 tablespoon kosher salt, or to taste

¾ teaspoon freshly ground black pepper, or to taste
2 teaspoons sherry vinegar
3 cups bite-size pieces of stale whole-grain country bread
4 ounces Stilton blue cheese, thinly sliced by your cheesemonger, or very coarsely crumbled

continued

Put the onions, oil, and butter in a stockpot set over medium heat and toss them all together. Cook, stirring occasionally, until the onions are meltingly soft and deeply caramelized, 1 to 1½ hours. As they start to caramelize, they'll begin sticking to the bottom of the pot, which is good, but be sure to scrape it often and decrease the heat as needed to prevent burning.

When the onions are ready, pour in the sherry and deglaze the pot, scraping up any browned bits. Simmer over medium heat until the sherry is mostly evaporated, 2 to 3 minutes. Stir in the broth, thyme, salt, and pepper. Decrease the heat, partially cover, and cook at a gentle simmer until the flavors marry, 20 to 25 minutes. Stir in the vinegar and wait about 1 minute, then taste and adjust the seasoning. (The soup will keep, covered, in the refrigerator for up to 3 days. It can be frozen for up to 6 months.)

Divide the hot soup among oven-safe crocks or bowls. Add a handful of the bread chunks to each and gently push them down so they're fully submerged but still at the top of the soup. Lay a slice of cheese (or a handful of crumbles) over the top. Broil until melted, bubbly, and browned in spots, about 2 minutes, then serve.

MENU

Antipasti
Chop Chop Salad
Sunday Sauce
Polenta

Sicilian Reds

Producers to Look For

Azienda Agricola Arianna Occhipinti
Azienda Agricola COS
Benanti
Francesco Guccione

Frank Cornelissen
I Vigneri delle vigne dell'Etna
Il Censo
Vino di Anna

The history of Sicilian wine is fraught with everything from interloping mafia to massive production of bianca carta—juice that tasted as plain and boring as white paper looks. Marsala was often made with the addition of caramel coloring. Winery cooperatives with more than two thousand members owned 5 percent of Sicily's vineyards, and the island was a major contributor to Europe's bulk-wine market. But there are many heroes in Sicily's wine story: those who have worked tirelessly to celebrate the diversity of the island's terroir and to reshape what we know as Sicilian wine today. It is now possible to drink tremendously well-made wine from the mainland as well as the beautiful satellite islands of Pantelleria and Lipari. The western side of Sicily is known for more international varieties, such as cabernet sauvignon and chardonnay, which don't really speak to the unique history and soils of the area, so keep an eye out for the native varieties instead.

The wine producers we've suggested for our Sunday Sauce are all revolutionaries in one way or another, and represent three distinctive parts of Sicily: the greenest and coldest corner that climbs over 3,500 feet up Mount Etna is home to nerello mascalese (neh-ray-LO mah-scah-LAY-zsay), a grape that is at once light and bright as well as powerfully tannic. The rocky outcroppings of Palermo and its surroundings have given birth to the peppery fruitiness of inky perricone (pear-ih-COH-nay). And the idyllic country roads of the southwest nestle up to vineyards teeming with lithe, floral frappato and juicy nero d'avola. Although part of Italy, Sicily has a culture and history all its own, being that it sits so close to North Africa, and is still considered "wild" by many who love the island. The wines here are undoubtedly Italian, with their rusticity and boldness, but they are also distinctively different from anything else in the world with their off-the-beaten-path flavors. While there are tremendous white wines made across the expanse of Sicily, a platter of rich polenta topped with meltingly tender meat calls for nothing other than a parade of red wines from every corner of the island.

Our version of the Sicilian-American Sunday Sauce is a dramatic feast fit for Don Corleone himself. Hand-rolled beef braciole (bra-JOAL), spicy Italian sausages, and pork riblets simmer away in a pot of garlic-scented red sauce until they're fall-apart tender and ready to be scooped onto a heap of soft polenta. Start with a platter of antipasti, including hot soppressata, olives, pepperoncini, marinated artichoke hearts, caponata, and cheeses like buffalo mozzarella and sliced caciocavallo. Toss together a chopped Italian salad and you have a seriously delicious Sunday supper.

SUNDAY SAUCE

Chop Chop (page 92)

Sunday Sauce on Polenta
(page 208)

Antipasti Platter with Giardiniera,
Marinated Artichokes, Olives,
Cured Meats, and Cheeses

SUNDAY SAUCE ON POLENTA

Makes 8 to 10 servings

wine food

Braciole

10 (¼-inch-thick) slices beef top round
    (cut on a meat slicer by your butcher)
Kosher salt
Freshly ground black pepper
4 cloves garlic, minced
⅓ cup finely chopped fresh flat-leaf parsley
10 slices provolone cheese

Sauce

¼ cup extra-virgin olive oil
1 head garlic, separated into cloves,
    smashed, and peeled
5 hot Italian sausages, halved crosswise
2 racks (2 pounds) baby back pork ribs, cut
    into individual ribs or 2-rib sections
3 (28-ounce) cans whole peeled tomatoes,
    partially crushed with your hands
½ teaspoons red pepper flakes
Kosher salt
Freshly ground black pepper

Polenta

9 cups water
Kosher salt
2½ cups polenta or coarse cornmeal
2 tablespoons unsalted butter
4 ounces finely grated Parmigiano-
    Reggiano cheese

About 20 basil leaves
2 ounces finely grated Parmigiano-
    Reggiano cheese

To make the braciole: One at a time, place the beef slices between 2 large sheets of plastic wrap. Using a meat mallet or rolling pin, lightly pound the beef to an even thickness, just a little thicker than ⅛ inch. Season both sides of the beef slices with salt and pepper. Sprinkle one side of each with the garlic and parsley and divide the cheese among the short ends. Roll up from one short end to the other, tucking in the sides to prevent the cheese from melting out during cooking. Tie with twine crosswise at each end and once lengthwise. Set aside.

To make the sauce: Set a large rimmed baking sheet next to your stove. In a large Dutch oven (at least 6½ quarts), warm the oil over medium-low heat. Add the garlic and cook until golden brown, 2 to 3 minutes. Transfer the garlic to the baking sheet. Add the sausages to the Dutch oven and sear until deeply browned, 4 to 5 minutes per side. While cooking the meat, adjust the heat as needed to prevent burning, but keep it hot enough to develop a rich brown color. Transfer the sausages to the baking sheet with the garlic. Add the ribs to the pot, in two batches if needed, and sear until deeply browned, 4 to 5 minutes per side. Transfer the ribs to the baking sheet with the sausages and garlic. Finally, add the braciole, again working in batches if needed; it's okay if they fit snugly as long as they're in one layer. Sear the braciole until deeply browned, 4 to 5 minutes per side. Transfer the braciole to the baking sheet with the other meats and garlic.

Now add the tomatoes and red pepper flakes and return the cooked garlic to the pot. Bring it to a simmer over medium-high heat, scraping the bottom to release all the meaty bits. Season with a few big pinches of salt and several grinds of pepper.

Add the braciole and ribs back to the pot, nestling them into the sauce, along with any accumulated juices from the baking sheet. Partially cover and cook at a gentle simmer for 1½ hours. Add the sausages and continue simmering, partially covered, until the braciole is exceptionally tender and the meat easily shreds, the ribs are falling-off-the-bone tender, the sausages are fully cooked, and the sauce is full of amazing flavor, 30 minutes to 1 hour more. (The sauce will keep, covered, in the refrigerator for up to 3 days.)

To make the polenta: In a 3-quart heavy-bottomed pot, bring the water with several big pinches of salt to a boil over high heat. Slowly pour in the polenta while whisking. Bring it to a simmer, whisking often. Decrease the heat to maintain a simmer and cook until the polenta begins to spit, about 15 minutes. Decrease the heat

and continue cooking, stirring and scraping the bottom often with a sturdy wooden spoon, until the polenta is tender and pulls away from the sides of the pot, 45 minutes to 1 hour. You're looking for it to be very thick and creamy, but not too stiff and dry. (If the polenta is too firm at any stage of cooking, add a little more water.) When it's at a good consistency, stir in the butter and Parmigiano-Reggiano cheese. Taste and adjust the seasoning.

Just before serving, stir the basil leaves into the sauce and meat and allow them to wilt in, about 5 minutes. Pour the polenta into a very large, shallow serving bowl. Allow it to set up, about 1 minute, then make a giant well in the center and spoon in the meat and some of the sauce. Present your festa Siciliana with the remaining sauce and Parmigiano at the table.

Pairing Cheat Sheet
The World Is Your Meatball

SANGIOVESE / ITALIAN-AMERICAN

ZWEIGELT / LAMB KOFTE

PRIORAT / MOROCCAN KEFTA

OREGON PINOT NOIR / SWEDISH WITH LINGONBERRY

GARNACHA / ALBONDIGAS

CHÂTEAUNEUF-DU-PAPE / ROMANIAN MICI

SOUTH AFRICAN CHENIN BLANC / VIETNAMESE
LEMONGRASS CHICKEN

OFF-DRY RIESLING / SPICY THAI GREEN CURRY

FINO SHERRY / DIM SUM SHRIMP + PORK

GAMAY / TSUKUNE

Cozy Night In

White Burgundy

OUR CHICKEN POT PIE

Makes 6 to 8 servings

Producers to Look For

Domaine Clos des Rocs
Domaine de Roally
Domaine Guillot-Broux
Domaine Henri & Gilles
Buisson

Chicken and chardonnay may very well be the greatest wine pairing in the history of food and wine being consumed together. What's more, chicken, Dijon mustard, and chardonnay are like a rogue ménage à trois, which makes sense since Dijon comes from . . . Dijon, as in Burgundy, as in one of the most significant places in the world for chardonnay and chicken. So, how can this match-up be bad? It can't. But do look for white Burgundy that isn't overtly oaky; a little oak can go a long way with the chardonnay grape, giving it body and texture without making it taste like a two-by-four. Keep in mind that you can find extremely delicious, affordable white Burgundy by looking for "village" wines from Mâcon, for example, or wines simply labeled *Bourgogne*, and avoiding Premier Cru or Grand Cru bottlings. Unless, of course, you like the idea of a lowbrow dish with a highbrow wine as much as we do.

Before you think we're crazy for including a recipe for chicken pot pie that doesn't have a bottom crust, allow us to explain. This is a rustic pie loaded with chunks of juicy chicken, fragrant celery root, and ruffly mustard greens, all packed into a cast-iron skillet and designed to feed a small crowd. We like the layers of mustard flavor, using both the condiment and the greens, while the buttery crust begs for another sip of crisp white Burgundy. It's a family-style meal guaranteed to earn you some serious ooohs and ahhhs as you pull it from the oven. The sauce will be bubbling, the deeply golden crust will be crackly, and your house will smell like Grandma came to make dinner, with lots of butter. Simply put, this pot pie is so delicious that no one will ever miss a bottom crust.

Crust

2 cups all-purpose flour, plus more
    for dusting
½ teaspoon kosher salt
13 tablespoons cold unsalted butter, cubed
6 tablespoons sour cream
6 tablespoons ice water
1 tablespoon apple cider vinegar

2½ pounds bone-in, skin-on chicken breasts
    and thighs, patted dry
3½ teaspoons kosher salt
Freshly ground black pepper
¼ cup extra-virgin olive oil, plus more
    as needed
1½ pounds cremini mushrooms, quartered
¼ cup dry white wine
1 large leek, white and light green parts,
    halved lengthwise and sliced

1 large yellow onion, diced
3½ cups low-sodium chicken broth
½ cup sour cream
1½ tablespoons Dijon mustard
2 teaspoons fresh thyme leaves
1 bay leaf
6 tablespoons all-purpose flour, plus more
    for dusting
1 small (about 12 ounces) celery root, peeled
    and cut into ½-inch cubes
1 bunch (about 8 ounces) mustard greens,
    thick stems removed, leaves and
    tender stems cut crosswise into
    ½-inch strips
1 large egg
1 teaspoon water
Flaky sea salt, for topping

continued

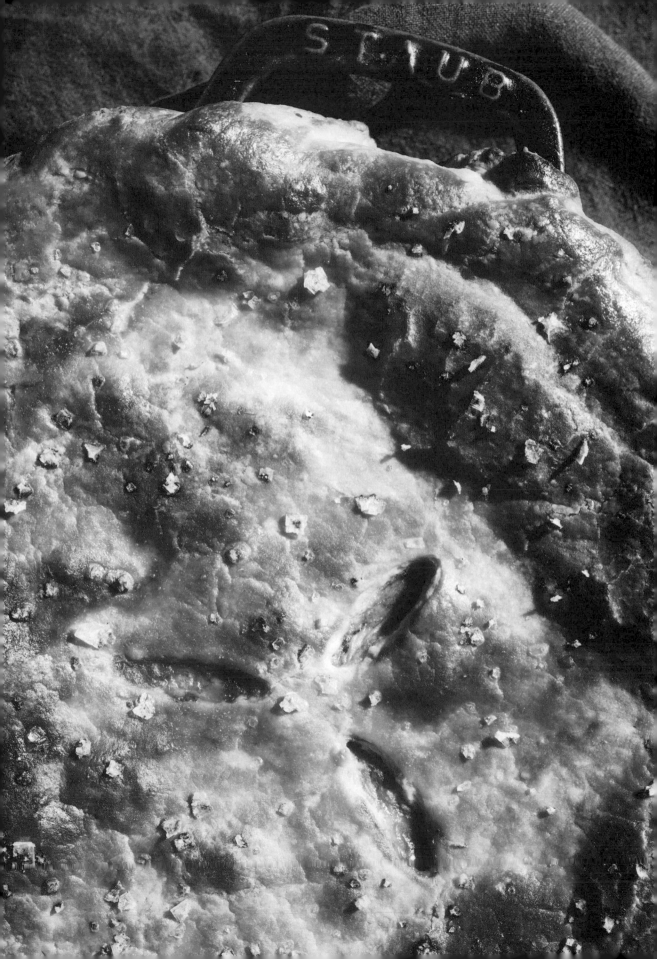

To make the crust: In a large bowl, whisk the flour and kosher salt. Using your fingertips, work the butter into the flour mixture until it looks mealy, with no pieces larger than the size of a pea. In a small bowl, whisk the sour cream, ice water, and vinegar. Add the sour cream mixture to the flour mixture. Mix with a fork to combine until a shaggy mass forms. Dump the mixture out onto a countertop and press and pat it together to form a ball, dusting with flour as needed if it's sticky. Press it into a smooth disk about 1 inch thick. Wrap the disk tightly in plastic wrap and refrigerate until well chilled, at least 1 hour. The dough can be made up to 2 days in advance and kept in the refrigerator.

Season the chicken pieces all over with 1½ teaspoons of the salt and several grinds of pepper. Warm 2 tablespoons of the oil in a 12-inch heavy skillet (preferably cast-iron) over medium-high heat. Brown the chicken, working in two batches, if needed, until golden and crisp on both sides, 10 to 15 minutes total. Transfer the chicken to a plate and set aside. Add the mushrooms to the remaining fat in the pan and cook until they are deeply browned and kind of crusty at the edges, 10 to 12 minutes. Pour in the wine and scrape the bits up from the bottom of the pan. Season with ½ teaspoon salt and a few grinds of pepper. Transfer the mushrooms to a bowl and set aside.

With the pan still over medium-high heat, add the remaining 2 tablespoons oil and the leek and onion. Season with ½ teaspoon salt and cook until softened and lightly browned, 6 to 8 minutes. Stir in the broth, sour cream, Dijon mustard, thyme, bay leaf, and remaining 1 teaspoon salt and bring to a simmer. Nestle the browned chicken and juices into the sauce, cover, and gently simmer until the chicken is cooked through and shreddable, about 30 minutes. Transfer the chicken to a cutting board and discard the bay leaf. Set the pan of sauce aside until the fat rises to the surface, about 20 minutes.

Preheat the oven to 425°F with a rack positioned in the middle.

When the chicken is cool enough to handle, use two forks to shred it into large bite-size pieces, discarding the skin and bones. Skim the chicken fat from the sauce using a wide spoon and reserve it. Measure the fat and add enough additional olive oil to equal a total of ¼ cup. In a medium bowl, use a fork to mix the fat with the flour until a cohesive paste forms. Pour in a ladleful of the warm sauce and whisk until smooth with no lumps. Now whisk in another ladleful to loosen the paste and then set aside.

Bring the pan of sauce to a simmer over medium-high heat. Stir in the celery root, then add the mustard greens a handful at a time, tossing the greens into the sauce to wilt. Stir in the fat-flour paste, followed by the cooked mushrooms and pulled chicken and any juices. Bring to a gentle simmer as the mixture thickens. Taste and adjust the seasoning. (The filling can be made up to 2 days in advance; rewarm before continuing with the recipe.)

In a small bowl, whisk together the egg and water to make an egg wash. On a lightly floured surface, roll out the dough to a large circle that is wide enough to cover the pan with about 1 inch of overhang on all sides. Brush the outside edges of the pan with some of the egg wash and place the dough over the top, pressing gently to adhere it to the egg wash. Working quickly, so the dough doesn't melt into the warm filling, cut a few 1-inch slits in the dough for venting and brush the top and edges with the remaining egg wash. Sprinkle the crust generously with flaky salt. Bake until the crust is a rich golden brown and flaky and you can see that the filling is bubbling through the vent holes, about 30 minutes.

Remove the pot pie from the oven and set aside to rest for at least 5 minutes. It will stay warm for about 30 minutes before serving.

Serve the pot pie in warm shallow bowls, scooping out spoonfuls of the filling, along with some of the crust along the edges of the pan.

Store, covered, in the refrigerator for up to 1 day. Reheat in a 350°F oven until hot and bubbling, 30 to 45 minutes.

Orange Wine

PORCINI MUSHROOM STROGANOFF

Makes 4 servings

Producers to Look For

Bodegas Bernabé Navarro
La Garagista
La Stoppa
Paolo Bea
Radikon
Škerk

Orange wine, aka amber wine, aka skin-contact white wine, is, without a doubt, some of the most interesting (and delicious) wine on the planet. With flavors of overripe autumn apples and pears, sun-baked hay, toasted nuts, and wild herbs, orange wines are a touch like cider, quite savory, and very special. Their history goes back thousands of years to our friends in the Republic of Georgia, who took whole clusters of white grapes, put them into *qvevri* (underground clay vessels), and left everything to macerate and ferment. The juice that was pulled from the qvevri had a distinctive deep amber color that came from long months of the juice and skins hanging out together. Think of them as white wines made like a red wine: white grape skins have color, tannin, and texture, too, so if you leave them in contact with the juice, you're bound to end up with something much more complex than a typical white wine. There are a wide variety of orange wines made throughout Italy, concentrated in Friuli, which shares a border with Slovenia, also known for its beautiful skin-contact whites. Georgia, of course, has maintained its tradition of making amber wines for the past four thousand years. France, Spain, the United States, and Australia also boast a handful of exceptional orange wines. We encourage you to seek out these wines and drink them with lots of different savory foods. They go well with grilled meats, sauces, and umami-rich foods like wild mushrooms and aged hard cheeses. Orange wines can be challenging to drink on their own; they taste entirely different when enjoyed with food. Even just a simple wedge of cheese will do in a pinch. We like to serve orange wine somewhere between completely chilled and room temperature, and a decanter will be your friend. Allowing your orange wine to really open up will be a much better experience than drinking it straight from the bottle.

Given that porcini mushrooms push the savory and umami buttons, we decided to stew them into a dreamy, soul-satisfying stroganoff. Our sauce is rich in shallots, garlic, and thyme, but also uses fresh porcini as well as porcini powder to accentuate the mushroominess. The powder is available at many specialty stores, but it's also very simple to make at home: just buzz a handful of dried porcinis to a fine powder in a food processor. It not only amps up the porcini flavor, creating layers and depth in the final dish, but it also acts as a thickener for the sauce. You could substitute all-purpose flour, but you'll be missing out on that serious kick of earthy, mushroomy goodness. Fresh porcinis come into season in the fall, which makes this the ultimate cozy stew to coat a bowl of old-school egg noodles.

¼ cup unsalted butter

4 ounces shallots, thinly sliced

3 cloves garlic, thinly sliced

2 pounds fresh porcini mushrooms,
cut into bite-size chunks

2 tablespoons porcini mushroom powder
or 1 tablespoon all-purpose flour
(if you must substitute)

½ cup orange wine or dry white wine

1 cup mushroom or vegetable broth

2 teaspoons fresh thyme leaves

2 teaspoons kosher salt, or to taste

Freshly ground black pepper

½ cup crème fraîche or sour cream

¼ cup chopped fresh flat-leaf parsley,
plus more for garnish

12 ounces extra-wide or wide egg noodles

Melt the butter in a large skillet over medium-high heat. Add the shallots and garlic and cook until lightly browned, 2 to 3 minutes. Add the mushrooms and cook, stirring, until they have softened and released most of their liquid, then turned nicely brown, 5 to 8 minutes. Add the mushroom powder and stir it into the mixture. Pour in the wine and cook until it's mostly absorbed, scraping the bottom and sides of the pan, about 1 minute. Add the broth, thyme, salt, and several grinds of pepper and bring to a simmer. Allow the sauce to gently simmer until thickened slightly, 2 to 3 minutes. Remove the pan from the heat and stir in ¼ cup of the crème fraîche or sour cream and the parsley. Taste and adjust the seasoning.

Meanwhile, bring a large pot of water to a boil over high heat, season generously with salt, and stir in the noodles. Cook the noodles, stirring occasionally, until al dente according to the package instructions. Drain, reserving about ½ cup of the cooking water.

Add the noodles to the sauce and toss to combine. Warm briefly over low heat to blend the flavors, adding just enough of the cooking water to loosen the sauce and coat the noodles. Serve in warm bowls, topped with a dollop of the remaining crème fraîche and a sprinkling of parsley.

Red Burgundy

A GIANT STUFFED PUMPKIN FOR HARVEST TIME

Makes 6 to 8 servings

Producers to Look For

Catherine & Claude Maréchal

Domaine Henri & Gilles Buisson

Domaine Simon Bize et Fils

Fanny Sabre

Sylvain Pataille

It's nearly impossible to encapsulate one of the world's undisputed great wine regions in a paragraph or two. So, we'll give you the abridged version. Burgundy is the home of pinot noir and chardonnay, and is the place that most people look to for benchmark wines made from those grapes. Sitting in Eastern France running south from the city of Dijon to the village of Mâcon, Burgundy is full of bucolic rolling hills, quaint villages, and gently sloping vineyards as far as the eye can see. Soils are mostly limestone based, with some clay and small stones, and evidence of sea creatures from millions of years ago can be found in many vineyards. There are four main parts of Burgundy (excluding Chablis), including the Côte de Nuits, heralded for its pinot noir, the Côte de Beaune, celebrated for chardonnay, the Côte Chalonnaise, for less expensive reds and whites, and the Mâconnais, known for its affordable and beautiful chardonnay. Some of the most expensive wines on the planet come from the grand cru vineyards dotted along the Côte de Nuits and Côte de Beaune, and those are probably out of reach for a harvest dinner of stuffed pumpkin. Instead, look for more reasonably priced red Burgundy labeled as Bourgogne AOP, or for village-labeled reds from the Côte Chalonnaise. Of course, if you feel like splurging, or you have some red Burgundy aging away in your cellar, by all means, go for it. Think about these wines as "feminine" pinot noirs with bright cherry, dry summer dust, and mushroom aromatics. No jammy, big New World pinot flavors here.

A giant stuffed pumpkin is a fantastic conversation piece, and so much fun to serve for a gathering of friends on a chilly fall evening. After watching an episode of Anthony Bourdain's *Parts Unknown* in which famed chef Daniel Boulud roasted a whole stuffed pumpkin in a wood-burning oven on his family's farm in Burgundy, Andrea was determined to create this recipe. She served it with copious bottles of red Burgundy for a birthday celebration, and we dare say the pumpkin was the star of the evening. It would make an excellent vegetarian centerpiece on the Thanksgiving table, too. You'll want to find a big heirloom pumpkin, which will roast up with much more flavor than a plain orange jack-o'-lantern style. The stuffing is a bit like a savory bread pudding, with multiple layers of crusty country bread, sautéed mushrooms and kale, nutty alpine cheese, and warm spices. You'll press everything into the squash, cover it with its lid, and let it roast until the pumpkin starts to slump just a tiny bit and the stuffing is melty and steaming. Carry it to the table and scoop the filling and sweet flesh right from the pumpkin. Your house will smell so good that your neighbors will be wondering what's going on, so you should probably have a little extra Burgundy on hand.

continued

1 tablespoon extra-virgin olive oil,
    plus more for rubbing
8 ounces wild mushrooms, torn into
    bite-size pieces
2 cloves garlic, minced
¼ cup water
1 large bunch kale, stemmed and
    coarsely chopped
3½ teaspoons kosher salt
1 (11- to 12-pound) pumpkin, such as
    Long Island Cheese or Cinderella,
    or a Sweet Meat squash
1¼ cups heavy cream
1¼ cups milk
2 teaspoons sweet paprika
½ teaspoon freshly grated nutmeg
½ teaspoon freshly ground black pepper
½ loaf of levain bread, or crusty sourdough,
    sliced and toasted
12 ounces Comté or Gruyère cheese,
    or a combination, grated
3 tablespoons thinly sliced fresh chives

Preheat the oven to 350°F. Line a baking sheet with aluminum foil.

Warm the oil in a large, deep skillet or wide saucepan over medium-high heat. Add the mushrooms and cook until tender and beginning to brown, 5 to 6 minutes. Stir in the garlic and cook 1 minute more. Pour in the water, then add the kale and ½ teaspoon of the salt. Use tongs to toss the leaves into the mixture. Cover and cook, stirring occasionally, until the kale is wilted and just tender, 5 to 7 minutes. Remove the cover and continue cooking until any liquid in the bottom of the pan is evaporated, 1 to 2 minutes. Remove the pan from the heat and set aside, uncovered, to cool slightly.

Cut a cap off the top of the pumpkin that gives a large enough opening to fill it, 8 to 10 inches in diameter. Scoop out and discard the interior stringy bits and seeds. Place the pumpkin on the prepared baking sheet and rub all over the outside with oil. Sprinkle the inside with 2½ teaspoons salt.

In a large bowl, whisk the cream, milk, paprika, nutmeg, pepper, and remaining ½ teaspoon salt.

Fill the pumpkin beginning with a layer of about one-third of the toasted bread slices, followed by one-third of the cheese, then half of the chives, and half of the cooked mushrooms and kale. Pour in about one-third of the cream mixture. Add another one-third of the bread slices and firmly press them down to pack the filling a little tighter. Repeat layering with another one-third of the cheese and the remaining half of the chives and mushrooms and kale. Pour in another one-third of the cream mixture. Top with the remaining one-third of the bread slices, pressing down as needed to fit in as much as possible. Top with the remaining one-third of the cheese. Pour the remaining cream mixture over the top. (Don't be surprised if all of the filling doesn't quite fit in the pumpkin. Pumpkins differ in thickness, which will affect how much you can pack inside.) Replace the cap, trimming excess flesh from the bottom of it, if needed, so that it fits snuggly. The pumpkin can be stuffed up to 1 day in advance and kept in the refrigerator. Bring to room temperature before roasting.

Roast the pumpkin until the filling is hot in the center, the pumpkin flesh is very tender, and the exterior looks browned and wrinkly, 2½ to 3 hours. Remove the pumpkin from the oven and set aside to rest for about 10 minutes. With the cap on, it will stay hot for about 30 minutes before serving.

Serve the pumpkin at the table, scooping out spoonfuls of the filling, along with some of the interior flesh, into warm shallow bowls.

Trousseau

COQ AU VIN JURA

Makes 6 servings

Producers to Look For

Domaine André et
Mireille Tissot
Domaine de L' Octavin
Domaine des Cavarodes
Domaine Labet
Domaine Pêcheur

The Jura is Eastern France's mountainous region that butts right up along the border of Switzerland. It's known for pastoral views, brown-and-white cows with clangy bells around their necks, and one of our favorite cheeses, Comté. The Jura is also home to some of the world's most exotic and sommelier-sought-after wines. The whites are often nutty and oxidized, and the reds are fruit juicy with flavors of cranberry, currants, raspberries, and mountain herbs. They're high-altitude reds at their finest: tangy acidity, light in color, and delicious with typical white-wine foods such as poultry and fish. There are two main reds grown in the Jura: poulsard and trousseau. While either will be tasty with this dish, we think trousseau is the winner. It's got more body and savory notes than poulsard, which can look almost like a dark rosé, and it definitely fits the bill for a warm dinner on a cold, dark evening. Because of their unusual nature, wines from the Jura cost a little bit more than a Tuesday-night wine, and they really do want to be enjoyed with food, especially something savory.

Chicken and wine have gone together since the beginning of time, or so it seems. Long before Julia Child touted the magic of coq au vin in *Mastering the Art of French Cooking*, wine-braised chicken was a rustic peasant dish, meant to use the last dregs in the bottom of a jug and an old rooster from the yard. A long, slow braise turned that tired bird into fall-apart tenderness, surrounded by a luxurious sauce. Fast-forward a few generations, and chicken cooked in wine isn't much more complex than it used to be. A few details, like giving the chicken a crackly, golden crust before braising, and drinking it with a really great wine from the Jura, make a huge difference. Don't skimp on the mushrooms and bacon, as they add just the right amount of earthy smokiness to make your trousseau sing. And since this is a dish for a cozy night, we recommend serving it over silky pureed potatoes or buttered egg noodles for soaking up that seductive sauce.

6 chicken hindquarters

Kosher salt

Freshly ground black pepper

2 tablespoons fresh thyme leaves,
plus 3 sprigs

¼ cup chopped fresh flat-leaf parsley

¼ cup extra-virgin olive oil

3 ribs celery, chopped

1 large carrot, chopped

½ large onion, chopped

½ ounce dried porcini mushrooms

2 large cloves garlic, smashed

2 bay leaves

2 tablespoons tomato paste

2 cups dry light red wine, preferably
trousseau

1 quart chicken broth

1 pound pearl onions

8 ounces slab bacon, cut into ½ by
½ by 2-inch rectangles (lardons)

1 pound cremini mushrooms, halved

continued

Season the chicken hindquarters all over with salt and pepper, followed by the thyme leaves and parsley. Arrange the herby chicken in a single layer in a large baking dish, cover, and chill for at least 4 hours and up to overnight. Set them out to come to room temperature about 1 hour before cooking.

Select a large, shallow braising pan or skillet that will hold the chicken in a snug single layer and set it over medium-high heat. Add 2 tablespoons of the oil. When you just begin to see wisps of smoke, add half of the chicken hindquarters, skin-side down. Cook until a deep golden crust forms, 8 to 10 minutes. Turn and cook on the other side until crusty, about 5 minutes more. Transfer the seared chicken to a platter and cook the remaining chicken in the same way in the rendered fat in the pan. Transfer the second batch to the platter and set the seared chicken aside.

Pour off all but about 2 tablespoons of the rendered fat in the pan, reserving the excess. Set the pan over medium heat and add the celery, carrot, chopped onion, dried porcini mushrooms, garlic, and bay leaves and cook, stirring often, until the vegetables take on a little color, 6 to 8 minutes. Add the tomato paste and cook while stirring to coat the vegetables, about 2 minutes. Pour in the wine and scrape up the bits from the bottom of the pan, then increase the heat to high and bring it to a boil. Continue boiling until the wine is reduced by about half. Pour in the broth and bring to a boil. Nestle the seared chicken into the braising liquid and vegetables. Cover tightly with a lid or aluminum foil and adjust the heat to cook at a gentle simmer until the meat is tender and pulls away from the bone easily, 1½ to 1¾ hours.

Meanwhile, preheat the oven to 450°F. Toss the pearl onions (unpeeled) in a bowl with the remaining 2 tablespoons oil and the thyme sprigs. Season with a couple big pinches of salt and several grinds of pepper. Spread them out on a rimmed baking sheet and roast until tender, 15 to 20 minutes. When they are cool enough to handle, pinch the onions to slip off their skins. Set aside.

Once the chicken is done, take it out of the braising liquid and set it aside. Strain the liquid into a large wide saucepan, pressing the solids to extract as much liquid as possible. If the layer of fat that rises to the surface of the liquid seems excessive, you can skim it with a large spoon, but leave a thin layer of fat. Bring the braising liquid to a boil over high heat and cook until it is reduced to a thin sauce that just barely coats the back of a spoon, 10 to 15 minutes.

While the sauce reduces, add 1 tablespoon of the reserved chicken fat to the braising pan and set it over medium-high heat. Add the bacon and cook until it's lightly browned but still fatty and meaty, 3 to 4 minutes. Add the cremini mushrooms and cook until they are tender and browned at the edges and the bacon is a rich reddish brown color, about 5 minutes.

Pour the reduced sauce into the pan of bacon and mushrooms. Nestle in the chicken and pearl onions and bring it to a gentle simmer over medium heat, cooking just until the chicken is warmed through. Serve the chicken in warm shallow bowls, with plenty of the sauce, bacon, mushrooms, and onions all around.

Store, covered, in the refrigerator for up to 3 days. Reheat before serving.

Corsican Red

SEAFOOD STEW WITH AROMAS OF THE MAQUIS

Makes 6 servings

Producers to Look For

Antoine Arena
Clos Canarelli
Clos Signadore
Nicolas Mariotti Bindi
Yves Leccia

Corsica sits southeast of France, and although it's a French island, it hovers much closer to Western Italy and nearly touches Northern Sardinia. It's one of the most beautiful islands in the world with rocky plateaus, snow-capped mountain peaks, crystal-clear water, and the scent of *maquis*, wild evergreen underbrush, in the air. Often referred to as "the scented isle," Corsica is home to more than 2,500 species of wildflowers as well as scrub brush and native trees. Imagine the scents of eucalyptus, rosemary, sage, thyme, rose, wild fennel, marjoram, and lavender wafting along the ocean breeze in the heat of summer. That is the essence of the maquis. Intoxicating. And that's basically how we feel about Corsica and her wines. Some of the world's most energizing and stunning wines come from the island where the vines grow straight from the granite and schist bedrock and the maquis-laced winds cool the Mediterranean heat. Red varieties include nielluccio (neel-OO-chee-yo), which is genetically identical to sangiovese, and sciaccarellu (sha-ca-RAY-lyoo), which is the same grape as Tuscany's mammolo. Given Corsica's proximity to Tuscany, it makes sense that these two grapes have a home here, although they couldn't taste more different than their Italian counterparts. Nielluccio tends to be planted more predominantly on the northern part of the island, and makes medium-bodied wines that are at once deeply fruited and earthy, but replete with the maquis aroma. The southern part of Corsica is where sciaccarellu is king, and makes wines with more elegance and finesse. Think medium-bodied wines with brighter, fresher red fruits and dusty notes.

We would normally suggest white wine with a seafood-heavy dish, but this is a red wine stew, without a doubt. Given the fact that Corsica is completely surrounded by water, and that they produce such incredible reds on the island, Corsican-inspired food is naturally a great way to experience red wine with seafood. Be sure to get the freshest, nicest mussels, clams, shrimp, and squid you can find. It might require buying them at a few different stores, but it's worth the effort. Our stew is all about texture with the creamy chickpeas, tender fennel, and meaty squid. And it's equally flavorful from as much maquis-inspiration as we could interject. Fennel pollen and marjoram play large, with saffron and tomato rounding out the aromatics. Fregola looks quite similar to Israeli couscous, but is the toasty version that comes from Sardinia and adds a toothsome bite to the dish. The seafood cooks in just minutes but adds so much depth of flavor. We've enjoyed this dish in both summer and winter, but there's something about a richly flavored seafood stew in wintertime that transports us to the wilds of Corsica.

continued

5 tablespoons extra-virgin olive oil, plus more for drizzling

1½ cups fregola sarda or Israeli (pearl) couscous (see Note)

3 cups hot water

1 tablespoon plus 1 teaspoon sea salt

1 leek, trimmed, white and light green parts halved and thinly sliced

½ sweet yellow onion, diced

4 cloves garlic, slivered

2 bay leaves

½ cup dry white wine

4 cups seafood or fish stock

1 (14.5-ounce) can diced tomatoes and their juices

Juice of 1 orange

1 large fennel bulb, trimmed, reserving fronds, halved lengthwise, cored, and sliced crosswise

1 teaspoon fennel pollen or ground fennel seeds

1 teaspoon saffron threads

Freshly ground black pepper

1 cup canned chickpeas, drained and rinsed

2 tablespoons chopped fresh marjoram or oregano

1 pound clams, scrubbed

1 pound mussels, scrubbed and debearded

18 extra-large (about 1 pound) shrimp

12 ounces squid tubes and tentacles, tubes cut into ½-inch-thick rings

Baguette or country bread, for serving

Warm 2 tablespoons of the oil in a medium saucepan over medium heat. Stir in the fregola until well coated, then pour in the hot water. Season with 1 teaspoon of the salt. Bring to a simmer over high heat, stirring occasionally. Continue simmering until the fregola is slightly firmer than al dente (when you bite into one, it should have just a slight crunch in the very center), 6 to 8 minutes. Drain and rinse the fregola under cold water to stop the cooking. Leave in the colander to drain until needed.

Warm the remaining 3 tablespoons oil in a 6-quart Dutch oven or stockpot over medium heat. Add the leek, onion, garlic, and bay leaves and cook until softened, 6 to 7 minutes.

Pour in the wine, increase the heat to medium-high, and cook until it's mostly evaporated, about 2 minutes. Add the stock, tomatoes and juices, and orange juice. Stir in the fennel, fennel pollen, saffron, remaining 1 tablespoon salt, and several grinds of pepper. Increase the heat to high and bring to a boil. Decrease the heat to medium to maintain a gentle simmer, cover, and cook until the fennel is tender, about 5 minutes.

Uncover the pot and stir in the chickpeas and marjoram. Increase the heat to medium-high and return the broth to a simmer. Add the clams and mussels, cover, and cook at a rapid simmer. After 2 minutes, uncover and add the shrimp and squid. Return the lid and continue cooking at a gentle simmer until the mussels and clams are open and the shrimp and squid are opaque throughout, 3 to 4 minutes more. Discard any mussels or clams that don't open. Stir in the fregola sarda and remove the pot from the heat.

Ladle the stew into warmed bowls. Drizzle each portion with oil and garnish with fennel fronds. Serve with bread for sopping up the fragrant broth.

Note

Fregola sarda is a Sardinian pasta that is very similar to Israeli-style pearled couscous, but it is toasted, which gives it a nutty flavor. If it's unavailable, substitute toasted Israeli couscous. To toast the couscous, follow the instructions in the recipe for cooking fregola, but after the couscous is added to the oil, continue cooking it, stirring almost constantly, until the couscous is lightly toasted, 4 to 5 minutes. Proceed with adding the water and cooking the couscous as the recipe instructs.

Balkan Red

ROMANIAN CABBAGE ROLLS WITH LOTS OF DILL

Makes 6 to 8 servings

Producers to Look For

Brkić
Miloš Winery
Piquentum
Vinarija Križ
Vina Štoka

Dana spent three and a half years in the Peace Corps in Romania, and she ate approximately 637 cabbage rolls during that time. The chitter-chatter of her Romanian neighbors and the aroma of dill are burned in her memory, as are the hands-on lessons in how to roll the parcels just right. Cabbage rolls are a common part of nearly every Eastern European festivity, and *sarmale*, as they're called in Romania, are stuffed with an aromatic mixture of pork, rice, paprika, and dill and slow-braised in a bacon-enriched tomato sauce until tender. Traditionally served with a dollop of thin soured cream and a firm polenta, they are eaten by the dozens to celebrate weddings, holidays, and community gatherings. Washed down with homemade palincă, Romania's famed fruit brandy, cabbage rolls are as soulful and delicious as food gets.

They drink wine in Romania too, but unfortunately very little of it comes to the States. So we turn to neighboring countries that are making exceptional wines to accompany the stewed, smoky flavor of these cabbage rolls. With miles and miles of coastline, one might assume Croatian wines are all white, but they make absolutely beautiful reds from grapes such as refošk (RAY-foshk; the same grape as Italy's refosco) and plavac mali (PLA-vacks mah-ly). You can expect them to be medium-bodied, peppery, and slightly tannic. If you can find blatina (BLAH-tee-nah), grown in Bosnia and Herzegovina, you'll have a wonderful pairing in its spicy, almost coffee notes. Teran (TEH-rahn), which is related to refosco and grown throughout the region, is wonderful when it comes from Slovenia, bursting with a distinctive iron mineral note and juicy dark berries. This is a fantastic recipe for splurging on a few different bottles so you can experiment, tasting multiple wines with the same dish.

¼ cup distilled white vinegar

¼ cup kosher salt

1 large (2½- to 3-pound) head green cabbage, cored but left whole

½ cup long-grain white rice

1¼ pounds ground pork

½ yellow onion, finely chopped

1 cup coarsely chopped fresh dill, plus 6 sprigs

⅔ cup chopped fresh flat-leaf parsley

2 tablespoons fresh thyme leaves

3 cloves garlic, minced

2 tablespoons sweet paprika

1 teaspoon freshly ground black pepper

8 ounces thick-cut bacon, cut crosswise into ¼-inch strips

1 (28-ounce) can crushed tomatoes

Crème fraîche, for serving

Fill a large stockpot with 4 quarts water and add the vinegar and 3 tablespoons of the salt. Bring it to a boil over high heat.

Preheat the oven to 350°F. Place a large rimmed baking sheet lined with a clean kitchen towel next to the stove.

Submerge the whole cabbage in the boiling water, cover, and cook at a gentle simmer until the outer leaves are tender and begin loosening from the head, about 2 minutes. Using tongs, begin peeling off the outer leaves as they become loose and pliable and transfer them to the baking sheet. Continue cooking the cabbage until all of the leaves that are large enough to fill have been removed. Remove the ball of smaller leaves from the water and set aside. Pat the larger leaves dry with the towel. Trim away any remaining core attached to the leaves. Cut the largest leaves in half, but keep most whole. You should end up with about 18 leaves. Cut the ball of smaller leaves into ½-inch-thick shreds. Set the cabbage leaves and shreds aside.

Fill a small saucepan about two-thirds full of water and bring it to a boil over high heat. Add the rice and cook at a gentle simmer for 5 minutes. Drain the par-cooked rice in a strainer and rinse under cold water to cool; drain well.

In a large bowl, combine the cooled rice with the pork, onion, ⅔ cup of the dill, the parsley, thyme, garlic, paprika, remaining 1 tablespoon salt, and pepper. Using your hands, mix the ingredients until everything is well incorporated and the mixture sticks together (like meatballs), but don't overwork it to the point that the meat becomes mushy.

Working with one cabbage leaf at a time, fill each leaf with about ¼ cup of the filling mixture. Lay a leaf in front of you with the cup-shaped side facing up and the core end closest to you and place the filling in the center of the leaf. Fold the sides over the filling and then roll it up toward the tip end to completely encase the filling. Repeat to use up all of the leaves and the filling. If there are excess leaves, just shred them and add that to the rest of the shredded leaves.

Scatter half of the shredded cabbage in the bottom of a large Dutch oven. Arrange half of the cabbage rolls in a single, snug layer over the shredded cabbage. Top with 3 of the dill sprigs and half of the bacon. Add another layer of cabbage rolls. Top those with the remaining dill sprigs and bacon. Pour the crushed tomatoes over the cabbage rolls and tap and wiggle the pan to get them to sink down between the layers. Spread the remaining shredded cabbage over the top. Cover the pot and place it in the oven to bake the cabbage rolls until the rice and meat are cooked through and the cabbage is very tender, 1½ to 2 hours.

Spoon the cabbage rolls into warm shallow bowls, along with plenty of the shredded cabbage, bacon, and sauce. Top with crème fraîche and garnish with the remaining ⅓ cup chopped dill. Serve immediately.

The stuffed cabbage is even better the next day; allow leftovers to cool in the pot, then cover and refrigerate for up to 4 days. Reheat, covered, in a 350°F oven for 10 to 20 minutes.

Barolo

SLOW-BRAISED LAMB RAGÙ WITH RIGATONI AND WHIPPED RICOTTA

Makes 6 servings

Producers to Look For

Brovia
Cappellano
Cavallotto
Comm. G.B. Burlotto
Giovanni Canonica

Barolo is a very special wine, and one that's worth the extra money it costs to enjoy. Made entirely from nebbiolo grown in Italy's Piedmont region, it's a wine of strength but also of elegance. While nebbiolo has a long history in the Piedmont, Barolo only poked its head into the spotlight in the forties, and it's had a tumultuous and interesting seventy years since then. Barolo has traditionally been made by allowing the nebbiolo grapes to macerate on their skins for extended periods of time, sometimes for weeks, and then slowly aging in large, old barrels to help calm the harsh tannins. But the eighties and nineties gave rise to the Barolo Boys, a group of young winemakers who wanted to revolutionize how Barolo was made. Consumers across the world were drinking rich, juicy, oaky red wines, and the Boys decided to upend the old style of nebbiolo production for something more modern and international. This ignited a storm of controversy with the traditionalists in the region. The Barolo Boys used a host of methods to make their wines more immediately drinkable, including shorter maceration periods and aging in new, small barrels, and the international market took notice. They completely flipped custom on its head, and money poured into the region. Today, you can find wines made in both styles. Traditional wines will have a good grip of tannin to them when young, plus floral and savory characteristics and notes of warm cherries. In modern Barolo, you'll find richer, darker berry fruits, softer tannins, and vanilla and baking spice notes from new oak barrels. Our preference lies with the traditionalists. By law, Barolo must be aged a minimum of three years before release. Young Barolo will drink with a mouth-puckering dryness, lively red cherries, and berries, and it really benefits from decanting. If you can find a bottle that has ten years or more of age on it, you'll be in for a treat. As Barolo ages, you can expect the fresh fruit notes to settle into flavors of black tea, wet leaves, and dried roses. Look for wines simply labeled *Barolo* if you're trying to mind your budget. Bottles with vineyard names listed will open your wallet a bit more. And those labeled *Riserva* are a definite splurge.

Nothing says "comfort food" like a bowl of pasta in a long-cooked lamb ragù with a spoonful of creamy ricotta. The meat has braised to textbook tenderness so it pulls apart with a fork, the pasta is perfectly al dente, and the tomato sauce is deeply fragrant with oregano and rosemary. Combined with a splurge-y bottle of Barolo and a movie on the couch, you'd almost wish every night was a cozy night in. This pasta is a go-to for us because it checks off all of the boxes: hearty, flavorful, textural, and soul-satisfying. When we cooked this for our guys, they admitted that if it were healthy to eat a third bowl, they would.

continued

1 (2-pound) boneless lamb shoulder roast, halved (see Note)

2½ teaspoons kosher salt, or to taste

1 tablespoon extra-virgin olive oil, plus more for finishing

1 large yellow onion, finely diced

1 (6-ounce) can tomato paste

1 cup dry red wine

1 (28-ounce) can whole peeled tomatoes

½ cup water

¼ cup plus 2 tablespoons fresh oregano leaves

6 cloves garlic, minced

1 teaspoon red pepper flakes

1½ pounds dried rigatoni

1 tablespoon minced rosemary

1 tablespoon red wine vinegar

Whipped Ricotta

1 cup whole-milk ricotta

½ cup whole milk

½ cup packed freshly grated Pecorino Romano cheese

½ teaspoon freshly ground black pepper

½ teaspoon kosher salt

Season the lamb on all sides with 2 teaspoons of the salt. Warm a large Dutch oven over medium-high heat. Add the oil, and when you just begin to see wisps of smoke, add the lamb. Sear on all sides until a deep brown crust forms, 7 to 10 minutes. Transfer the lamb to a plate and set aside.

Add the onion to the pot and cook until just softened and lightly browned, adjusting the heat as needed, about 4 minutes. Add the tomato paste and cook, stirring almost constantly, until it darkens slightly and a deep brown crust forms on the bottom of the pot, about 2 minutes. Pour in the wine and scrape up the bits from the bottom of the pot. Stir in the tomatoes, water, ¼ cup of the oregano, the garlic, red pepper flakes, and remaining ½ teaspoon salt. Nestle the seared lamb back into the pot and bring to a rapid simmer. Decrease the

heat to maintain a gentle simmer, cover, and braise until the lamb is tender and easily shreds apart, about 2 hours.

Remove the lamb from the sauce and shred it into bite-size pieces using two forks. Return the shredded lamb to the sauce. (It will be quite thick now, but will be thinned with pasta water later.) Taste and adjust the seasoning. (At this point the ragù can be cooled to room temperature, then covered and refrigerated for up to 3 days before serving.) Return the ragù to a gentle simmer and keep it warm over low heat.

Cook the rigatoni in boiling salted water until al dente according to the package directions. Drain, reserving 2 cups of the cooking water, and return the rigatoni to its pot.

Stir some of the cooking water into the ragù to loosen it and add the remaining 2 tablespoons oregano, the rosemary, and vinegar. Add a few ladlefuls of the ragù to the pot of rigatoni to lightly coat. Place the rigatoni pot over medium-low heat and cook, stirring often, to allow the pasta to absorb some of the sauce, about 2 minutes.

To make the whipped ricotta: In a medium bowl, whisk the ricotta with the milk, cheese, pepper, and salt until it is loose and creamy, about 30 seconds. Use immediately, or cover and refrigerate for up to 3 days.

Serve the rigatoni in warm bowls, with a ladleful of the ragù spooned over each portion. Top with the whipped ricotta and a drizzle of oil.

Note
Special-order a boneless lamb shoulder roast from your butcher, or substitute cubed stew meat and decrease the braising time by up to 30 minutes.

Cahors

VIETNAMESE BEEF STEW (BÒ KHO)

Makes 4 to 6 servings

Producers to Look For

Château Combel-la-Serre
Château La Grave
Clos La Coutale
Domaine Cosse
Maisonneuve
Simon Busser

Spicy foods often have limited pairing options. Riesling and gewürztraminer are go-tos, as their fruitiness can help balance the heat of chiles, pepper, and curry. But what about a full-bodied red wine? It's kind of a no-brainer with beef. So we turned to the dark, floral broodiness of malbec to match with this stew's spices. While you could choose a juicy malbec from Argentina, we suggest seeking out Cahors for its deep fruitiness, crunchy tannins, and beautiful limestone minerality, not to mention lower alcohol than its Argentine counterpart. Cahors is only required to be 70 percent malbec (also known as côt), with the balance comprising tannat and merlot; however, many producers choose to use 100 percent malbec.

Long-cooked hunks of fall-apart meat, vegetables simmered to just-this-side-of-tenderness, and a rich sauce meant to be sopped up with crusty bread or ladled over a tangle of noodles. But sometimes even the homiest dishes can be rediscovered. While writing this book, Andrea spent her birthday in Vietnam eating her way from north to south, and discovered the deliciousness that is bò kho: the Vietnamese version of the worldwide favorite, beef stew. Back in the States, she sought out the dish and found a delicious version at her neighborhood Vietnamese restaurant. She turned to her friend Andrea Nguyen, author of *Into the Vietnamese Kitchen*, for further inspiration on our take on bò kho. Paired with a deeply rich malbec-based wine from Southwest France's Cahors region, the warm star anise and fragrant lemongrass really sing.

2¼ pounds boneless beef chuck, trimmed of excess fat and cut into 1½-inch cubes

¼ cup matchsticks of peeled ginger

2 tablespoons fish sauce, plus more for serving

2 teaspoons light brown sugar

5 tablespoons vegetable oil

2 tablespoons annatto seeds

1 medium onion, chopped

2 cloves garlic, minced

1 tablespoon Vietnamese or Indian yellow curry powder

3 cups beef broth

2 tablespoons soy sauce

2 lemongrass stalks, loose outer leaves and dry tops discarded, cut into 3-inch lengths and crushed with the side of a large knife

1 bay leaf

1 pound carrots, cut 1 inch thick on a bias

1 large shallot, thinly sliced

1 red jalapeño, Fresno, or cherry bomb chile, seeded and sliced

2 star anise, ground

½ cup fresh Asian basil leaves

Asian wheat-and-egg noodles or French bread, for serving

Small cilantro sprigs, for serving

continued

In a bowl, combine the beef with the ginger, fish sauce, and brown sugar; toss to coat; and leave to marinate for about 30 minutes.

Meanwhile, warm the oil in a small saucepan over medium-low heat. Add the annatto seeds and stir briefly to coat, then remove from the heat and set aside for 10 minutes to infuse the oil. Strain and discard the seeds, reserving the oil.

In a 5-quart (or larger) Dutch oven, warm about 2 tablespoons of the annatto oil over medium-high heat. Sear half of the marinated beef until a light crust forms, turning once, 4 to 5 minutes total. Transfer the seared beef to a plate and repeat to sear the remaining beef. Transfer that to the plate and set aside.

Decrease the heat to medium and add the onion and about half of the garlic. Cook until softened and fragrant, scraping up the bits from the bottom of the pan, 4 to 5 minutes. Add the curry powder and stir briefly until fragrant and well combined. Add the seared beef and any accumulated juices, the broth, soy sauce, lemongrass, and bay leaf. Increase the heat to bring to a boil, lower it to maintain a gentle simmer, cover, and cook until the meat is chewy-tender, about 1½ hours. Add the carrots and cook until both the beef and carrots are tender but not falling apart, 15 to 20 minutes more. Taste and adjust the seasoning. (The stew will keep, covered in the refrigerator, for up to 3 days.)

Meanwhile, put the remaining annatto oil back into the small saucepan over medium heat. Add the remaining garlic, the shallot, chile, and star anise and cook until the shallot is just beginning to soften and the mixture is fragrant, about 1 minute.

Just before serving, stir the aromatic shallot mixture and about half of the basil into the hot stew. Serve in big warm bowls, poured over noodles or with bread on the side (or both!). Pass the rest of the basil, the cilantro sprigs, and additional fish sauce at the table.

Red Bordeaux

INDIAN-SPICED DUCK BREAST WITH BURST GRAPES AND GLAZED CIPOLLINI

Makes 4 to 6 servings

Producers to Look For

Château de Bellevue
Château le Puy
Château Meylet
Clos du Jaugueyron
Clos Saint-André
Le Colombier de la Métarie

The styles of red Bordeaux can be split by the Gironde River, which separates the region into two distinct parts: the left bank, with its gravelly soils, is dominated by cabernet sauvignon and the right bank is planted mostly with merlot on clay. Left-bank wines include those from Pauillac, Saint-Julien, Saint-Estèphe, and Maurguax, and tend to be deeper and richer, and with a healthy backbone of tannin. Right-bank villages, including Pomerol, Fronsac, and Saint-Émilion, are renowned for softer, fruitier wines with plenty of brightness and minerality. Regardless of which side of the river the wine comes from, it is most likely blended with some combination of cabernet franc, malbec, or petit verdot. We love the way right-bank wines taste with this recipe. The acidity of merlot-based Bordeaux nicely cuts through the richness of the duck, and the clove and peppercorn spiciness of the garam masala almost mirrors the notes of the wine.

Duck is one of those foods that most home cooks shy away from cooking. A perfectly cooked duck breast or fall-apart-tender confit leg can seem like restaurant-only fare. But you can cook duck at home! It primarily comes down to searing the fatty skin of the duck so that it renders crispy and the meat is a perfect rosy pink. Rubbed with the warm Indian spices of garam masala, these duck breasts become something slightly exotic when served with browned cipollini onions and sweet, saucy grapes. And while Bordeaux is certainly one of the textbook pairings for duck, this is a bit of a twist on classic French cooking.

4 (8- to 10-ounce) duck breasts
Kosher salt
2 teaspoons garam masala
8 ounces small cipollini onions, preferably red ones
1 cup dry red wine
1 cup chicken broth
2 cups seedless black or red grapes
2 tablespoons unsalted butter
2 teaspoons fresh thyme leaves

Pat the duck breasts dry with a paper towel. Using a sharp knife, cut a ½-inch crosshatch pattern into the fatty skin, taking care not to penetrate the flesh. Season generously with salt all over. Sprinkle the meat sides only with 1 teaspoon of the garam masala. Set aside with the skin side up for 30 minutes to 1 hour to marinate as they come to room temperature.

Fill a large saucepan with water and bring it to a boil. Add the onions and cook for 30 seconds, then drain and rinse them under cold water to stop the cooking. Trim the roots, but keep them intact, and slip off the skins. Halve each onion through the root and set them aside.

Place the duck breasts, skin-side down, in a cold large skillet. Set the skillet over medium-high heat and cook until the skin is crisp and most of the fat is rendered, 6 to 9 minutes. Turn and cook on the meat side until the thickest part of each breast registers 125°F on an instant-read thermometer for medium-rare doneness, 2 to 3 minutes more. Transfer the duck breasts to a cutting board to rest, skin-side up, while you finish the dish.

Pour off all but about 1 tablespoon of the fat from the pan (reserve the excess duck fat for another use). Add the onions to the pan with their cut sides down and cook over medium-high heat, without turning, until deeply browned, about 2 minutes. Turn the onions over and pour in the wine (it will spatter).

Simmer until the wine is reduced by about half, 2 to 4 minutes. Add the broth and bring to a simmer. Cook for about 3 minutes, then add the grapes and a pinch of salt. Continue to simmer until the grapes burst but hold their shape and the sauce is slightly thickened, 3 to 5 minutes more. Decrease the heat to medium-low and add the butter, thyme, and remaining
1 teaspoon garam masala. Swirl the pan over the heat until the butter is melted, then remove it from the heat and taste and adjust the seasoning.

Cut the duck into slices against the grain. Spoon the sauce, grapes, and onions into warm shallow bowls. Fan the duck slices over top and serve.

Champagne

Producers to Look For

Benoît Lahaye   Champagne Tarlant
Cédric Bouchard   Marie-Noel Ledru
Champagne Agrapart   Thomas Perseval
Champagne Marie Courtin

If we were left on a desert island with only one bottle of wine to drink, it would undoubtedly be Champagne, and it would definitely be in magnum so that we'd have twice as much. (And, no, that's not cheating.) While it can be expensive for an everyday wine, it's at the top of our list for a special dinner or celebration of any sort. We'd like you to think of Champagne as wine for food, not just for toasting, as good Champagne is incredibly layered and complex in both flavor and mouthfeel, and should be enjoyed with a meal. (For more information about Champagne production, see page 30).

If you're throwing a party that's centered around a special occasion, perhaps a birthday or winter holiday, there's no reason not to go big with the wine. Magnums are awesome for a few reasons: (1) they look impressive, (2) they evoke more excitement than a standard bottle, and (3) they're fantastic for aging. Let's talk about that last one. Consider the little space of oxygen in the neck of a bottle, between the wine and the cork. That space, or ullage, is necessary for the wine to contract and expand during temperature changes, but it also has an effect on the wine itself: the more oxygen the wine is exposed to, the quicker it ages. Therefore magnums, and their bigger brothers and sisters (see page 18 for a list of bottle sizes), with their higher ratio of wine to oxygen exposure, are a great size for the precise, mature aging of special wines. But, for our purposes, they're just fun to have on the table.

The spicy and colorful flavors of this menu respond well to wines that are just a touch sweet. You'll want to choose bottles that are labeled *extra-dry*, *brut*, or *extra-brut*, all styles that have a small amount of sugar in them. Extra-dry and brut Champagnes may not even taste the faintest bit sweet, but they'll have the right amount of fruitiness to stand up to the food. Avoid anything labeled *nature*, *brut nature*, *cuvée zero*, or other Champagnes made without dosage—the sugar mixture added to the wine in various amounts—they'll be much too dry for this complex food.

This is a dinner that celebrates the West Coast's sweet-meat Dungeness crabs, the intoxicating flavors of Southeast Asian cuisine, and the fabulousness of big bottles of Champagne. Andrea's birthday falls in December, right at the start of crabbing season, so every year she celebrates with crabs and Champagne and requests that friends bring it in magnum form. Because, well, it's her birthday. One year, the party took a turn from a Stateside crab boil with vats of drawn butter to a Southeast Asian feast with big bowls of noodles and lots of fish sauce, and it's never gone back. The high-low of popping Champagne and cracking crab legs, alongside vibrant salads inspired by Vietnamese street stalls, was exactly what the party needed to make it even more fun. It's informal, it's messy, but it also feels special.

CRABS AND MAGS

Golden Eggs (page 30)

Sweet-Sour-Salty-Crunchy Citrus Salad
(page 94)

Dungeness Crab Boil with Lemongrass
and Lime (page 242)

Green Mango Rice Noodles with Coconut
Milk and Fish Sauce (page 243)

A Bowl of Shrimp Chips

DUNGENESS CRAB BOIL WITH LEMONGRASS AND LIME

Makes 8 to 10 servings

8 stalks lemongrass
4 limes
2 tablespoons black peppercorns
¼ cup sea salt
5 or 6 (12 to 14 pounds) live
    Dungeness crabs

Fill a 16- to 20-quart seafood boiling pot with 10 quarts water (or divide the water between two large stockpots). Trim the lemongrass stalks and remove the dry outer leaves. Cut each stalk into thirds and bash the segments with a mallet or the back of a knife. Toss the bruised lemongrass into the pot of water. Halve the limes, squeeze the juice into the pot, and drop in the peels. Very lightly crush the peppercorns in a mortar with a pestle or with the back of a knife, and add them to the pot, along with the salt. Set the pot over high heat, cover, and bring the water to a boil.

One at a time, grasp the crabs from the tail end, between the legs, and plunge them headfirst into the boiling water. Cover and cook for 15 minutes, adjusting the heat as needed to maintain a steady simmer.

Set a large rimmed baking sheet near the stove. Using tongs, remove the crabs from the pot and place them on the baking sheet. (Reserve 2 cups of the crab-boiling broth for the rice noodles [see facing page]).

With the aid of a kitchen towel to protect your hands from the heat, begin cleaning the crabs on a cutting board with a moat to collect the juices. One at a time, turn a crab on its back with the belly side facing up. Pull back the triangular flap on the belly and discard it. From the tail end, pull the body away from the top shell, taking care to reserve the golden "crab butter" that will pool in the bowl-shaped shell. From the body section, clean away any of the remaining reddish membrane and pull off and discard the gills. Cut the bodies in half to get two sets of legs. Pour the crab butter into a bowl and reserve it. Scrub the top shells under hot water, then return the crab butter to the cleaned shells.

You can choose to pre-crack the crab claws and legs with a mallet or hammer, or serve the crab with sets of crackers for everyone to crack their own at the table. Pile the crab on two large platters and serve family-style, with the crab butter for dipping the meat.

GREEN MANGO RICE NOODLES WITH COCONUT MILK AND FISH SAUCE

Makes 8 to 10 servings

Noodles

1½ pounds rice stick noodles
Sea salt
½ cup dried shrimp
1½ pounds green mangos (see Note)
1 seedless cucumber, thinly sliced
    on the bias
2 cups mung bean sprouts
1 bunch green onions, thinly sliced
    on the bias
1 cup fresh Vietnamese cilantro leaves
    (rau ram), or regular cilantro
1 cup fresh Asian basil leaves
1 cup fresh mint leaves
1 batch Fried Garlic (see page 164)

Sauce

1 cup coconut cream (see Note, page 67)
½ cup fish sauce
⅓ cup fresh lime juice
1 tablespoon plus 1 teaspoon sugar
6 cloves garlic, minced
4 to 6 green Thai chiles, minced, or 2 to
    3 serrano chiles, seeded and minced

To Serve

Vietnamese cilantro sprigs (rau ram),
    or regular cilantro
Asian basil sprigs
Mint sprigs
Mung bean sprouts
Sliced red and green Thai chiles
Fish sauce
Up to 2 cups hot crab-boiling broth

To make the noodles: Place the rice noodles in a large bowl and pour in enough hot water to cover them by 1 inch. Allow the noodles to soak for 15 minutes to soften, then drain.

Meanwhile, fill a large pot with 4 quarts water and bring it to a boil. Salt the water and add the softened noodles. Cook until just tender, about 1 minute, stirring to prevent the noodles from sticking together. Drain the noodles in a colander and rinse them under cold water to stop the cooking. Transfer the drained noodles to an extra-large, wide serving bowl (or two bowls, if needed) and set aside.

Put the dried shrimp in a large, dry skillet and place it over medium heat. Toast the shrimp, stirring often, until they appear dry and crackly on the outside and some take on a golden color, about 5 minutes. Transfer the shrimp to a mortar and pound with a pestle to break them up into a very coarse, crumbly powder. Alternatively, put them in a zip-top bag and pound them with a rolling pin. Set aside.

Peel the green mangos. Using the fine julienne attachment on a mandoline, cut the mango flesh into long, thin shreds, working down to the pit on both sides. Alternatively, you can cut the flesh away from the pit and process it through a spiralizer.

continued

Top the rice noodles with the shredded mango, cucumber, bean sprouts, green onions, cilantro, basil, and mint, keeping each item separated in piles around the perimeter of the bowl. Pile the toasted shrimp and fried garlic in the center of the bowl. Cover and set aside at room temperature for up to 2 hours, or refrigerate for up to 8 hours. Bring to room temperature for 1 hour before serving.

To make the sauce: In a medium bowl, whisk the coconut cream, fish sauce, lime juice, sugar, and garlic. Add the smaller quantity of chiles to start. Taste and adjust the seasoning, adding more chiles if you'd like the sauce a little spicier. The sauce will keep in a covered container in the refrigerator for up to 3 days.

To serve: Arrange the herb sprigs and bean sprouts on platters. Put the sliced chiles and fish sauce in small bowls and nestle them on the platters too.

Place the noodle bowl in the center of the table to finish the dish as your guests look on. Pour the sauce over the ingredients in the bowl and toss with salad servers to coat and distribute everything well. Add a ladleful of the hot crab-boiling broth and toss again. Add another ladleful of the broth if you think it needs it; the goal is to just slightly warm the dish and create a loose, brothy sauce. Pass the herbs, chiles, and fish sauce at the table.

Note

Green mangos are crunchy, tart mangos that are grown specifically to be eaten when underripe. They can be found at most Asian markets, but if you can't locate them, Granny Smith apples would be an interesting substitute.

Pairing Cheat Sheet
Sweet Endings

BANYULS / CHOCOLATE TART

MUSCAT DE BEAUME DE VENISE /
A BOWL OF FRESH PEACHES

JURANÇON / CARROT CAKE

VIN SANTO / ALMOND BISCOTTI

TOKAJI / LINZER TORTE

GERMAN EISWEIN / PINEAPPLE UPSIDE DOWN CAKE

TAWNY PORT / CHOCOLATE–HAZELNUT SEMIFREDDO

AGED MARSALA / ORANGE–OLIVE OIL CAKE

PEDRO XIMÉNEZ / ROASTED FIGS WITH VANILLA ICE CREAM

MOSCATO D'ASTI / PANNA COTTA WITH TROPICAL FRUIT

Resources

Retailers

California

Los Angeles

Domaine LA
domainela.com

Helen's Wines
helenswines.com

Lou Wine Shop
louwineshop.com

Psychic Wines
psychicwines.com

Silverlake Wine
silverlakewine.com

Oakland

Bay Grape
baygrapewine.com

Minimo
minimowine.com

Ordinaire
ordinairewine.com

The Punchdown
punchdownwine.com

San Francisco

Bi-Rite Market
biritemarket.com

Flatiron Wines
flatiron-wines.com

Ruby Wine
rubywinesf.com

Terroir Natural Wine Bar &
Merchant
terroirsf.com

Santa Monica

Esters Wine Shop & Bar
esterswineshop.com

Colorado

Denver

The Proper Pour
theproperpour.com

Florida

Naples

Natural Wine Naples
naturalwinesnaples.com

Georgia

Atlanta

Cakes and Ale
cakesandalerestaurant.com

Perrine's Wine Shop
perrineswine.com

Illinois

Chicago

57th Street Wines
Wines57.com

Red & White
redandwhitewineschicago.com

Louisiana

New Orleans

Bacchanal Wine
bacchanalwine.com

Faubourg Wines
faubourgwines.com

Keife & Co.
keifeandco.com

Maine

Portland

Maine & Loire
maineandloire.com

Massachusetts

Boston

The Wine Bottega
thewinebottega.com

Cambridge

Central Bottle Wine & Provisions
centralbottle.com

Michigan

Ann Arbor

Spencer
spencerannarbor.com

Detroit

The Royce
theroycedetroit.com

Western Market
westernmkt.com

Minnesota

Minneapolis

Henry & Son
shophenryandson.com

Nebraska

Omaha

La Buvette
labuvetteomaha.com

New York

Brooklyn

Dandelion Wine
dandelionwineshop.tumblr.com

Leon & Son
leonandsonwine.com

Uva
uvawines.com

Vine Wine
vine-wine.com

Buffalo

Paradise Wine
paradisewinebuffalo.com

Hudson

Hudson Wine Merchants
hudsonwinemerchants.com

Kingston

Kingston Wine Co.
kingstonwine.com

New York City

Chambers Street Wines
chambersstwines.com

Discovery Wines
discoverywines.com

Flatiron Wines
flatiron-wines.com

Troy

22 2nd St. Wine Co.
winetroy.com

Oregon

Portland

Ardor Natural Wines
ardornaturalwines.com

Bar Norman
barnorman.com

Division Wines
divisionwines.com

South Carolina

Charleston

Monarch Wine Merchants
monarchwinemerchants.com

Tennessee

Nashville

Woodland Wine Merchant
woodlandwinemerchant.com

Texas

Dallas

Bar and Garden Dallas
barandgardendallas.com

Houston

Houston Wine Merchant
houstonwines.com

Waco

Wine Shoppe
wacowineshoppe.com

Vermont

Stowe

Cork Wine Bar & Market
corkvt.com

Waterbury

Cork Wine Bar & Market
corkvt.com

Washington

Orcas Island

The Bodega at
Champagne Champagne
champagnechampagne.me

Doe Bay Wine Co.
doebaywinecompany.com

Seattle

Marine Area 7
marinearea7.com

Vif Wine | Coffee
vifseattle.com

Vita Uva
shopvitauva.com

Wisconsin

Madison

Square Wine Co.
squarewineco.com

Importers to Know

Blue Danube

Chris Terrell Wines

Grand Coeur Wines

Jenny & Francois

José Pastor Selections

Kermit Lynch Wine Merchant

Louis/Dressner Selections

The Piedmont Guy

Polaner Selections

PortoVino

Rosenthal Wine Merchant

Selection Massale

SelectioNaturel

Selections de la Viña

Scuola di Vino

VomBoden

Zev Rovine Selections

Further Reading

The Feiring Line
alicefeiring.com

PUNCH
punchdrink.com

SevenFifty Daily
daily.sevenfifty.com

Sprudge Wine
wine.sprudge.com

Wine Folly
winefolly.com

resources

Acknowledgments

Writing this book would have been no fun at all without the incredible support and unquenchable appetites of our menfolk, Scott Frank and Thomas Monroe. (Guys, we love you.) Their thoughtful input on nearly all of these recipes and wines was invaluable. Orly's insightful commentary was much appreciated for many reasons. (And we love you, too.)

Lorena Jones, our editor and publisher, who believed in this before we'd even written the proposal, heard our ideas about what a book on modern wine and food pairing should be and let us run with it. We're honored to have your name printed on the book's spine.

Kara Plikaitis listened to our story, read the words, and made them come to life with her brilliant design. It's been such a pleasure to work together.

Thanks, too, to Senior Production Editor Doug Ogan, Production Manager Jane Chinn, Senior Publicity and Marketing Manager Erin Welke, Associate Marketing Director Allison Renzulli, and everyone else at Ten Speed.

Our literary agent Alia Habib's kindness and enthusiasm is matched only by her tenacity.

Camille Shu. We've been crushing on her illustrations for a long time and can't believe we are so fortunate to have them in our book.

An all-star dream team of talented women helped us create the stunning images for this book. Eva Kolenko, whose energy for this project and creative genius on set made the photography perfectly match the passion we feel for the subject. She is an absolute delight and a friend for life. Soraya Matos painted her nails, unpainted her nails, went through countless wardrobe changes, held heavy lighting equipment in the rain, fanned the campfire smoke, placed her hands in innumerable compromising positions for an ungodly amount of time, and did it all with poise. We're beyond grateful for Kira Corbin's immense talent for arranging beautiful things and feel so fortunate to have her as a friend and collaborator. No one can put together two back-to-back parties with the humor, style, and effortlessness that Jenna Winkler does. She has been the captain of the *Wine Food* cheerleading squad since the beginning.

Betty and Tom Pickell were our recipe testers, dishwashers, prep cooks, and errand runners. Their help, enthusiasm, and fun-loving attitudes carried us through.

Thanks to Joan Childs for arranging that fateful lunch at Luce. And for the deadline Negronis!

We have mad respect for Talia Baiocchi, editor in chief of PUNCH, for being such an important voice in wine writing and for helping us get this book off the ground.

Thank you to all of our friends, family, and colleagues in the Portland food and wine world (and beyond) who ate and drank with us in the name of research. Those experiences were the inspiration for this book.

Lastly, our most heartfelt gratitude to all of the growers and winemakers mentioned in this book (and some who we surely forgot to include) for providing more people with the opportunity to drink good wine.

Index

A

Agerre, 150
Aglianico, 200
Aguachile, Shrimp, 35–36
Aioli by Hand, 113
Albariño, 38
Albert Boxler, 90
Albert Mann, 66
Aleksi Tsikhelashvili, 142
Alexandre Bain, 103
Alfredo Maestro, 160, 190
Alice et Oliver De Moor, 40, 189
Aligoté, 189
Alsace, 61, 66, 90, 98
Altesse, 50
Alto Adige, 50, 98
Amity Vineyards, 77
Amontillado sherry, 46
Analemma, 44
Anchovies
    Pintxos Gilda, 178
    Roasted Shallot Pissaladière, 42
André-Michel Brégeon, 32
Antoine Arena, 106, 225
Apátsági Pince, 125
Apple Relish, Fennel-, 32–34
Apricot-Tarragon Mostarda, 53
Arcari + Danesi, 63
Arneis, 55, 92
Assyrtiko, 155
Athiri, 155
Azienda Agricola Arianna
    Occhipinti, 206
Azienda Agricola COS, 206
Azienda Agricola Musto
    Carmelitano, 200
Azienda Agricola Negro Angelo e
    Figli, 92
Azienda Agricola Pisano Danila, 162

B

Bagels and Lox, Pretzel, 68–71
Banyuls, 245
Barbaresco, 92, 181
Barbera, 92, 115, 195, 200
Barco del Corneto, 122
Barolo, 92, 230
Basilicata, 200
Beans
    Butternut Lamb Chili, 200
    Campfire Cassoulet, 167–69
    Paella de la Corona, 178–79
    See also Chickpeas
Beaujolais, 77, 87, 147, 164, 192
Beckham Estate Vineyard, 44
Bedrock Wine Co., 137
Beef
    Big Boule Sandwich with Roast
        Beef, Pickled Beets, and
        Gorgonzola, 162–63
    Borscht Risotto, 195–96

Khinkali (Georgian Soup
    Dumplings), 143–44
Leftover Beef Hash with Herby
    Poached Eggs, 75–76
Sunday Sauce on Polenta, 208–9
Tomahawk Steaks with Grilled
    Radicchio and Cherry
    Tapenade, 171–73
Vietnamese Beef Stew (Bò Kho),
    233–35
Beets
    Beets with Their Greens and Dried
        Cherries, 146
    Big Boule Sandwich with Roast
        Beef, Pickled Beets, and
        Gorgonzola, 162–63
    Borscht Risotto, 195–96
    Quick-Pickled Beets, 162–63
Bellwether Wine Cellars, 82
Benanti, 158, 206
Bengoetxe, 150
Benoît Lahaye, 240
Bernard Baudry, 132
Bernhard Ott, 153
Beurer, 94
Biscuits and Morel Gravy, 61–62
Bisson, 35
Blatina, 228
Bloomer Creek Vineyard, 90
Bodega Akutain, 190
Bodegas Albamar, 38
Bodegas Alba Viticultores, 46, 201
Bodegas Bernabé Navarro, 218
Bodegas César Florido, 201
Bodegas Corisca, 38
Bodegas el Viejo Almacén de
    Sauzal, 128
Bodegas Grant, 201
Bodegas Gutiérrez Colosía, 201
Bodegas Vega de Tera, 122
Bodega Vinificate, 164
Bordeaux, 61, 130, 132, 236
Borscht Risotto, 195–96
Bossäm with Riesling Ssäm Sauce,
    84–85
Bott Pince, 125
Boulud, Daniel, 220
Bourboulenc, 110
Bourdain, Anthony, 220
Bouzeron, 189
Bow & Arrow, 77, 103
Bread
    Big Boule Sandwich with Roast
        Beef, Pickled Beets, and
        Gorgonzola, 162–63
    Caramelized Onion and Bread
        Soup with Brûléed Blue
        Cheese, 201–3
    Fig Fattoush with Grilled
        Halloumi, 106–7
    Flatbread alla Norma, 158–59

Griddled Zucchini Bread with
    Moscato Peaches and Crème,
    58–60
Sherry-Cherry Chicken Liver
    Toast, 46–47
Brettanomyces (Brett), 24
Brick House Vineyard, 77
Brkić, 228
Broc Cellars, 137
Brovia, 230
Bugey-Cerdon, 68
Bura-Mrgudić Winery, 186
Burgundy, 17, 40, 61, 189
    red, 55, 220
    white, 147, 214
Burja Estate, 96
Butter
    Pancetta-Chive Butter, 40–41
    Whipped Chorizo Butter, 39

C

Cabbage
    Bossäm with Riesling Ssäm Sauce,
        84–85
    Romanian Cabbage Rolls with
        Lots of Dill, 228–29
    Two Quickie Kimchis, 86
Cabernet franc, 87, 132, 236
Cabernet sauvignon, 206, 236
Ca' dei Zago, 118
Cà del Vént, 63
Cà de Noci, 75
Cahors, 233
Calabretta, 158
California, 44, 77, 96, 128, 132, 137
Cameron Winery, 167
Camin Larredya, 104
Campania, 200
Campfire Cassoulet, 167–69
Canary Islands, 106
Cantina Giardino, 200
Cantina Paltrinieri, 75
Cappellano, 230
Cardedu, 35
Carić Vina, 186
Carignan, 128
Carricante, 158
Carrots
    Carrot-Ginger Dressing, 90–91
    Carrot-Zucchini Latkes, 125–27
    Pomegranate-Roasted Carrots
        with Lentils, Labneh, and
        Carrot-Top Zhoug, 134–36
Casa Coste Piane, 118
Cascina Barisel, 58
Cascina delle Rose, 195
Cascina 'Tavijn, 195
Cascina Val del Prete, 92
Cassoulet, Campfire, 167–69
Castello di Luzzano, 96
Catalonia, 28
Catherine & Claude Maréchal, 220

Catherine & Pierre Breton, 120

Cauliflower "Couscous," Roots
    Tagine with, 137–39

Cava, 28, 87

Cavallotto, 230

Cave Caloz, 50

Cédric Bouchard, 240

Celine & Laurent Tripoz, 61

Chablis, 40, 220

Champagne, 21, 28, 30, 55, 58, 240

Champagne Agrapart, 240

Champagne Marie Courtin, 240

Champagne Tarlant, 240

Chang, David, 82

Chardonnay, 55, 61, 63, 87, 206,
    214, 220

Chasselas, 50

Château Combel-la-Serre, 233

Château de Bellevue, 236

Château d'Oupia, 164

Château La Grave, 233

Château le Puy, 236

Château Meylet, 236

Châteauneuf-du-Pape, 211

Château Peyrassol, 42

Château Pradeaux, 110

Château Sainte-Anne, 110

Château Simone, 110

Cheese
    Big Boule Sandwich with Roast
        Beef, Pickled Beets, and
        Gorgonzola, 162–63
    Burrata with Strawberry Salad, 44
    Delicata Crostata with Fennel
        Sausage, Ricotta, and
        Buckwheat Honey, 198–99
    Fig Fattoush with Grilled
        Halloumi, 106-7
    Hot Melted Raclette, 52
    Neon Coconut Curry with Paneer
        (or Tofu) and Greens, 120–21
    pairing wine and, 55
    Pimento Cheese Soufflé, 77–79
    Slow-Braised Lamb Ragù with
        Rigatoni and Whipped Ricotta,
        230–32
    Spaghetti Squash Parmigiano,
        130–31
    Stuffed Peppers with Sweet Corn,
        Herby Rice, and Possibly Too
        Much Cheese, 122–24

Chenin blanc, 61, 101, 120, 211

Cherries
    Beets with Their Greens and Dried
        Cherries, 146
    Cherry-Olive Tapenade, 172
    Cherry Vinaigrette, 172
    Sherry-Cherry Chicken Liver
        Toast, 46–47

Chianti Classico, 87, 130

Chicken
    Coq au Vin Jura, 223–24
    Our Chicken Pot Pie, 214–17
    Paella de la Corona, 178–79
    Salt-and-Pepper Fried Chicken
        with General Tso's Dipping
        Sauce, 150–52

Sherry-Cherry Chicken Liver
    Toast, 46–47

Spatchcock Roast Chicken
    with Schmaltzy Potatoes and
    Cabbage, 192–94

Chickpeas
    Chop Chop, 92–93
    Falafel Waffles, 72–74
    Seafood Stew with Aromas of the
        Maquis, 225–27

Child, Julia, 223

Chili, Butternut Lamb, 200

Christian Tschida, 184

Chutney, Green, 100

Cinsault, 42, 110, 160

Ciro Picariello, 200

Clairette, 110

Clams
    Cod and Clams en Papillote,
        186–88
    Seafood Stew with Aromas of the
        Maquis, 225–27

Clos Canarelli, 106, 225

Clos de la Roilette, 192

Clos du Jaugueyron, 236

Clos La Coutale, 233

Clos Marfisi, 35

Clos Saint-André, 236

Clos Signadore, 225

Coconut
    Green Mango Rice with Coconut
        Milk and Fish Sauce, 243–44
    Neon Coconut Curry with Paneer
        (or Tofu) and Greens, 120–21
    Sweet-Sour-Salty-Crunchy Citrus
        Salad, 94–95
    Tropical Yogurt Parfaits with
        Seedy Cashew Crunch, 66–67

Cod and Clams en Papillote, 186–88

Colatura, 159

Commanderie de Peyrassol, 110

Comm. G.B. Burlotto, 230

Complemen'terre, 32

Corked wines, 24

Corkscrews, 21

Correcaminos, 190

Corsica, 106, 225

Costadilà, 118

Côte Chalonnaise, 220

Côte de Beaune, 220

Côte de Nuits, 220

Côtes du Rhône Villages, 134

Crab Boil, Dungeness, with
    Lemongrass and Lime, 242

Crémant, 61

Croatia, 9, 186, 228

Crowley Wines, 167

Crudités for Early Summer, 114

Cucumbers
    Cucumber-Grapefruit Granita,
        32–34
    Forbidden Rice Bowls with Slow-
        Roasted Salmon and Those
        Sweet-and-Sour Cucumbers
        Everyone Loves, 184–85

Curry, Neon Coconut, with Paneer
    (or Tofu) and Greens, 120–21

D

Daniel Ramos, 176

Dard & Ribo, 171

Daterra Viticultores, 176

Day Wines, 72

Decanting, 22

Desserts, pairing wine and, 245

Didier Montchovet, 189

Didimi, 142

Die, 61

Dips
    Pistachio-Yogurt Dip, 39
    Tonnato Dip, 39

Division Winemaking Company,
    77, 167

Dolcetto, 92, 198

Dolores Cabrera Fernández, 106

Domaine A. et P. de Villaine, 189

Domaine André et Mireille
    Tissot, 223

Domaine aux Moines, 101

Domaine Balivet, 68

Domaine Bechtold, 98

Domaine Benoit Courault, 132

Domaine Bernard Levet, 171

Domaine Bott-Geyl, 98

Domaine Bru-Baché, 104

Domaine Castera, 104

Domaine Clos des Rocs, 214

Domaine Comte Abbatucci, 106

Domaine Cosse Maisonneuve, 233

Domaine de Bellivière, 101

Domaine de Juchepie, 101

Domaine de la Dentelle, 68

Domaine de la Ferme Saint-
    Martin, 134

Domaine de la Grand 'Cour, 192

Domaine de L' Amandier, 134

Domaine de la Pépière, 32

Domaine de L' Octavin, 223

Domaine de Majas, 35

Domaine de Piaugier, 134

Domaine de Roally, 214

Domaine des Cavarodes, 223

Domaine des Marnes Blanche, 61

Domaine de Souch, 104

Domaine des Terres Dorées, 192

Domaine de Sulauze, 42, 110

Domaine de Terrebrune, 42

Domaine du Bagnol, 42

Domaine du Closel-Château des
    Vaults, 101

Domaine du Clos Naudin, 120

Domaine du Joncier, 134

Domaine du Mortier, 132

Domaine Gèrard Duplessis, 40

Domaine Gilbert Picq et Fils, 40

Domaine Guillaume Gilles, 171

Domaine Guillot-Broux, 214

Domaine Hauvette, 42

Domaine Henri & Gilles Buisson,
    214, 220

Domaine Karanika, 155

Domaine Labet, 223

Domaine Landron, 32

Domaine Léon Boesch, 66, 90

Domaine les Fouques, 110
Domaine les Roches, 132
Domaine L'Oratoire St. Martin, 134
Domaine Louis Magnin, 50
Domaine Luneau-Papin, 32
Domaine Matassa, 128
Domaine Maxime Magnon, 128
Domaine Naudin-Ferrand, 189
Domaine Olivier Pithon, 128
Domaine Ostertag, 66
Domaine Pattes Loup, 40
Domaine Pêcheur, 223
Domaine Philippe Tessier, 61
Domaine Pierre Frick, 61
Domaine Renardat-Fâche, 68
Domaine Romaneaux-Destezet, 171
Domaine Simon Bize et Fils, 220
Domaine Tempier, 110
Domaine Trapet, 98
Domaine Vincent Carême, 120
Domaine Vincent Paris, 171
Domaine Weinbach, 90
Dominio del Urogallo, 176
Dominique Belluard, 50
Doniene Gorrondona, 150
Duck Breast, Indian-Spiced, with
    Burst Grapes and Glazed
    Cipollini, 236–37
Dumplings, Georgian Soup
    (Khinkali), 143–44

E

Edelzwicker, 90
Eggplant
    Flatbread alla Norma, 158–59
    Ratatouille Gratin, 128–29
Eggs
    Falafel Waffles, 72–74
    Golden Eggs, 30–31
    Leftover Beef Hash with Herby
        Poached Eggs, 75–76
    Pimento Cheese Soufflé, 77–79
    soft-cooked, 74
    Summer Piperade with Fried
        Eggs, 190–91
    Torta di Frittata with Spring
        Mushrooms and Stinging
        Nettles, 63
    Wild Mushrooms and Baked Eggs,
        or Breakfast of Champignons,
        132–33
Eiswein, 245
Elisabetta Abrami, 63
El Maestro Sierra, 46, 201
Emilia-Romagna, 75
Emilio Hidalgo, 46
Eminence Road Farm
    Winery, 77, 132
Enjingi, 186
Envinate, 176
Erbaluce, 147
Eric Texier, 171
Ermes Pavese, 50
Ethyl acetate (EA), 24
The Eyrie Vineyards, 44
Ezio T., 195

F

Falafel Waffles, 72–74
Fanny Sabre, 220
Fattoush, Fig, with Grilled Halloumi,
    106–7
Fausse Piste, 160
Fekete Pince, 125
Fennel
    Fennel-Apple Relish, 32–34
    Whole Grilled Fish with Herby
        Fennel Relish, 155–57
Fig Fattoush with Grilled Halloumi,
    106–7
Fino sherry, 211
Fish
    Forbidden Rice Bowls with Slow-
        Roasted Salmon and Those
        Sweet-and-Sour Cucumbers
        Everyone Loves, 184–85
    The New Tuna Noodle, 189
    Olive Oil–Poached Tuna with
        Herbes de Provence, 112
    Pintxos Gilda, 178
    Pretzel Bagels and Lox, 68–71
    Roasted Shallot Pissaladière, 42
    Roots Rémoulade with Smoked
        Trout, 104
    Tonnato Dip, 39
    Whole Grilled Fish with Herby
        Fennel Relish, 155–57
Foradori, 50
Forlorn Hope Wines, 153
Francesco Guccione, 206
Franciacorta, 63
François Pinon, 120
Franco Noussan, 50
Frank Cornelissen, 206
Frank, Scott, 77
Frantz Saumon, 72
Frappato, 206
Freisa, 115
Friuli, 181, 218
Fruits
    Tropical Yogurt Parfaits with
        Seedy Cashew Crunch, 66–67
    See also individual fruits
Fuchs und Hase, 72
Furmint, 125

G

Gamay, 68, 77, 164, 192, 211
Garlic
    Aioli by Hand, 113
    Fried Garlic and Garlic Oil, 164–66
    Green Garlic Vinaigrette, 153–54
Garnacha, 211
G.D. Vajra, 58
Gemischter satz, 153
General Tso's Dipping Sauce, 150–52
Gentle Folk, 44
Georgia, 142, 160, 218
Gewürztraminer, 90, 98, 115, 233
Ginger Mignonette, 32–34
Giovanni Canonica, 230
Giuseppe Mascarello, 198
Glassware, 21
Glera, 118

Glou-glou, 164
Goyo Garcia Viadero, 176, 190
Grapefruit
    Cucumber-Grapefruit Granita,
        32–34
    Sweet-Sour-Salty-Crunchy Citrus
        Salad, 94–95
Graševina, 186
Greco di Tufo, 181
Greek wines, 155, 160
Grenache, 42, 110, 134, 160
Gringet, 50
Grk, 186
Gros manseng, 104
Grüner veltliner, 87, 184

H

Ham
    Deviled Ham Hand Pies, 160–61
    Jamón and Peas, 28–29
    Melon and Prosciutto with
        Radishes, Avocado, and
        Mint, 96
Hand Pies, Deviled Ham, 160–61
Hárslevelü, 115
Hatzidakis Winery, 155
Hazan, Marcella, 130
Hofgut Falkenstein, 94
Holden Wine Company, 164
Holmberg, Martha, 158
Hope Well Wine, 167

I

Iago's Wine, 142
Iberieli, 160
I Clivi, 96
I Custodi delle vigne dell'Etna, 158
Idlewild, 92
I Fabbri, 130
Il Censo, 206
Il Palazzino, 130
Ingrid Groiss, 153
Irouleguy, 55
Isaac Cantalapiedra, 122
Iuli, 195
I Vigneri delle vigne dell'Etna, 206

J

Jacques Lassaigne, 30
Jamón and Peas, 28–29
Jauma Wine, 164
J.B. Becker, 94
Jean Foillard, 192
Jerez, 46
Joe Jack's Fish Shack, 35
Julien Pineau, 103
Julien Sunier, 192
Jura, 223
Jurançon, 104, 245
Jurg, 61

K

Kelley Fox Wines, 167
Kerner, 50, 181
Ketterman, Scott and Emily, 176
Khinkali (Georgian Soup Dumplings),
    143–44

wine food

Kimchis, Two Quickie, 86
Kisi, 142
Kohlrabi
    A Sophisticated Hippie Salad,
        90–91
    Two Quickie Kimchis, 86

L

Labels, 18–19
Labneh
    making, 136
    Pomegranate-Roasted Carrots
        with Lentils, Labneh, and
        Carrot-Top Zhough, 134–36
La Clarine Farm, 38
La Collina, 75
La Garagista, 218
Lagrein, 115
Lamb
    Butternut Lamb Chili, 200
    Slow-Braised Lamb Ragù with
        Rigatoni and Whipped Ricotta,
        230–32
Lambrusco, 75, 90
La Miraja, 195
Lamoreasca, 75
Languedoc-Roussillon, 17, 35, 115, 128
Larmandier-Bernier, 30
La Stoppa, 218
Latkes, Carrot-Zucchini, 125–27
Laurent Barth, 66, 90
Le Colombier de la Métarie, 236
Le Grange Tiphaine, 101
Lentils, Pomegranate-Roasted
    Carrots with Labneh, Carrot-
    Top Zhough, and, 134–36
Les Capriades, 72
Le Sot de L'Ange, 160
Les Vignes de Paradis, 50
Lett, David, 44
Le Vigne di Alice, 118
Liguria, 35, 162
Limoux, 61
Lo-Fi Wines, 77
Loire Valley, 61, 77, 101, 120, 132
Lombardy, 63
Louis-Antoine Luyt, 164
Lox, Pretzel Bagels and, 68–71
Lucy Margaux Vineyards, 72
Luigi Tecce, 200

M

Macebeo, 28
Mâconnais, 220
Maisulan, 190
Malagousia, 155
Malbec, 160, 233, 236
Malolactic fermentation (malo), 32
Malvasia, 96
Malvazija, 186
Mammolo, 225
Mandili, 142
Mandrágora Vinos de Pueblo, 176
Mango Rice, Green, with Coconut
    Milk and Fish Sauce, 243–44

Manni Nössing, 50
Marc Deschamps, 103
Marco Bianco, 58
Marc Pesnot, 32
Mariam Iosebidze, 142
Marie-Noel Ledru, 240
Marsala, 24, 206, 245
Martha Stoumen Wines, 128
Martin & Anna Arndorfer, 184
McFadden, Joshua, 158
Meatballs, pairing wine and, 211
Melon and Prosciutto with Radishes,
    Avocado, and Mint, 96
Mencia, 115
Menus
    Crabs and Mags, 240–41
    Fête de la Raclette, 50–51
    Georgian Supra, 140, 142
    Le Grand Aioli, 110–11
    Paella and Porrons, 176–77
    Somm-Ssäm Throwdown, 82–83
    Sunday Sauce, 206–7
Merlot, 236
Methode Sauvage, 132
Methymnaeos, 155
Meyer-Fonné, 66
Michael Gindl, 184
MicroBio, 122
Milan Nestarec, 184
Miloš Winery, 228
Minimus Wines, 160
Momofuku, 82
Monroe, Tom, 77
Montepulciano d'Abruzzo, 147
Montesecondo, 130
Moreau-Naudet, 40
Morgon, France, 9
Moscato d'Asti, 58, 245
Moscofilero, 155
Mosel, 94
Mostarda, Apricot-Tarragon, 53
Mourvèdre, 42, 110, 134
Mtsvane, 142
Muscadet, 32
Muscat, 90
Muscat de Beaume de Venise, 245
Mushrooms
    Biscuits and Morel Gravy, 61–62
    Coq au Vin Jura, 223–24
    A Giant Stuffed Pumpkin for
        Harvest Time, 220–22
    Our Chicken Pot Pie, 214–17
    Porcini Mushroom Stroganoff,
        218–19
    Spring Green Picnic Rolls, 153–54
    Torta di Frittata with Spring
        Mushrooms and Stinging
        Nettles, 63
    Wild Mushrooms and Baked Eggs,
        or Breakfast of Champignons,
        132–33
Mussels
    Cast-Iron Skillet Mussels with
        Pancetta-Chive Butter, 40–41
    Paella de la Corona, 178–79
    Seafood Stew with Aromas of the
        Maquis, 225–27

N

Nanclares y Prieto, 38
Natural wines, 14
Nebbiolo, 55, 92, 200, 230
Nerello Mascalese, 206
Nero d'Avola, 181, 206
Nettles, Stinging, Torta di Frittata
        with Spring Mushrooms and, 63
New York, 77, 82, 132
Nguyen, Andrea, 233
Nicolas Mariotti Bindi, 225
Nielluccio, 225
Nika Winery, 142
Nikolaihof, 82
Nikoloz Antadze, 142
Noodles. See Pasta and noodles
Northern Rhône, 11, 171
Nosiola, 50
Nuts, toasting, 29

O

Ochota Barrels, 98
Olives
    Cherry-Olive Tapenade, 172
    Pintxos Gilda, 178
Olivier Morin, 189
Oloroso sherry, 24, 201
Onions
    Caramelized Onion and Bread
        Soup with Brûléed Blue
        Cheese, 201–3
    Indian-Spiced Duck Breast with
        Burst Grapes and Glazed
        Cipollini, 236–37
    Pickled Red Onions, 122–24
Oranges
    Sweet-Sour-Salty-Crunchy Citrus
        Salad, 94–95
Orange wine, 181, 218
Oregon, 9, 44, 77, 167, 211
Ovum, 82, 98
Oxidation, 24
Oyster Bar, for a Shucking Good
        Time, 32–34

P

Pacina, 130
Paella de la Corona, 178–79
Pairing cheat sheets
    cheese, 55
    desserts, 245
    meatballs, 211
    pasta, 181
    quick dinners, 147
    soup, 115
    take-out food, 87
Pancetta-Chive Butter, 40–41
Paolo Bea, 218
Parellada, 28
Parfaits, Tropical Yogurt, with Seedy
        Cashew Crunch, 66–67
Pascal Doquet, 30
Pasta and noodles
    Green Mango Rice with Coconut
        Milk and Fish Sauce, 243–44
    The New Tuna Noodle, 189
    pairing wine and, 181

Pasta and noodles, *continued*
    Porcini Mushroom Stroganoff,
        218–19
    Seafood Stew with Aromas of the
        Maquis, 225–27
    Slow-Braised Lamb Ragù with
        Rigatoni and Whipped Ricotta,
        230–32
Peaches, Moscato, Griddled Zucchini
    Bread with Crème and, 58–60
Pears, Juniper-Pickled, 53
Peas, Jamón and, 28–29
Pecchenino, 198
Pedro Ximénez, 245
Peppers
    Blistered Padrón Peppers, 178
    Chop Chop, 92–93
    Paella de la Corona, 178–79
    Pimento Cheese Soufflé, 77–79
    Pintxos Gilda, 178
    Ratatouille Gratin, 128–29
    Stuffed Peppers with Sweet Corn,
        Herby Rice, and Possibly Too
        Much Cheese, 122–24
    Summer Piperade with Fried
        Eggs, 190–91
Perricone, 206
Pétillant naturel rosé, 72
Petit courbu, 104
Petite arvine, 50
Petit manseng, 104
Petit verdot, 236
Pheasant's Tears, 142
Piedmont, 92, 195, 230
Pierre Moncuit, 30
Pigato, 181
Pimento Cheese Soufflé, 77–79
Pinot blanc, 61, 63, 66, 90
Pinot grigio, 14, 147
Pinot gris, 90
Pinot noir, 44, 63, 167, 211, 220
Pintxos Gilda, 178
Piquentum, 228
Pissaladière, Roasted Shallot, 42
Pistachio-Yogurt Dip, 39
Plavac mali, 228
Podere le Boncie, 130
Poggerino, 130
Poggiosecco, 96
Polenta, Sunday Sauce on, 208–9
Pomegranate-Roasted Carrots with
    Lentils, Labneh, and Carrot-Top
    Zhoug, 134–36
Populis, 137
Pork
    Bossäm with Riesling Ssäm Sauce,
        84–85
    Glou-Glou Thai BBQ, 164–66
    Romanian Cabbage Rolls with
        Lots of Dill, 228–29
    Sunday Sauce on Polenta, 208–9
    See also Ham; Sausage
Port, 245
Potatoes
    Cod and Clams en Papillote,
        186–88
    Leftover Beef Hash with Herby
        Poached Eggs, 75–76

Persillade Potatoes, 52
Pot Pie, Our Chicken, 214–17
Poulsard, 68, 147, 223
Pretzel Bagels and Lox, 68–71
Prié blanc, 50
Primitivo, 137
Priorat, 211
Prosciutto and Melon with Radishes,
    Avocado, and Mint, 96
Prosecco, 118
Provence, 35, 42, 110
Puerto Vallarta, 35
Pumpkin, A Giant Stuffed, for
    Harvest Time, 220–22
Punta Crena, 162

R
Rabbit
    Paella de la Corona, 178–79
Radicchio
    Chop Chop, 92–93
    Tomahawk Steaks with Grilled
        Radicchio and Cherry
        Tapenade, 171–73
Radikon, 218
Raphaël Bartucci, 68
Ratatouille Gratin, 128–29
Recaredo, 28
Redford, Myron, 77
Reduction, 24
Refosco, 228
Refošk, 228
Relishes
    Fennel-Apple Relish, 32–34
    Herby Fennel Relish, 155–57
Retsina, 155
Rías Baixas, 38
Rice
    Borscht Risotto, 195–96
    Forbidden Rice Bowls with Slow-
        Roasted Salmon and Those
        Sweet-and-Sour Cucumbers
        Everyone Loves, 184–85
    Green Mango Rice with Coconut
        Milk and Fish Sauce, 243–44
    Paella de la Corona, 178–79
    Romanian Cabbage Rolls with
        Lots of Dill, 228–29
    Stuffed Peppers with Sweet Corn,
        Herby Rice, and Possibly Too
        Much Cheese, 122–24
Riesling, 55, 82, 87, 90, 94, 211, 233
Rioja, 55, 87
Rkatsiteli, 142
Roagna, 198
Robola, 155
Rosé, 90, 147
    Corsican or Canary Islands, 106
    full-bodied, 160
    pétillant naturel, 72
    of pinot noir, 44
    Provençal, 42, 110
Rossese, 162
Rueda, 122
Ruth Lewandowski, 92
Ryme Cellars, 35

S
Saetti, 75
Salad dressings
    Carrot-Ginger Dressing, 90–91
    Creamy Green Buttermilk
        Dressing, 101–2
    See also Vinaigrettes
Salads
    Burrata with Strawberry Salad, 44
    Chop Chop, 92–93
    Fig Fattoush with Grilled
        Halloumi, 106–7
    Little Louie Wedge, 101–2
    Melon and Prosciutto with
        Radishes, Avocado, and
        Mint, 96
    Our Ideal Green Salad, 103
    Roots Rémoulade with Smoked
        Trout, 104
    A Sophisticated Hippie Salad,
        90–91
    Sweet-Sour-Salty-Crunchy Citrus
        Salad, 94–95
    Tomato Chaat, 98–100
Salmon
    Forbidden Rice Bowls with Slow-
        Roasted Salmon and Those
        Sweet-and-Sour Cucumbers
        Everyone Loves, 184–85
    Pretzel Bagels and Lox, 68–71
Salvo Foti/I Vigneri, 158
Samuel Tinon, 125
Sancerre, 55
San Fereolo, 198
Sangiovese, 130, 160, 200, 211, 225
Sant'Or Winery, 155
Saperavi, 142, 160
Sardinia, 35
Sauces
    Aioli by Hand, 113
    General Tso's Dipping Sauce,
        150–52
    Ginger Mignonette, 32–34
    Riesling Ssäm Sauce, 84–85
    Sunday Sauce on Polenta, 208–9
    Tahini Sauce, 138–39
    Tamarind Dipping Sauce, 164–66
    Walnut Sauce, 145
Sausage
    Campfire Cassoulet, 167–69
    Delicata Crostata with Fennel
        Sausage, Ricotta, and
        Buckwheat Honey, 198–99
    Paella de la Corona, 178–79
    Sunday Sauce on Polenta, 208–9
    Whipped Chorizo Butter, 39
Sauternes, 55
Sauvignon blanc, 103
Savoie, 50
Scalvos Wines, 155
Sciaccarellu, 225
Scribe, 44
Serving suggestions, 21–22
Shallot Pissaladière, Roasted, 42
Sherry
    amontillado, 46
    fino, 211

oloroso, 24, 201
Shrimp
Little Louie Wedge, 101–2
Paella de la Corona, 178–79
Seafood Stew with Aromas of the
Maquis, 225–27
Shrimp Aguachile, 35–36
Sicily, 158, 206
Simon Busser, 233
Simone Scaletta, 198
Šipun, 186
Škerk, 218
Sky Vineyards, 137
Soave, 181
SoloUva, 63
Soufflé, Pimento Cheese, 77–79
Soups
Caramelized Onion and Bread
Soup with Brûléed Blue
Cheese, 201–3
pairing wine and, 115
Southern Rhône, 134, 160, 171
Spanish wines, 176
Squash
Butternut Lamb Chili, 200
Carrot-Zucchini Latkes, 125–27
Delicata Crostata with Fennel
Sausage, Ricotta, and
Buckwheat Honey, 198–99
Griddled Zucchini Bread with
Moscato Peaches and Crème,
58–60
Ratatouille Gratin, 128–29
Spaghetti Squash Parmigiano,
130–31
Squid
Seafood Stew with Aromas of the
Maquis, 225–27
Stilianou Winery, 155
Strawberry Salad, Burrata with, 44
Super Tuscan, 130
Suriol, 28
Sweet potatoes
Leftover Beef Hash with Herby
Poached Eggs, 75–76
Swick Wines, 44
Swiss chard
Spring Green Picnic Rolls, 153–54
Sylvain Pataille, 220
Sylvaner, 90, 147
Syrah, 11, 87, 110, 134, 171

T
Tahini Sauce, 138–39
Takaji Aszú, 125
Tamarind Dipping Sauce, 164–66
Tasting, 22–23
Tavel, 160
Tempranillo, 44, 160, 190
Teran, 228
Terenzuola, 35
Teroldego, 181
Terre Bianche, 162
Testalonga, 162
Teutonic Wine Company, 98
Thomas Perseval, 240
Tibouren, 42

Tokaji, 245
Tomato Chaat, 98–100
Torre dei Beati, 160
Trebbiano, 181
Trentino, 50
Tres Sabores, 137
Tribidrag, 137
Trousseau, 115, 223
Trout
Roots Rémoulade with Smoked
Trout, 104
Whole Grilled Fish with Herby
Fennel Relish, 155–57
Tsolikouri, 142
Tuna
The New Tuna Noodle, 189
Olive Oil–Poached Tuna with
Herbes de Provence, 112
Tonnato Dip, 39
Tuscany, 35, 130, 132, 200
Txakoli, 21, 150

U
Ugni blanc, 110
Ulibarri Winery, 176
Ulysse Collin, 30
Uriondo, 150

V
Valais, 50
Valdespino, 46
Valfaccenda, 92
Valle d'Aosta, 50
Valpolicella, 181
Vegetables
Crudités for Early Summer, 114
Dips and Sticks, 38–39
Glou-Glou Thai BBQ, 164–66
Roasted Vegetables in Walnut
Sauce, 145
Roots Rémoulade with Smoked
Trout, 104
Roots Tagine with Cauliflower
"Couscous," 137–39
Spring Fling, 118–19
See also individual vegetables
Verdejo, 122, 147
Vermentino, 35
Veyder-Malberg, 184
Via de la Plata, 28
Vienna, 153
Vinaigrettes
Cherry Vinaigrette, 172
Green Garlic Vinaigrette, 153–54
Vinarija Križ, 228
Vina Štoka, 72, 228
Viñátigo, 106
Vinho Verde, 115
Vino di Anna, 206
Vino Quantico, 158
Vin Santo, 245
Vinyes Singulars, 28
Vittorio Bera e Figli, 58
Vittorio Graziano, 75
Volatile acidity (VA), 24
Vouvray, 115, 120

W
Wachau, 82
Waffles, Falafel, 72–74
Walnuts
toasting, 29
Walnut Sauce, 145
Washington state, 132
Weingut Brand, 82, 94
Weingut Clemens Busch, 94
Weingut Hirsch, 82
Weingut Julian Haart, 82
Weingut Keller, 82
Weingut Peter Lauer, 94
Weingut Weiser-Künstler, 94
Wheat berries
A Sophisticated Hippie Salad,
90–91
Wieninger, 153
Willamette Valley, 44, 77
Wind Gap Wines, 164
Wine
additives in, 14
in bottles, 18
in boxes, 18
buying, 17
canned, 18
common faults in, 24–25
cooking with, 14
corked, 24
decanting, 22
in kegs, 18
labels on, 18–19
natural, 14
opening, 21
serving, 21–22
storing, 22
temperature of, 22
See also individual wines
Winegut Maria + Sepp Muster, 103

X
Xarel-lo, 28

Y
Yogurt
Pistachio-Yogurt Dip, 39
Tropical Yogurt Parfaits with
Seedy Cashew Crunch, 66–67
See also Labneh
Yves Leccia, 225

Z
Zanotto, 118
Zinfandel, 11, 137
Zlatan Otok, 186
Zucchini
Carrot-Zucchini Latkes, 125–27
Griddled Zucchini Bread with
Moscato Peaches and Crème,
58–60
Ratatouille Gratin, 128–29
Zweiglet, 211

Library of Congress Cataloging-in-Publication
Data

Names: Frank, Dana, author. | Slonecker, Andrea,
  author.
Title: Wine food : new adventures in drinking and
  cooking / Dana Frank and Andrea Slonecker.
Description: California : Ten Speed Press, [2018] |
  Includes bibliographical references and index.
Identifiers: LCCN 2017058757
Subjects: LCSH: Food and wine pairing. | Cooking.
  | LCGFT: Cookbooks.
Classification: LCC TX911.3.M45 F73 2018 |
  DDC 641.01/3—dc23
LC record available at https://lccn.loc.gov/
  2017058757
Hardcover ISBN: 978-0-399-57959-2
Ebook ISBN: 978-0-399-57960-8

Printed in China

10 9 8 7 6 5 4 3 2 1

First Edition

To Scott and Orly, my sweet little
family and my greatest loves
—Dana

To Tom, with love (l and h)
—Andrea